ILLUMINATIONS

The Geography of the Imagination

ILLUMINATIONS

Paintings Poems Drawings

by Steven Edwin Counsell

BLACK SWAN EDITIONS

Santa Fe, New Mexico

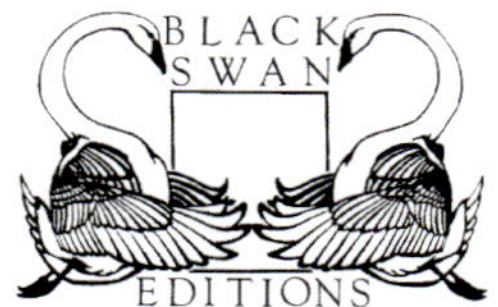

First Published in the United States by Black Swan Editions

© 2012 by Steve Edwards Counsell, Black Swan Editions
All rights reserved. No part of this book may be reproduced, stored in a retrieval system, or transferred in any form or by any means, electronic, mechanical, photocopying, recording or otherwise, without the prior written permission of the copyright owners, nor be otherwise circulated in any form of binding or cover other than that in which it is published and without a similar condition including this condition being imposed on the subsequent purchaser.

Conceived by Steven E Counsell, Santa Fe, NM
Designed by John Cole GRAPHIC DESIGNER, Santa Fe, NM
Edited by Lynne Holmes, Santa Fe, NM
Photography by High Desert Arts

FIRST EDITION
January 2012

Library of Congress Control Number: 2011905782

Counsell, Steven Edwin.
    Illuminations: Mythical, symbolic drawings and poetry/
Steven Edwin Counsell.

    ISBN 978-0-9835023-0-2
    1. Mythological imagery   2. Symbolic/Surrealist imagery
    3. poetry (word play)   4. Jungian Studies

Printed in China

BLACK SWAN EDITIONS
321 W. Cordova Road
Santa Fe, NM 87505
www.blackswaneditions.com

ACKNOWLEDGEMENTS

Robert Graves once said you cannot marry your muse, which is of course nonsense for thirty years ago I married Hope. This book is a love affair to all the people that have helped me.   My friend Buck who has been my friend for a lifetime, whose critical intelligence and sense of fun is without price. Jane Lipman and Janet Eigner, who have been my partners and midwives in poetry. John Cole's book design which you will soon be lucky enough to open. Monika Wikman, whose generous introduction makes me feel that I almost know what I am doing.

Thanks.

C O N T E N T S

WHAT LAND HAVE WE ENTERED

WITH STEVEN COUNSELL'S work doors open into the living imagination and invite us to walk through with him into its autonomous creative expressive landscape. And as we do the living question arises — what land have we entered?

From one point of view, we enter through his work via his paintings, drawings and accompanying poems, the landscape of the creation matrix itself erupting in ever fresh images revealing its own life from the depths as it informs contemporary daily reality.

In this land personal and transpersonal dimensions join hands and create the world anew. And we as witnesses may be opened, challenged, strummed and renewed in the process. For Counsell's work has as its bottom a courageous instinct that dares to drive a tap root down deeply into the living imagination, the strata beneath ordinary consciousness where image of its own volition moves, lives, transforms and asks for witnesses and participants.

As the pages turn and the depth, complexity and volume of his work take hold I also imagine we have been invited into Counsell's alchemical laboratory where the contemporary alchemist at work puts into our hands the living, changing waters from the depths of the psyche via his art and accompanying poems honed in the vessel of creative life.

The archetypal images provoke us to discover the world anew. This is by definition the mystery the artist opens, the door in the psyche where first man, first woman in each of us is taking its first breath, first step, first perception of the mysteries of the natural world and the dance between spirit and matter of which we are all a part. Counsell helps us open our lenses of perception to discover this mystery within.

Steven Counsell is also a culture carrier, for he explores and expresses currents of change that are happening collectively as well as individually. I would caution the reader to be prepared to be disturbed, surprised, stretched, shaken and taken into new territory. For Counsell's imagery portrays the dismantling post-modernist world view, where fresh life force disrupts form, erupts from some molten core beneath and inside all form.

Archetypal motifs play out as his shamanic visionary world view explodes traditional form and recasts life in new ways. In one of his images the tree of life itself, the axis mundi, is blast apart into many pieces and recast in new ways. It gives one the visceral experience of what Counsell's alchemical work has tapped — that sea of sulphuric transforming lava seething beneath the formed world that destroys the old and creates the new. Not a journey for the faint hearted…

His poem "Tree" is an exquisite example of this shamanic revisioning spirit that prevails in his work. The archetypal story of the world tree is taken into his poet hands and with this we as readers also hold the reality of the creation and destruction of the worlds as we all truly do hang in the balance these days. The reader is invited into the shamanic experience of the axis mundi (Yggdrasil) that connects us with our ancestors and all those we have ever known. Then the poem draws us, thaws us out of collective spells that freeze perception and life energy, and portrays the poignant meaningful role of the artist at the world tree. The poem hauntingly hangs in the air at the end over the abyss of creation and destruction of the worlds – just where the Norse creation myth saw it at the beginning of time, just as we know it to be so in our contemporary world —ending with the felt sense of the self portrait of the artist/poet;

Those interested in depth psychology will have a field day with this manuscript, for in it we find what Jung pointed to at the bottom of creation—the transformation of the divine, the changing god image. As we know, with the recent publication of Carl Jung's *The Red Book* by the Philemon Foundation, we now have access to Jung's own magnum opus, his own revelations poured forth onto the page in paintings, drawings, incantations, active imaginations and more. The exposure to the depths that Jung traveled, as portrayed in *The Red Book,* is daunting. And as Jung's opus takes its place as a contemporary alchemical book of revelation, it spotlights the hunger in the human soul to find places in the contemporary world where individual expressions of the mythological unconscious are lived and portrayed anew, both in our own lives and in the lives and work of others.

Steven Counsell's *Illuminations* reveal *his* 'Red Book', *his* magnum opus, *his* text of revelation where we witness the fruit of the work done in his alchemical vessel, the specific nature here, in this artist and poet of the divine transforming in the human soul.

As the pages turn and the depths stir, I wonder who will come to mind for you, dear reader, as kin to his work. As I found myself

musing on where *Illuminations* would find
kindred spirits in my library I saw the life
and work of Maria Remedio's Varo, Alex
Grey and Hieronymus Bosch. It is tricky
however, because Steven is part poet, artist,
alchemist, ethnographer and depth psychologist.
And the complexity of themes that run deep
in his writing and art deserve much more
than this brief introduction would allow.
They deserve to be studied in depth by
people of many fields of study. May that
be so, and may the world (for its own sake)
open its doors widely to the soul-stirring
work of this needed visionary as his light
from the depths shines for generations
to come.

> — Monika Wikman, Ph.D. Tesuque, New
> Mexico, March 2011. Jungian analyst and
> author of *Pregnant Darkness: Alchemy and
> the Rebirth of Consciousness* published by
> Nicolas Hays, 2005.

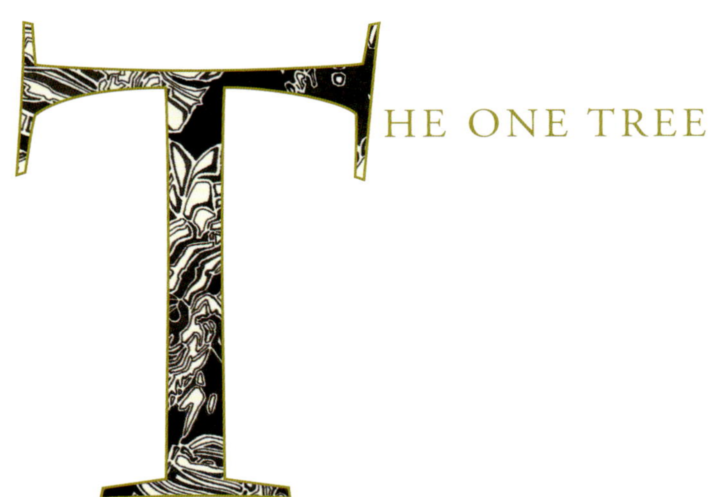

THE ONE TREE

XYLEM

THE LIFE STRUCTURE of trees, without showing
trees themselves — Xylem and Phloem. Biology
always gives budding young artists and poets
so many lovely and mysterious forms and words.

Altering context offers the gift of abstraction.
Scale, even a change in the grammar of objects,
causes them to pattern. Colors not expected
or a contrast not parsed. How glibly narrow

is the workaday script that makes reality just so.
The doors to larger rooms, to whole wings
of the unknown, start with looking, say, at the bark
of a tree, really looking until the mind blurs

to a lexicon of shapes. Once you enter the shape
of things, other symbols, and myth, the worlds
beyond the looking glass will open. To begin,
make form more than the function it follows.

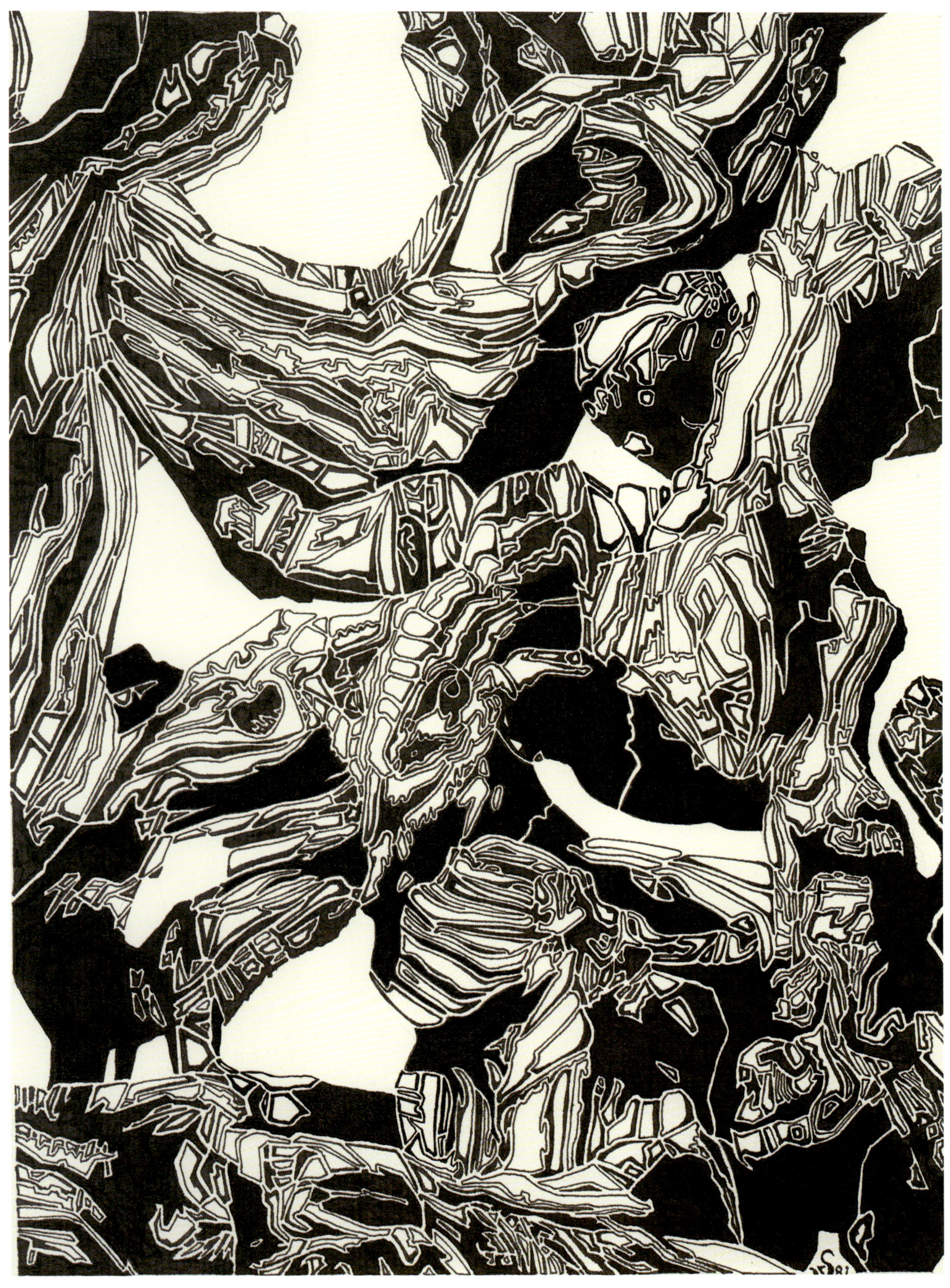

IN THE MORNING my hand, like the shape of this tree, is wooden.
Yet I know within the mind that seduces fingers to grip
brushes and chalk there are cubbies of space, windup wells
for stairs, and balconies for sailing kites and kittens from.

That the Pinocchio that lives inside the real boy is the one
who wants to get out. He's the one with all the adventures.
The Blue Fairy promised life but a sheet of flat paper
in a book offers escape beyond the prosody of simple song.

There may be more life in a painting, more to explore
than in a repeated trip to the same office, or a destiny
with the same meal, more soul or meaning than the
thrall of doxologies or the tyranny of current events.

The marionette that I am sits in a world of wonders.
When my painting session ends, the real boy returns
and has to pretend again that he knows what an adult is
and worst of all that he cares what an adult does.

After all, as the saying goes, history is the nightmare
from which I'm trying to awaken. However, daydreams
fogging into the frame of imagination, or stealing away
care, that's a wholly different mythopoesis.

You can walk a hundred miles in this painting, or a few feet,
follow a line of thought or a raggle of bark, or come to rest
upon its surface like a blue bottle fly, or simply turn the page,
it just depends, like Pinocchio, what kind of blockhead you are. 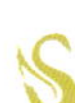

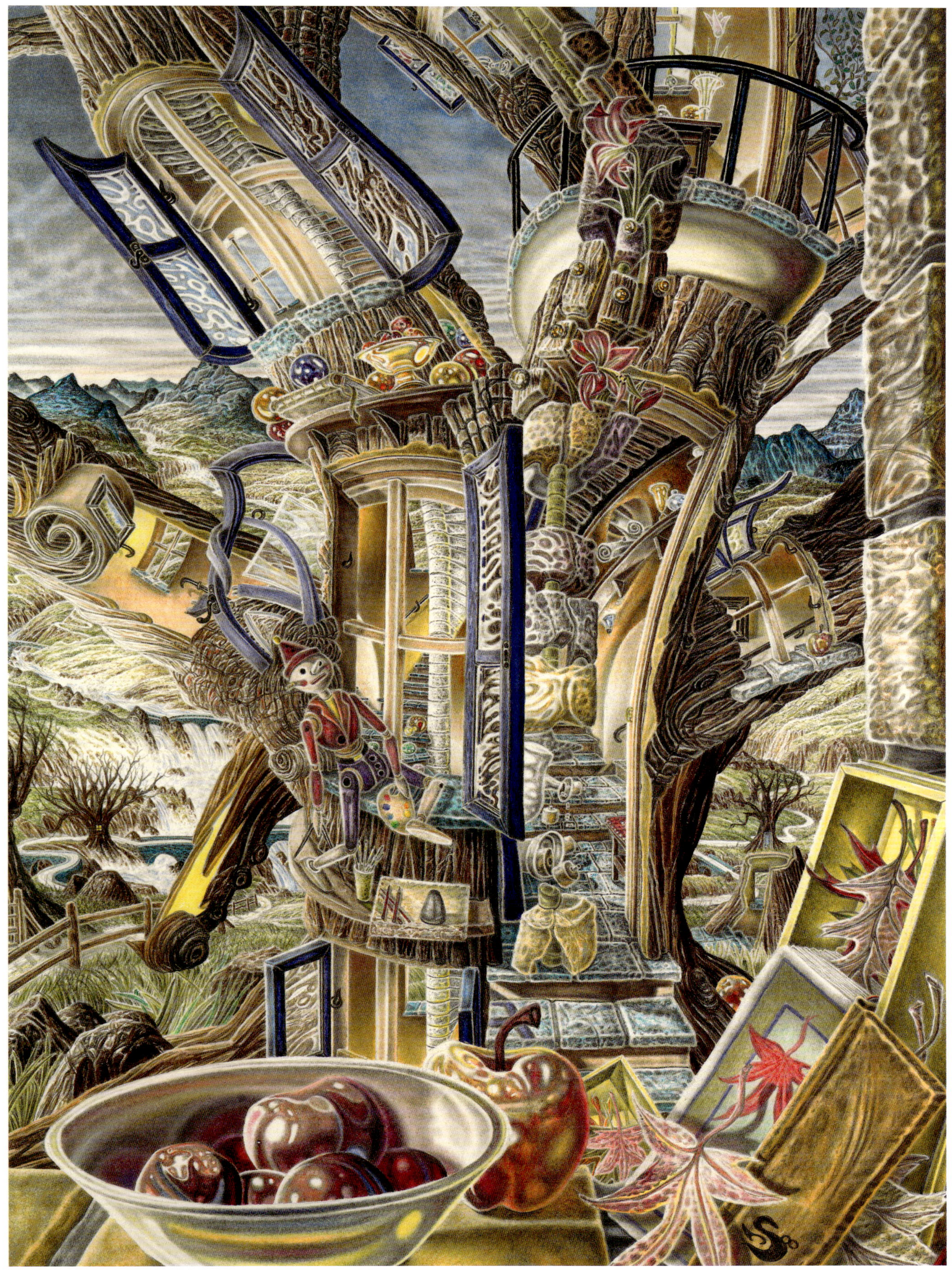

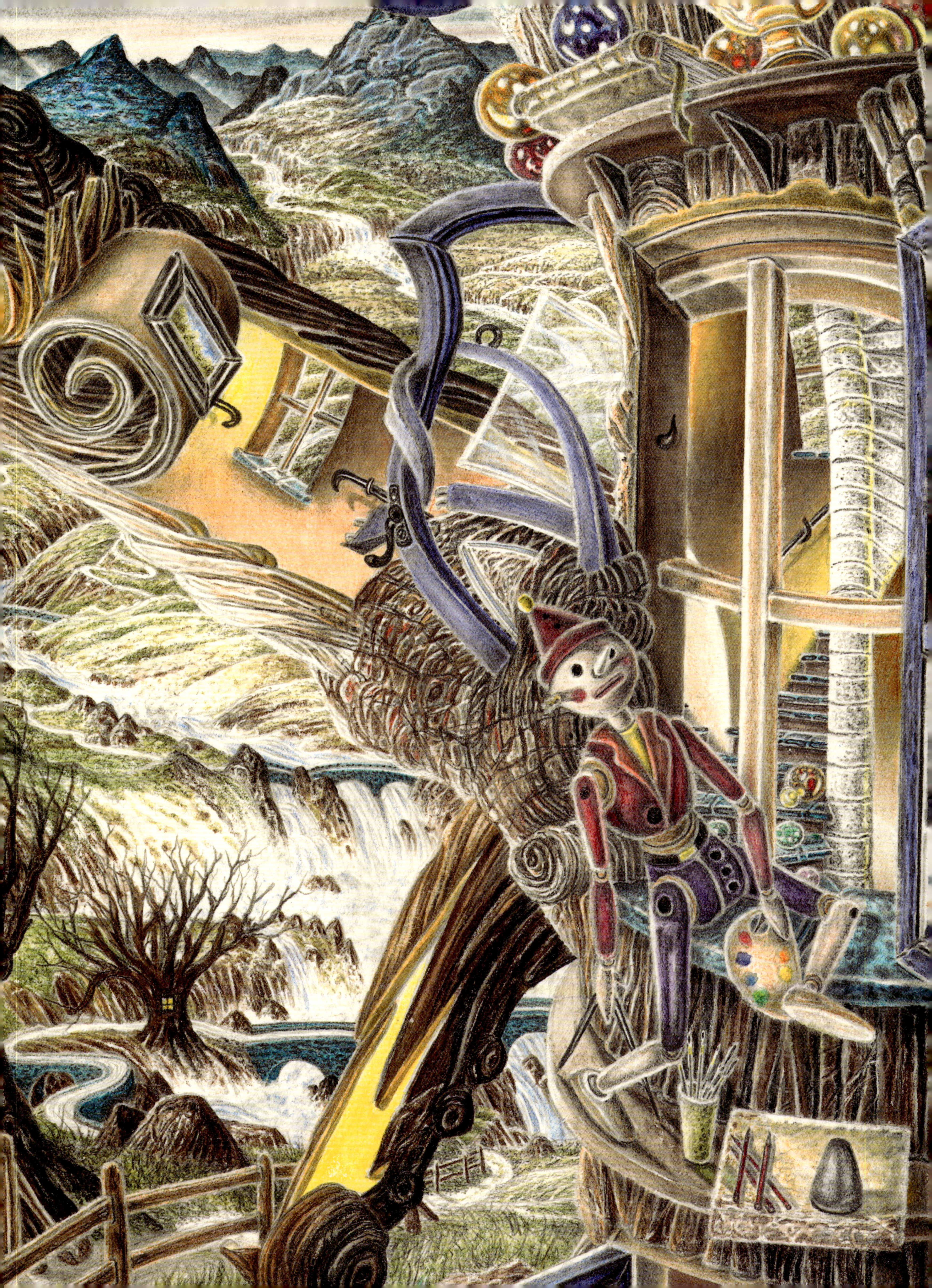

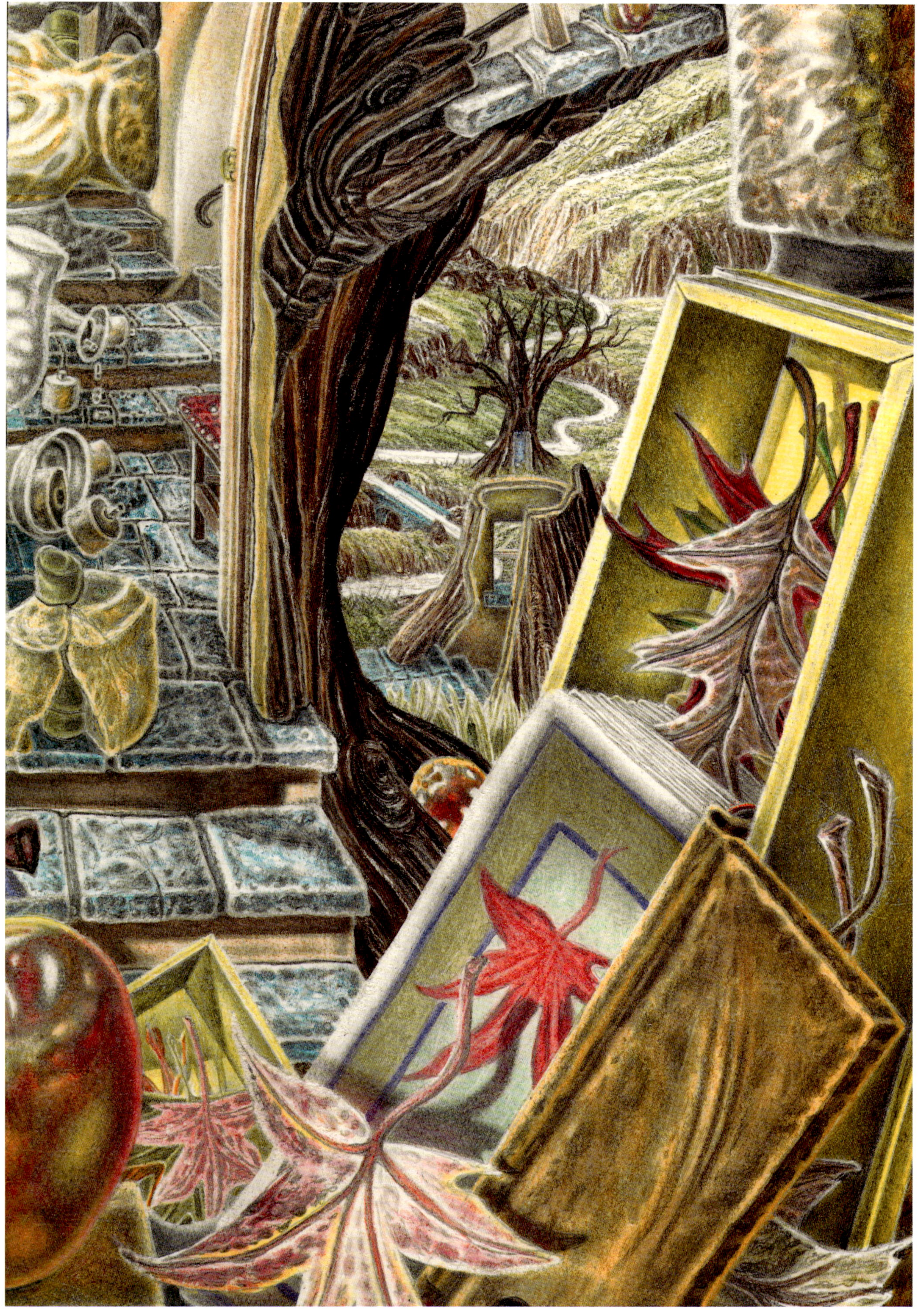

TREE

YGGDRASIL, the great world tree in Norse cosmology.
Its root in the underworld fed by the pool of wisdom,
its trunk in the realm of men, a column of life
and its branches in Asgard the home of the gods.

Look carefully in the fissures of any tree,
everyone you have ever known will be there.
The rooted nerves that match your own
and the watery blood rising through dry bark.

The grounding green wire, snapping and firing
is moist, as we remember being dragged up the trunk.
The crystal cathedrals of in-spired ambitions
lost in a frozen lattice of tasks and taskmasters…

Until recarved in the branch and the twig, our life
is rendered as art, masks, mannequins, torques
of gold filigree on children's blocks, or concave
mirrors of brass for seeing ourselves in the sky.

Proud adornments to a rendezvous with the gods
that reign above the tree, patiently waiting
upon our brief fountain, rising upward, to at last
craft a future before the bough breaks.

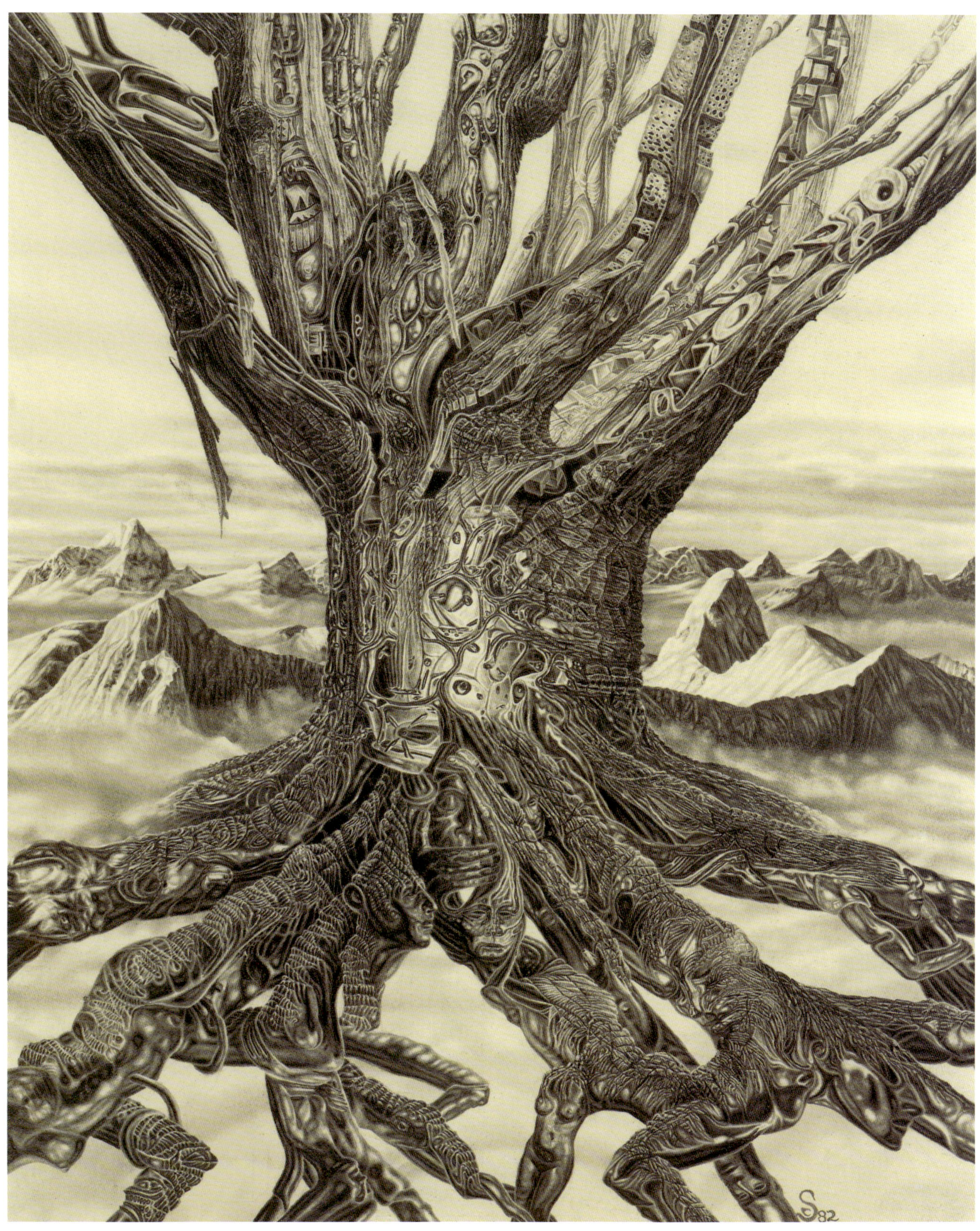

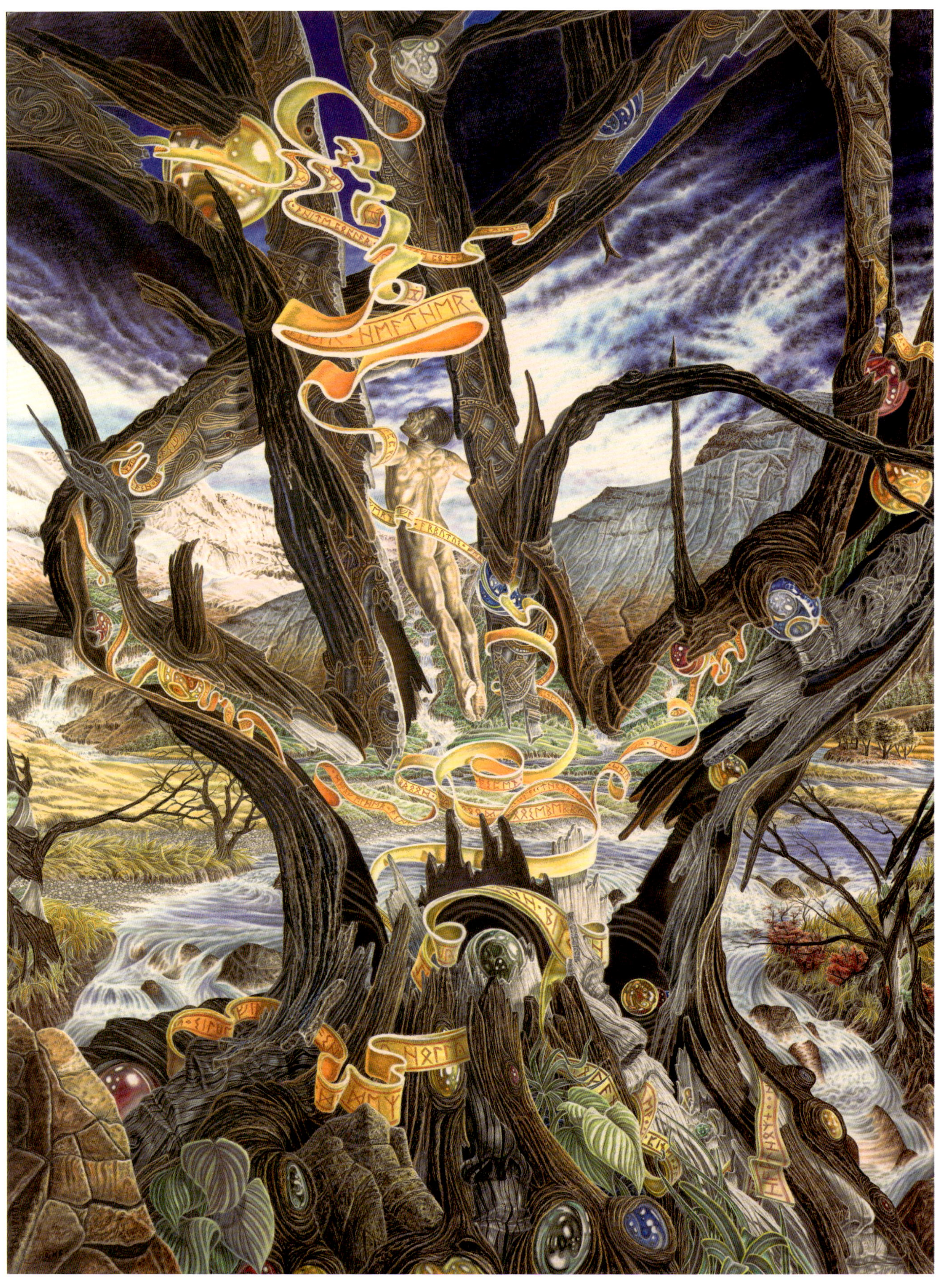

ROOTED BONES blanketed from birth
rattle and roil in the nurseried ground.
Faces emerge from knobs and cusps,
wooden tongues creak of seeded death.

Joints flex, knucklebones of root grasp
the hard creed of buried rock
the ruin of passing wracked in time
that is the trees' enduring name.

Under the gray sackcloth of leaves
the sun's martyrdom of broken light
miters the earth in a mottle of gold
and silvers and pearls the knot of eyes.

And limbs that shadow-dance and flame
skirling lines of lightning on bark
are steaming wet ground iridescently
in a witch trance of crowing dawn.

And the bright spell of the forest
would conjure a language ingrained in each
type of Oak, Yew, Hawthorn or Beech —
an Alphabet of the Trees, Beth-Luis-Nion it's called.

Or could woodwinds play our form anew?
Would the architect of the wood conjugate
our second skin of window and door, room
to underscore the earthbound rootedness in us?

Yggdrasil, tall Ash, fountain reborn
living through the dark rages of men.
Whether then or now, bled the same
the dead saw seasons that passed in you.

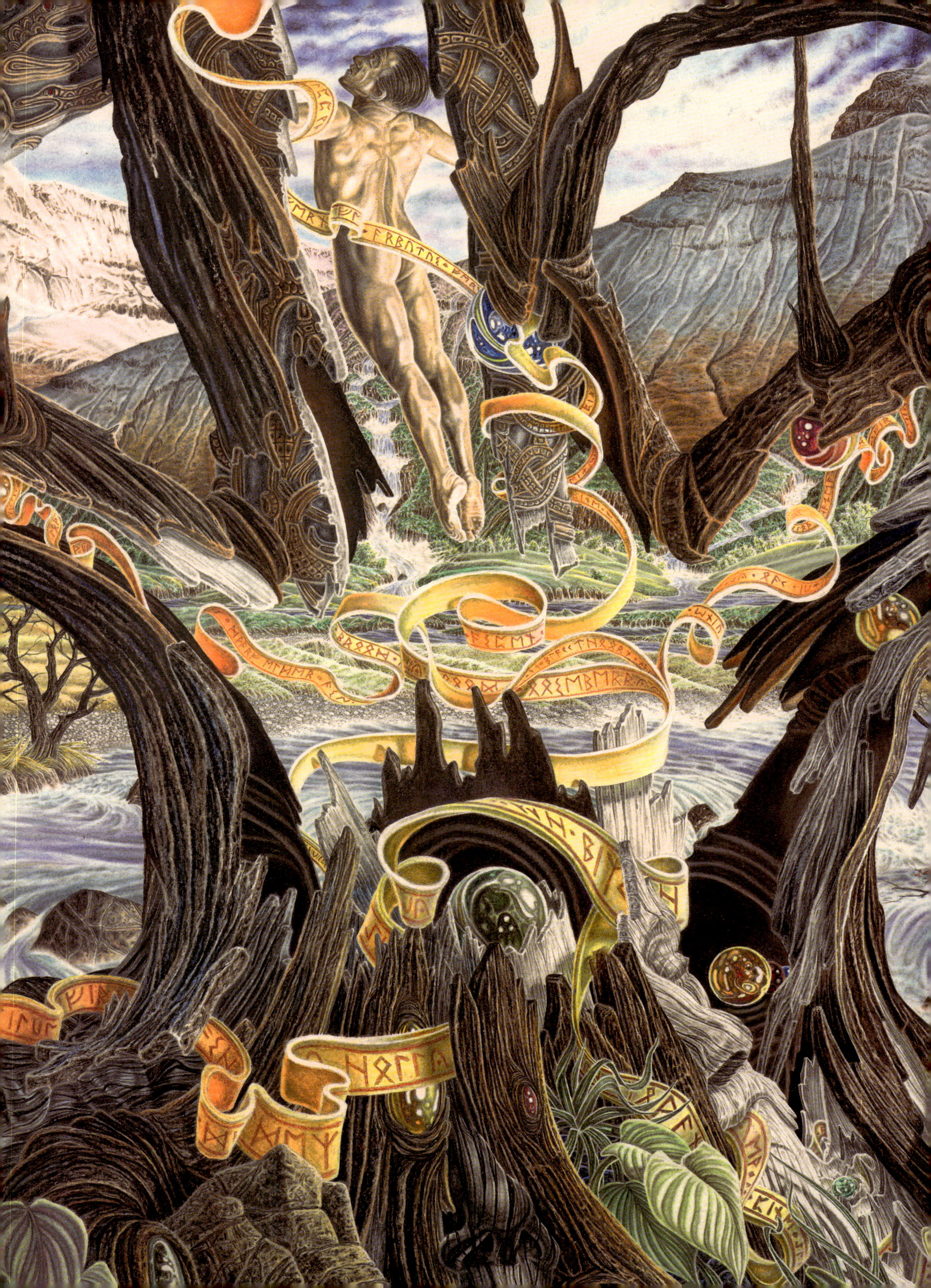

The living gnaw their splinter of light
slipping under the earth themselves
and you and I, lost in our final day,
sink beneath the waves of soil.

Minutes and hours make monuments of us
boxed up tight under branch and twig,
cap and bell, capillary and vein, we dry
under the heartwoods deepest drum.

Our high-strung, bird-quivered heart must stop.
The trees age so slowly they forget to die
and we die so quickly we forget to live.
We live in them, with them, and under them.

At the end of days the forest waits, rebudded
in space. The sting of violins in halls of jet —
one with the still silence of frozen night.
One by one the stars fall into disuse.

Yet in the forest's tall towers of life
as the starless shadows clot the world in kohl
the lime green leaves of spring emerge
and human fire is but a memory of smoke. 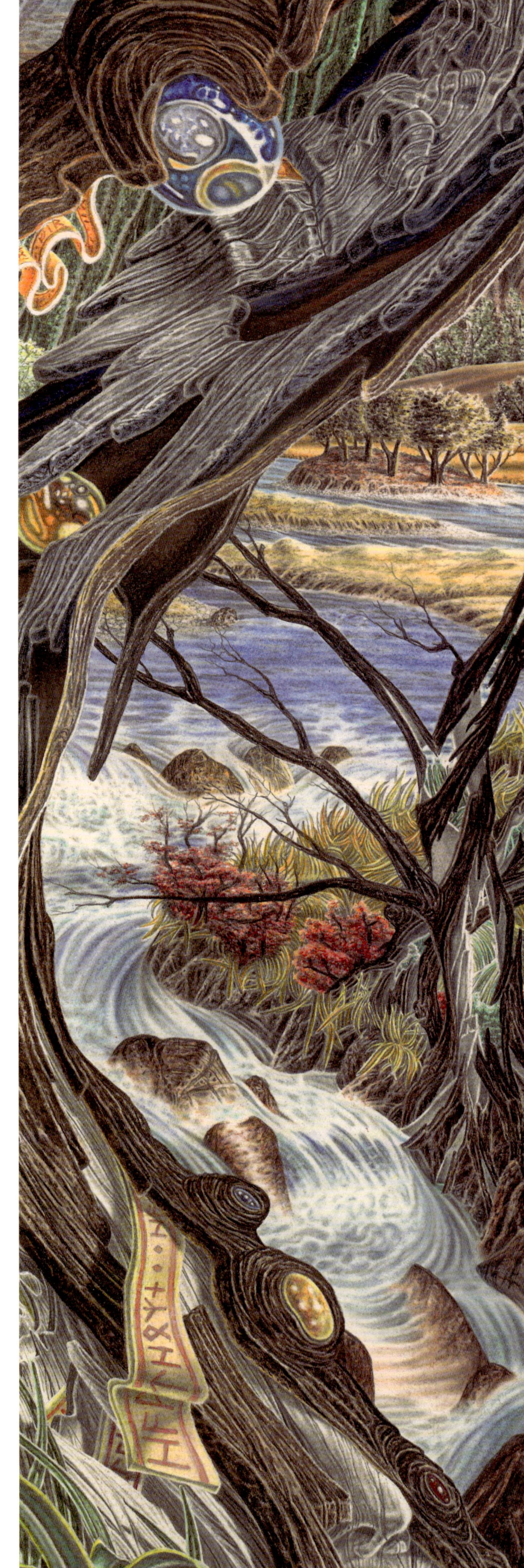

I. THE seasons pour through me
and flower buds lodge in my heart.
The dry regret and regard of fall —
   leaves in the book of my mind.

      A particular thrush trills its lust
into a spring greed, at the very
dawn of my time and, there,
that iridescent beetle nests in my palm.

II. We cannot escape the passage into rhyme.
Prose lives the volumes and passages,
in the gray space of memory without song.
Rhyme salts our skin in summer sweat.

We sink into the earth, names intact,
our winter cloak has humored the ground.
The bones form a cathedral for mice and moles.
We continue with a different voice, in fact

we know the biography of every stone,
daffodils grow right into our thoughts
glow and blush, we grow and rush out
the fingertips of she who will recycle us green.

Naive and grass-green again, it all happens;
belief is so unimportant for what we will become —
no matter what we were, we are everything again;
again and again, seasons pour through us.

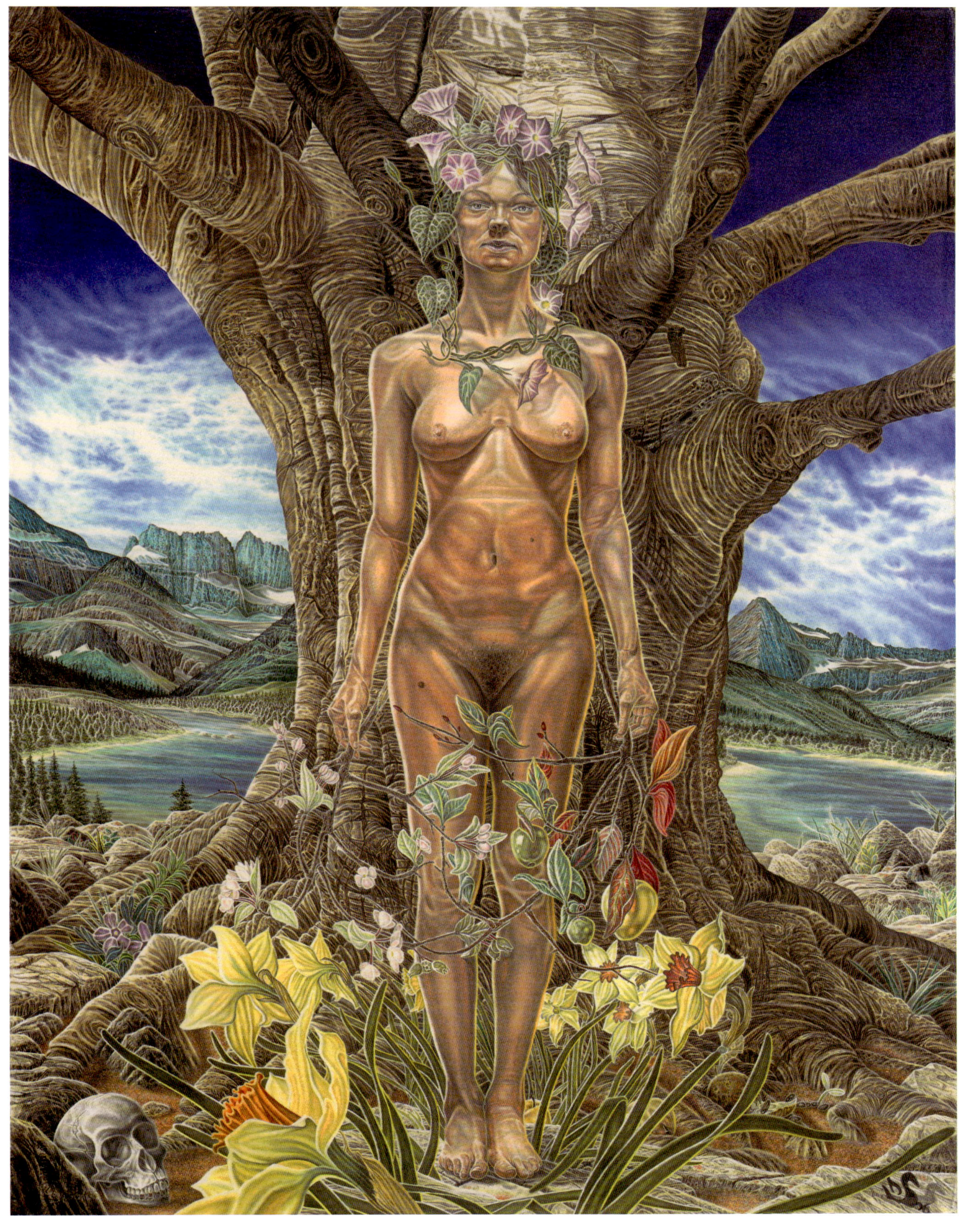

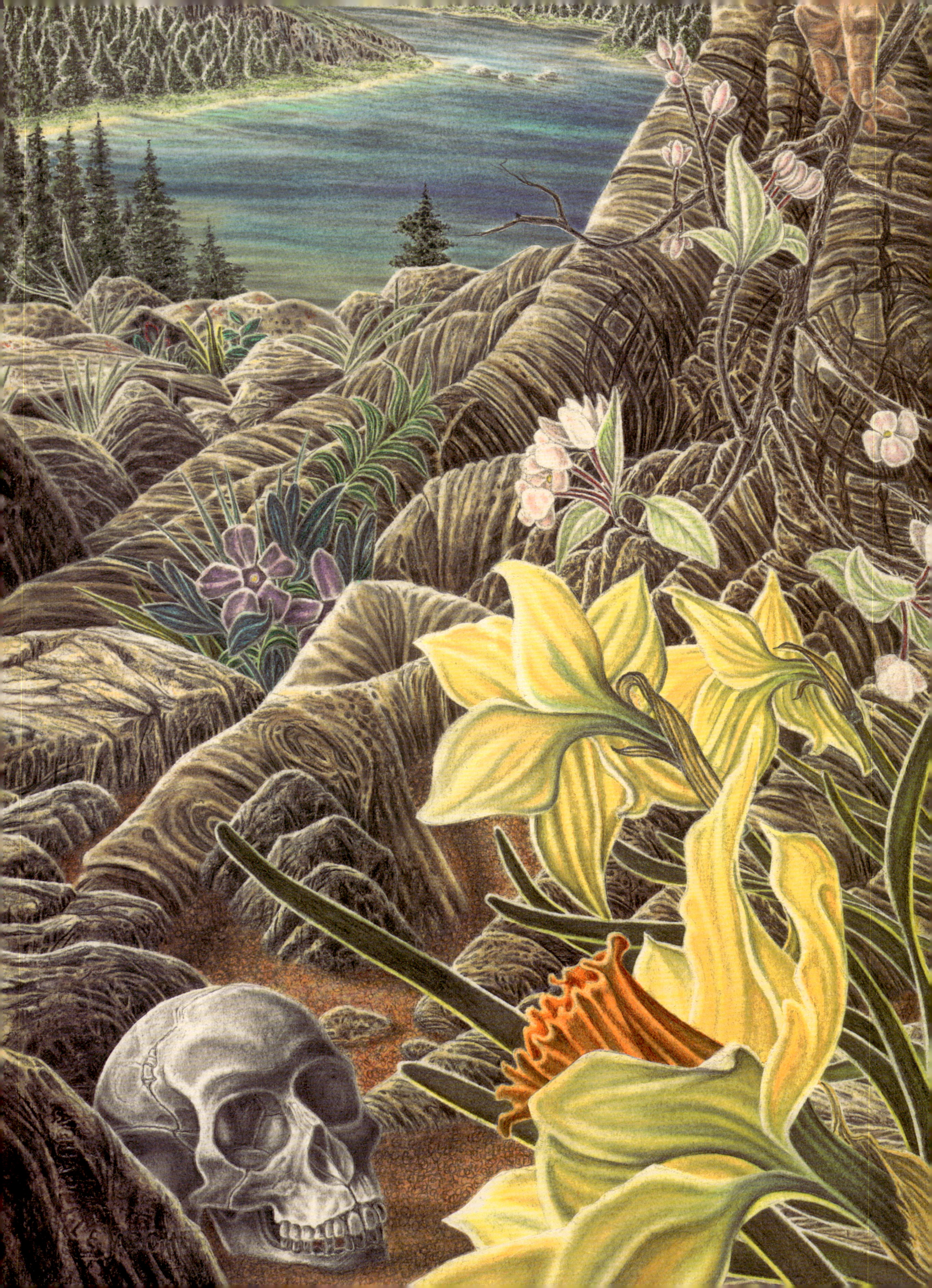

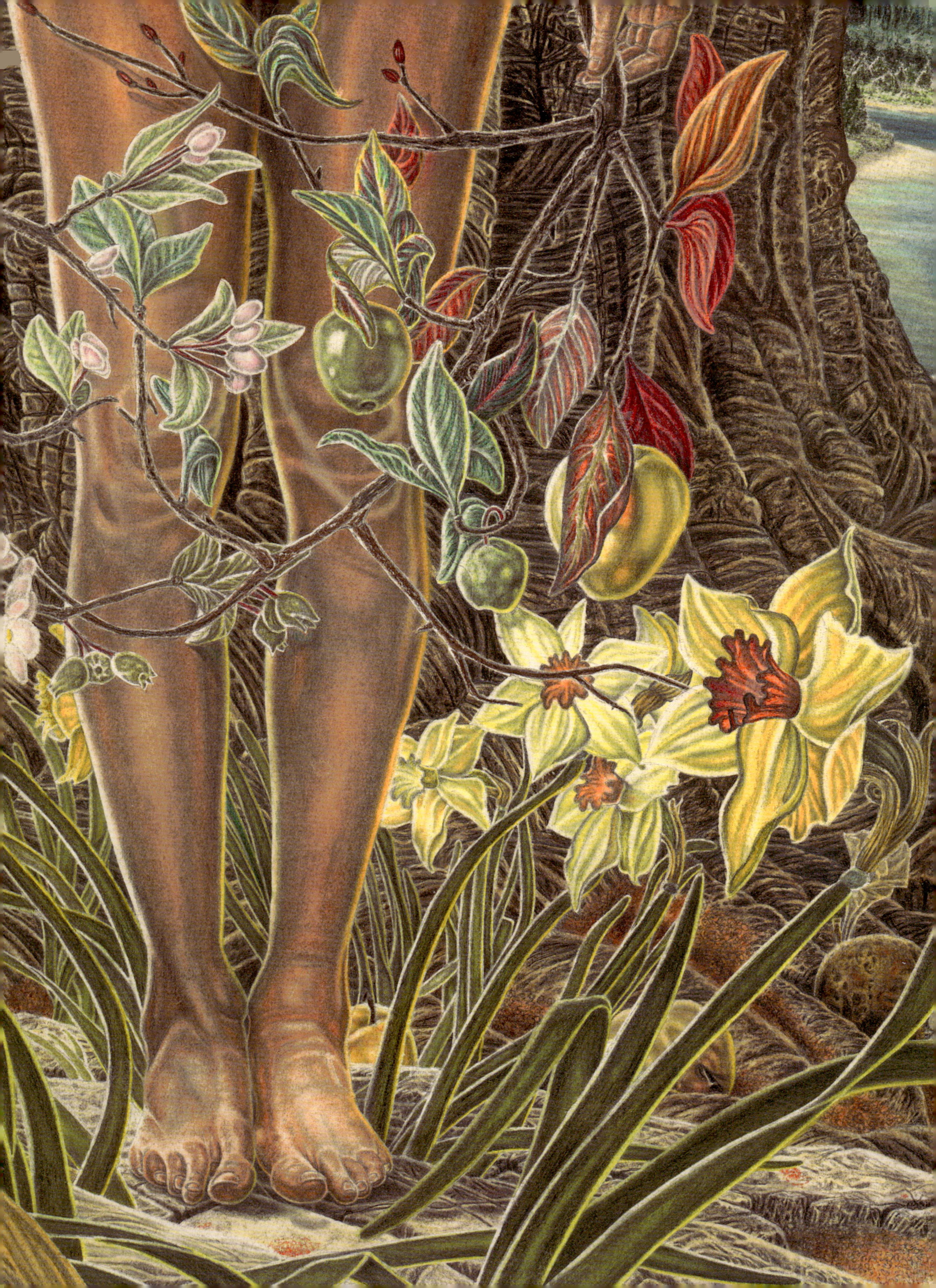

THE EARTHLY PARADISE

WHERE DO WE GO when we dream of Paradise?
In the halls of memory there are many palaces;
we must not settle for a gray cottage in an ashen sunrise.
In the shell of our meaning there are many gardens.

A small turn in a path takes its time in us.
The worlds that echo in us are shells of a different order;
they perch in the branches of our make-believe;
they sound, reverberate, and spiral in the loss of us.

When we return to ourselves in sanity, we know
the reality that was beaten into our obedience
is a faded tintype of Oz, Wonderland and Avalon.
Being an adult is forgetting how to return.

The Titmouse of Death is peeping in our pocket. When we
stay in the world we know we're easier to find; for the cheep-
cheep of finality to nest in our heart easily, do not go romping
in other worlds, wear your graybeard resignedly.

To wander so many paths, to cross so many bridges
why, if we're not careful, we may forget how to grow old.
If we're hopelessly young how can the light fade,
we may even forget we're mortal and live forever-

after. Happily, honestly, really have we ever
been truly sad in a garden? A slanty sun through
the hiss of wind, trees chiming gold as doubloons,
the Earthly Paradise spirals through the mind, all is well.

When we reach a mountaintop, and the coldly eternal
is all we see — breathe, descend, chlorophyll the blood,
diastole your worth, pulse through the exhale of Brahma.
Eden waits, Elysium beckons, even in our own backyard.

Squint a bit. Being grown up is not terminal.
It can be taken off like a cheap suit at a shabby wake
and resurrection is as simple as uncontrolled folly.
The Earthly Paradise reseeds endlessly in you.

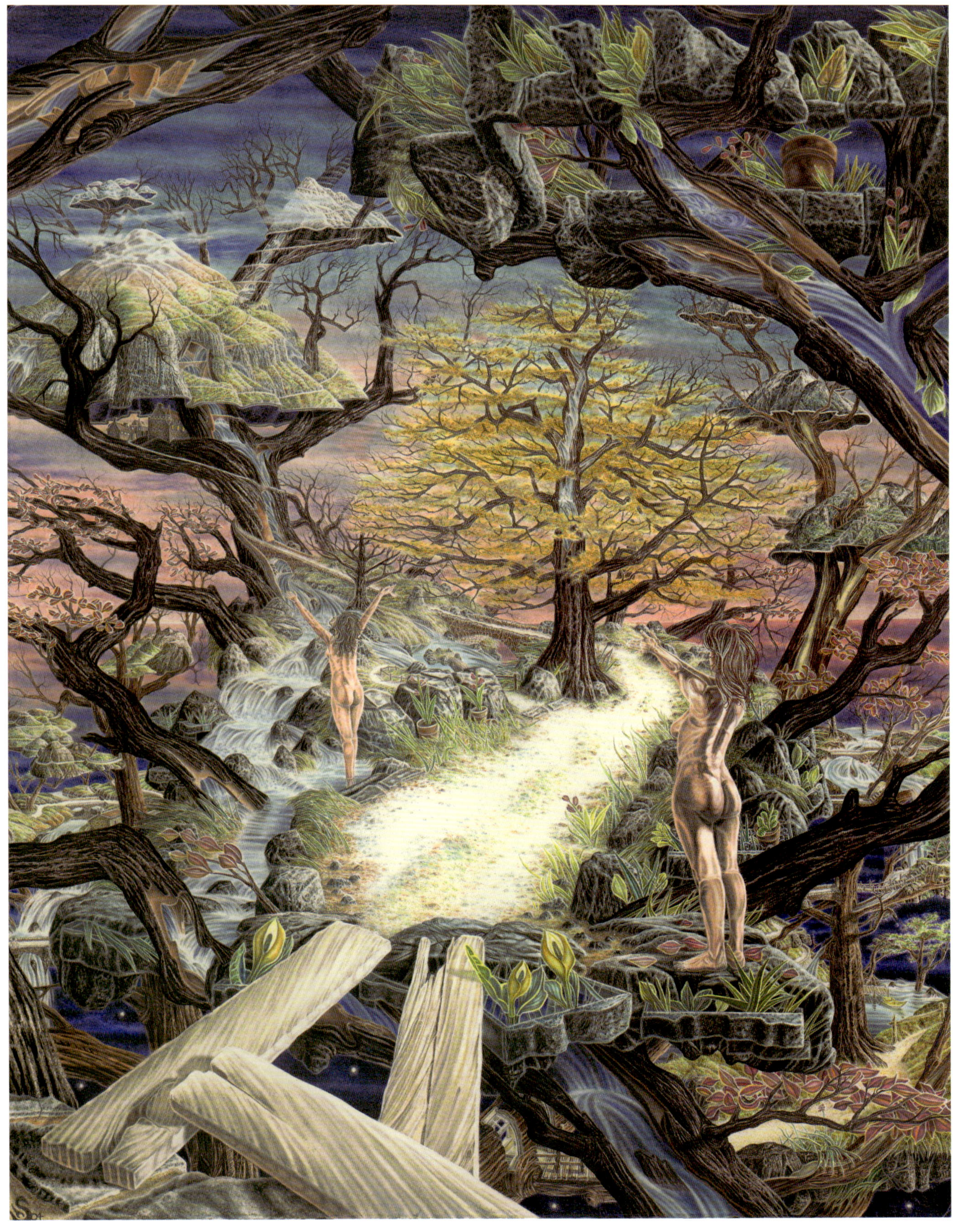

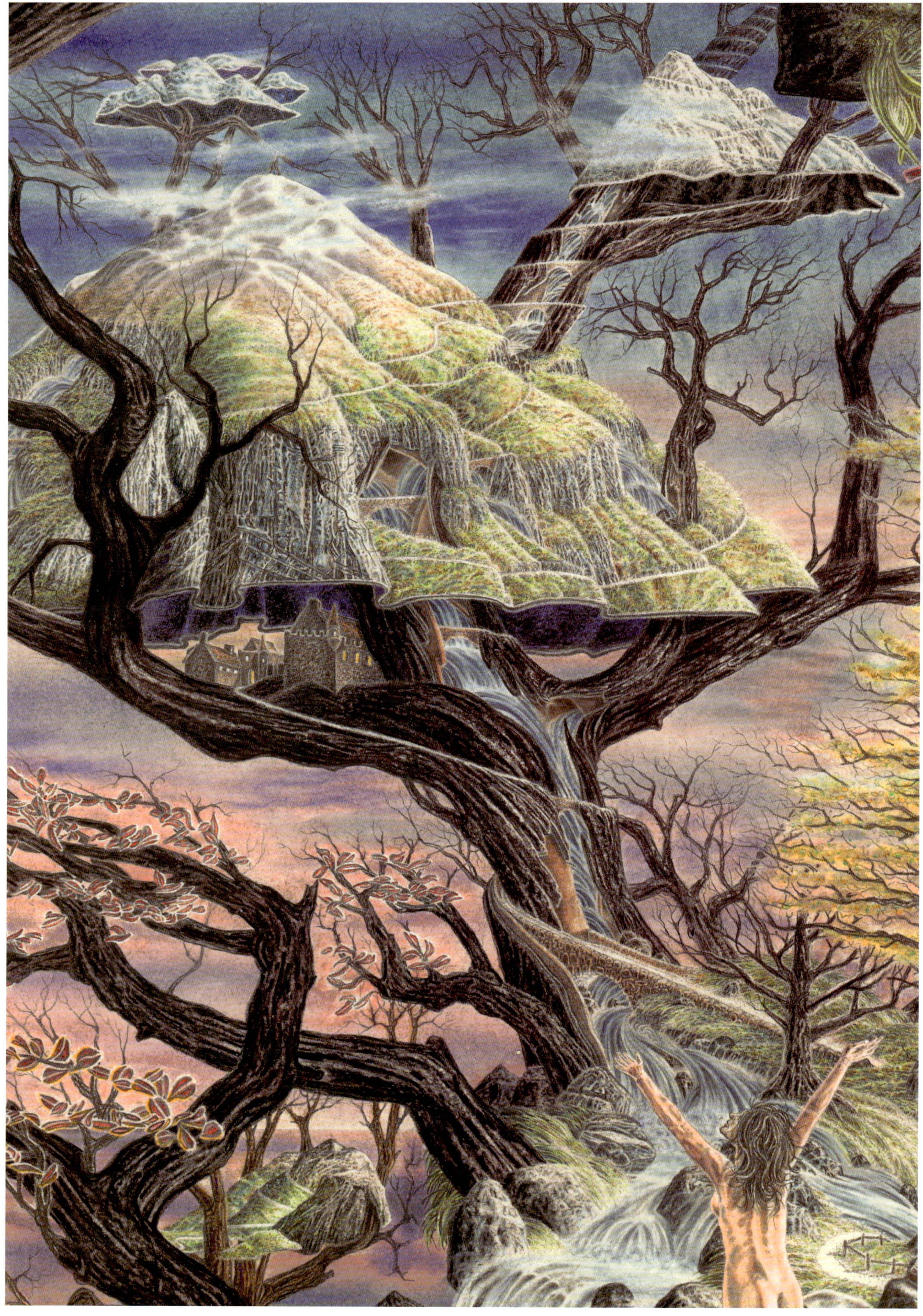

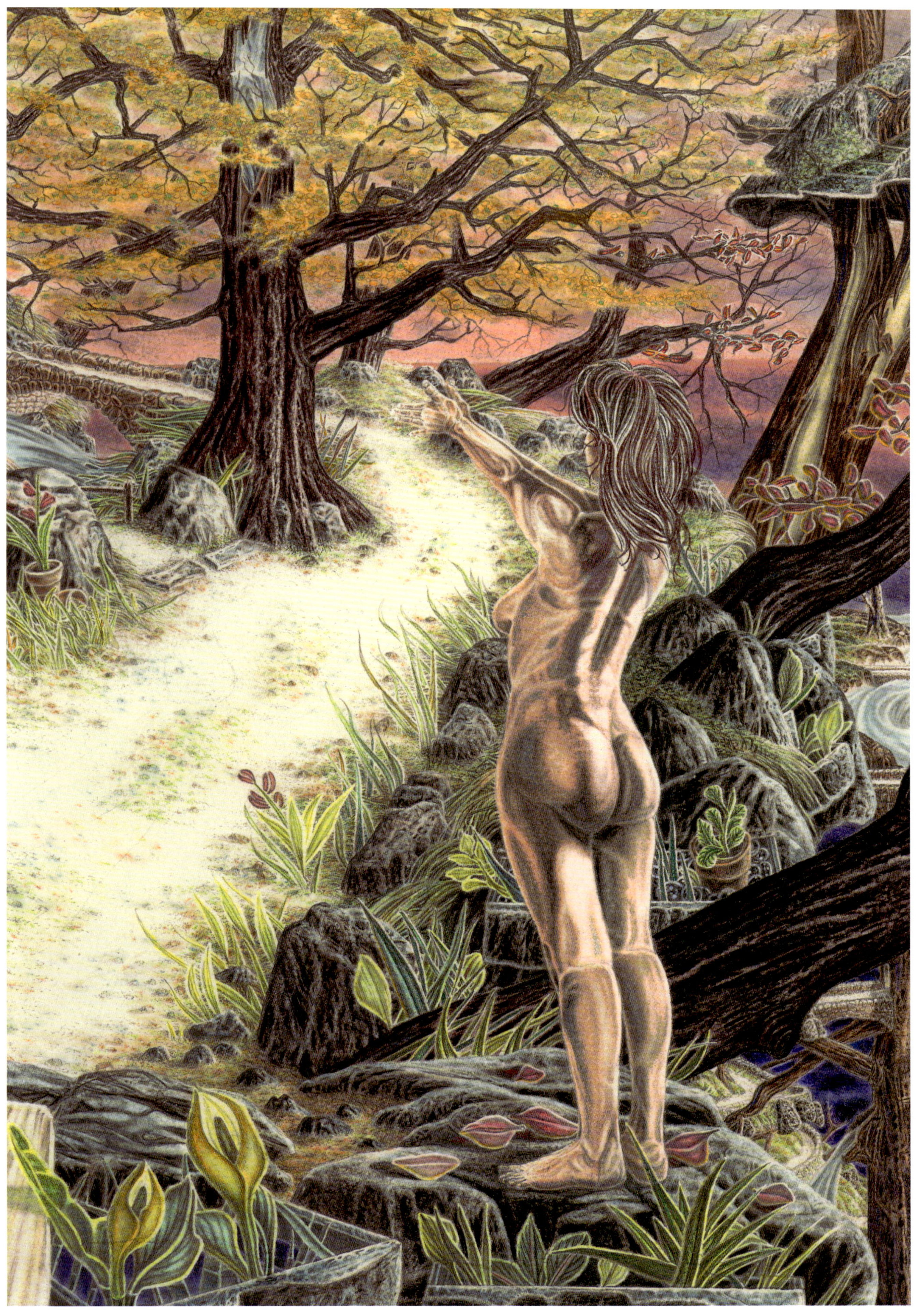

Winds are skirling up
the topsey turvey of clouds
confecting the sweet air
rounding the boil of waves.

Cork-screwing and hurly-burling
goblin-knots and mushroom-rings
and oaken root-webs cracking
up the chert gray mottled-rock.

The fever of it all returning, night-
crawlers swimming through dirt,
black beetles in jackdaw beaks,
sparrows exploded in talons of jet.

Nostrils twitched in the fire of speed,
drudged down in hunger by yellow eyes,
throats barking out living joys,
fears, confusion and mystery.

Fated within the dance
and mated with the hunt
gooseflesh and hot breath
a passion for here-and-now.

The tidal red salt rip
in the spiral of birth
wave washed in pain
and breathtaking hope.

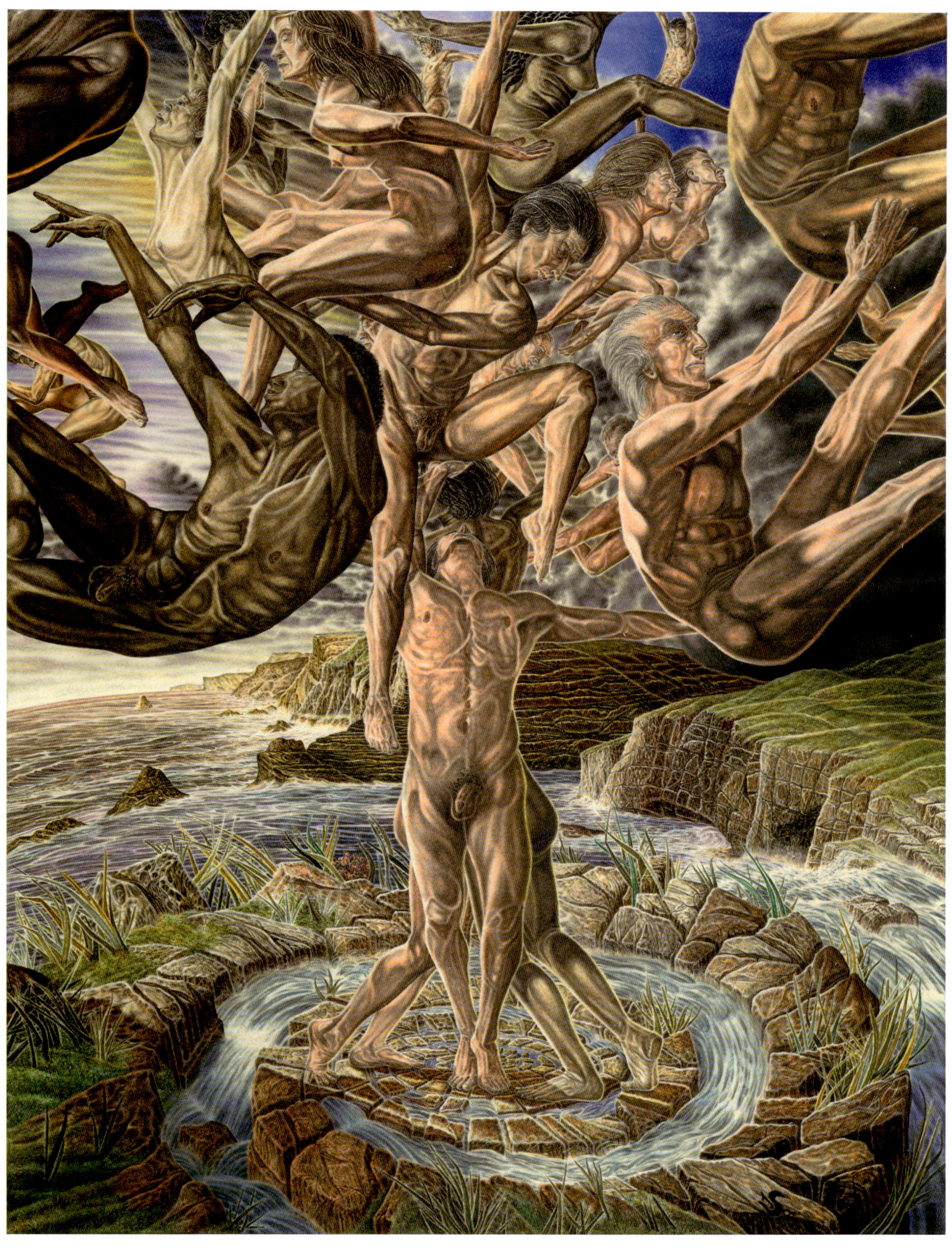

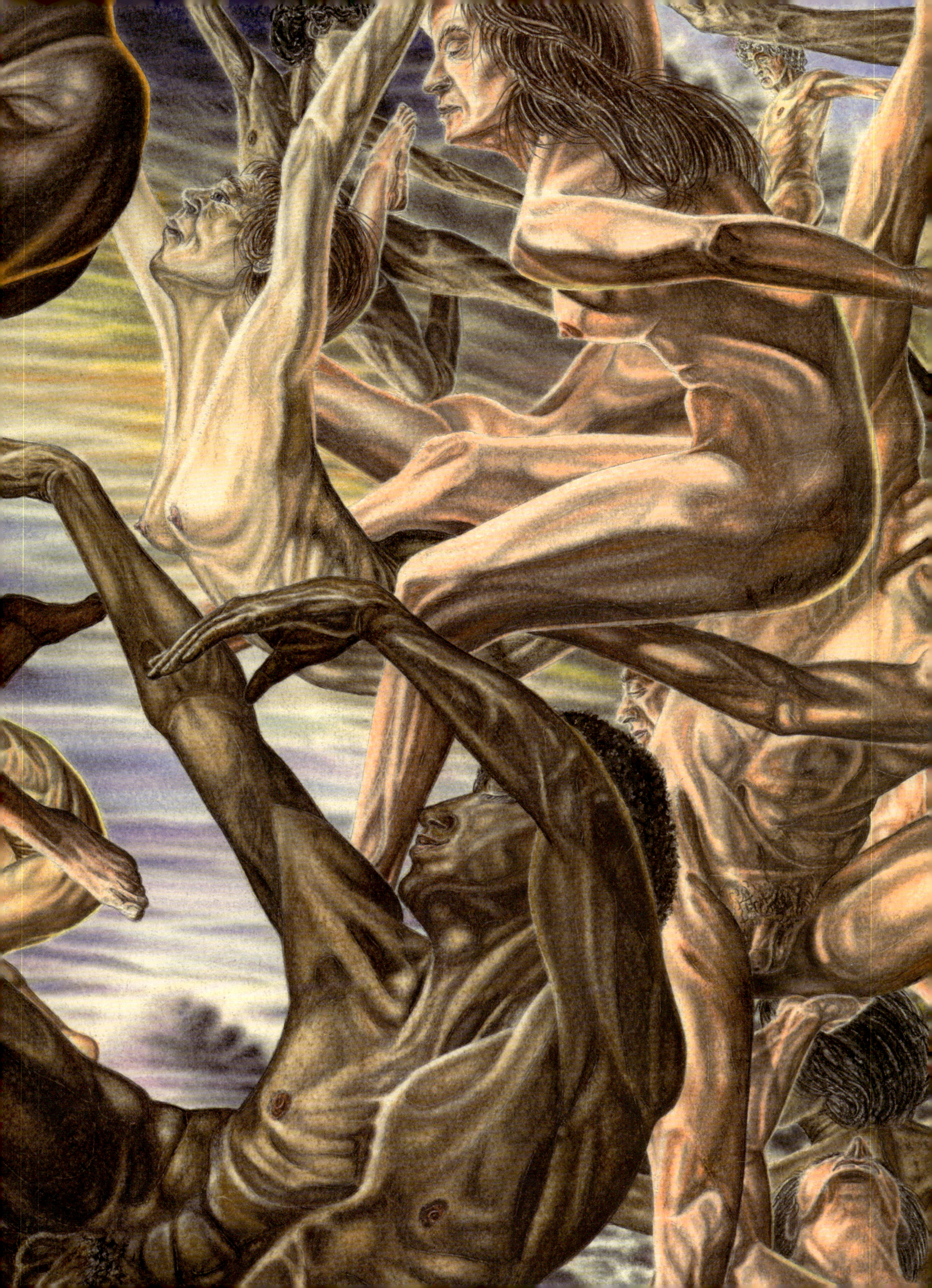

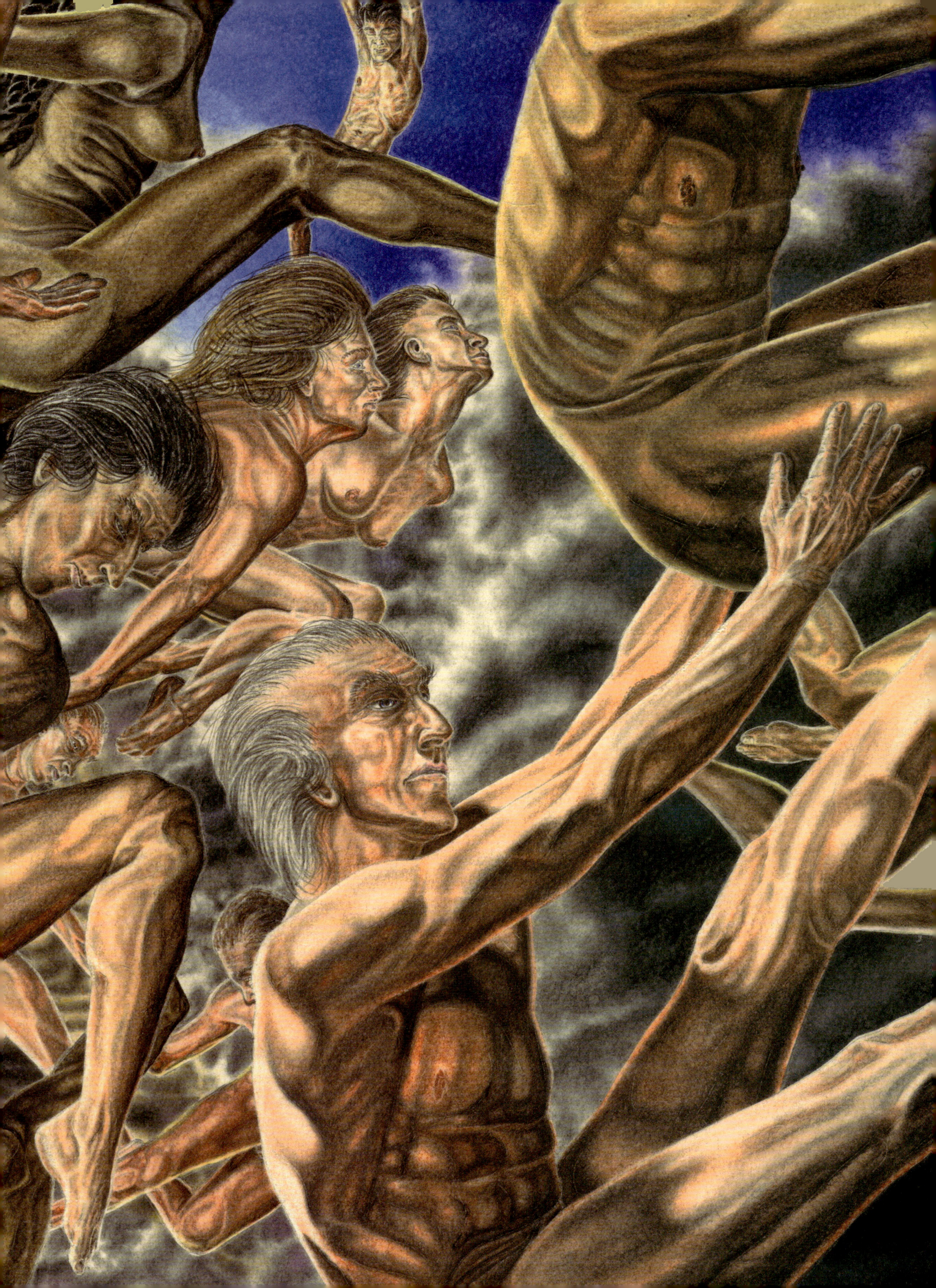

Upon this vast immediacy
a lunar brightness falls
upon the dark perfected earth.
The moon's lute-plucked clarity

cutting sharp all the shadow
like a glass bell. A clean strike
of silver singing the skin
ringing in the blood.

The slow slaying sun plays
upon a flinting of fire held
in the palm of the mind.
The world would change.

II. Before we made sense of ourselves
and dreamed the dream of reason
or knew enough to be wise
we knew enough to be.

We kept to the rhythm of daylight
and knew it would always return,
we kept to being and left
knowing in the long-to-be.

But there was something else.
The tree of knowledge had taken root
its canopy blacking the sun and moon.
Something else had come.

III. And now was the ordering of things;
the file, sort and placement
of kings and commoners
of uniforms and uniformities.

Rarities of worth, stacks
and stitching up time
the locked vaulting of MINE
the hoarding of golden stings.

The finger-ring of dying alone
the wills and forms of our past tense
complete with the number
of heartbeats left to beat.

Knowledge gave us a name
that we must live up to –
a history we will never
be allowed to forget.

An anxious tomorrow, a nervous
God empty of why and wherefore;
the universe and we passing away —
we only remember what leaves.

IV. Myth bubbles and squeaks
up through the ground
like mud through a thermal vent
or steam through a geyser –

crawls and leaks through
the vascular system of leaves,
a force of natural poetry
chlorophylling the air.

Analogies grow within and on
the roots and stems of rivers.
Similes salt up the oceans,
and like rime, always have.

The earth makes myth
the way it makes men.
The echo of us was here
before the voice it mocked.

We were bound to put
our ear to the ground
and hear our stories
and see the hear we saw.

On the blue-green pebble
of the world there were
always a few essential tales,
the great tree was one.

Not the last tree in Eden
the Tree of Knowledge,
but the lost tree –
the Tree of Life.

This tree rooted in old magic
locked in the spiral of renewal
and like the sparkling soot
of galaxies in space, eternal.

At this tree we recall
the delirium of desire;
the seed of this tree stays –
right to the end of us. ❦

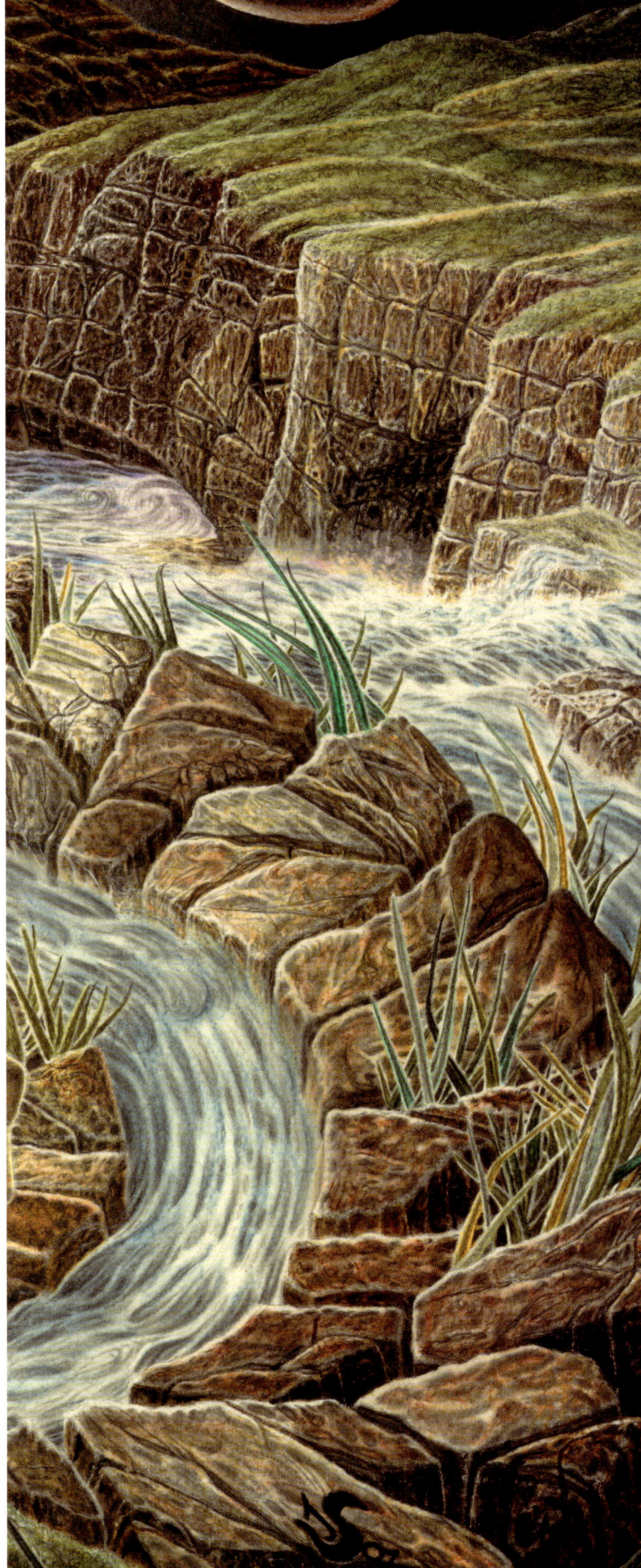

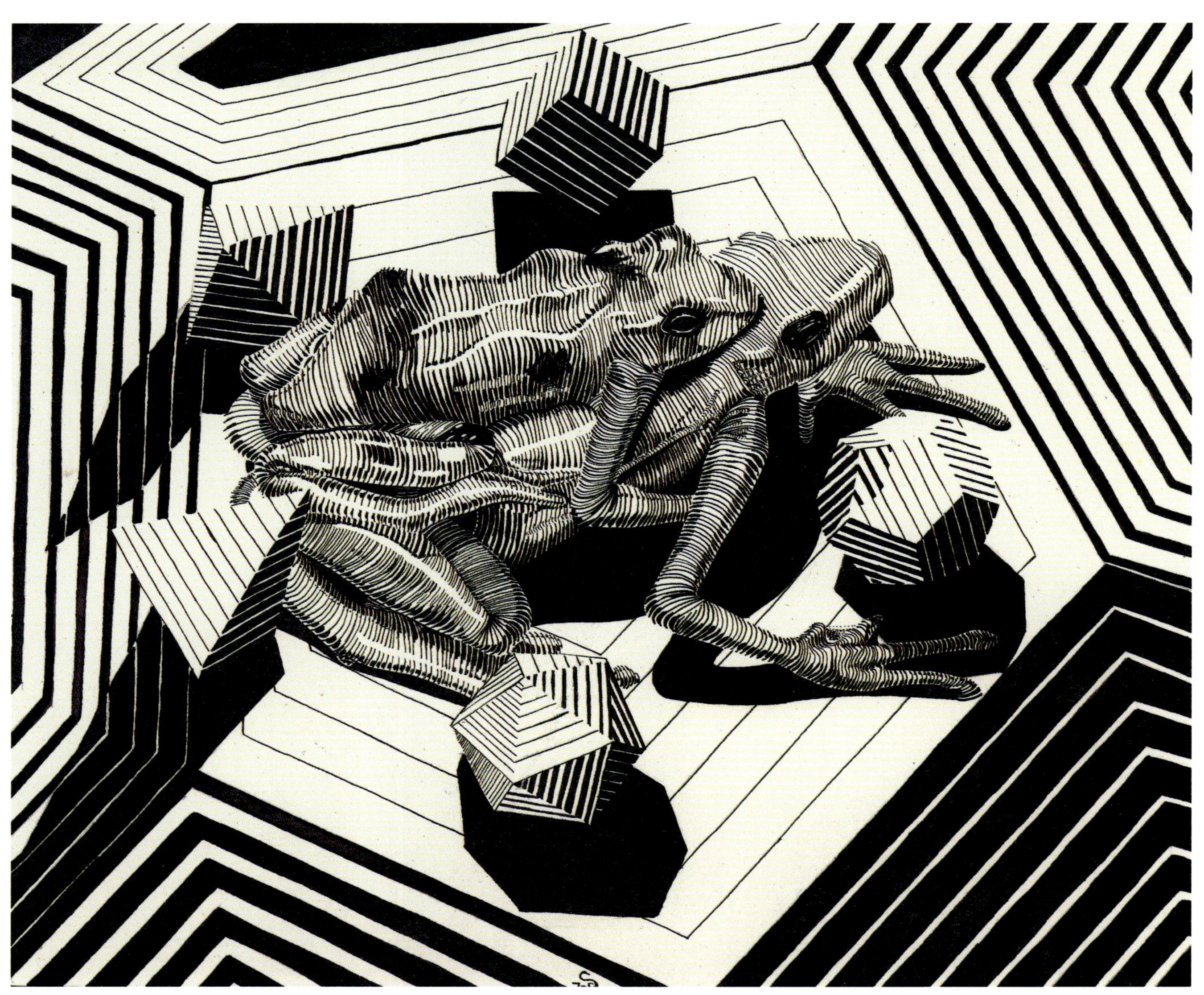

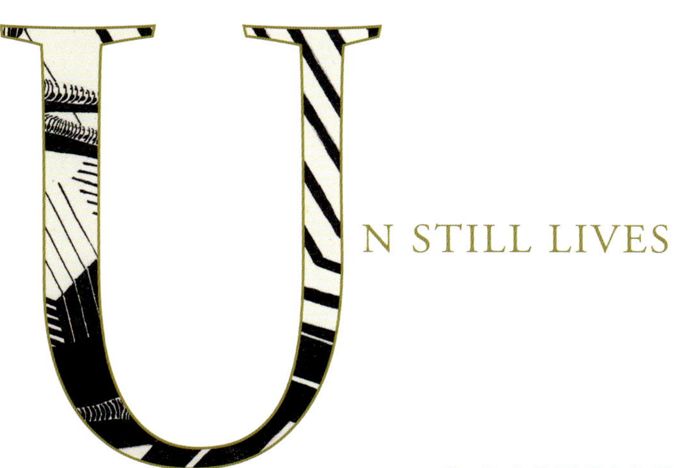

PART TWO

N STILL LIVES

CONFINEMENT

Upon the geometric stage of modern life
the awe full asymmetry of bodies
the awkward fragility of beating hearts.

Mother and child, surrounded and probably
menaced by the five platonic solids, don't they
truly menace us all the way to Hiroshima?

The moist life against the hard fact.
Done like a woodcut in homage to Escher,
with probably more existential dread.

There is a terrible fierce beauty
in perfect forms, the universal idea
and the oh so transitory we.

THE DUTCH Renaissance minted
the middle class. Ducats drawn
into the bloodstream of actual makers

of actual things, with a hunger
to prove their improvements
in that which mirrored their own rise.

They wanted the polish of art
but not inflated elegance. They lived
with small rooms, not imperial acreage.

Especially they wanted the things
that owned them painted to perfection.
Claesz, Von Aelst, Von Beijeren, Kalf,

invented still lives for unstill burghers;
crystal, fruit, lovely rooms, natural light
and perhaps a moral encomium or two.

Alas, centuries later all I can make are un-
still lives. I offer you Ripe where nothing
is at rest and everything expands.

Strawberries take over space contrapuntally,
play fugal variations on color, juice up and
quilt over the conventional taffy of glass.

In short, do all the things proper berries
are supposed to do. Only a dunce would expect
strawberries to wait patiently to be eaten.

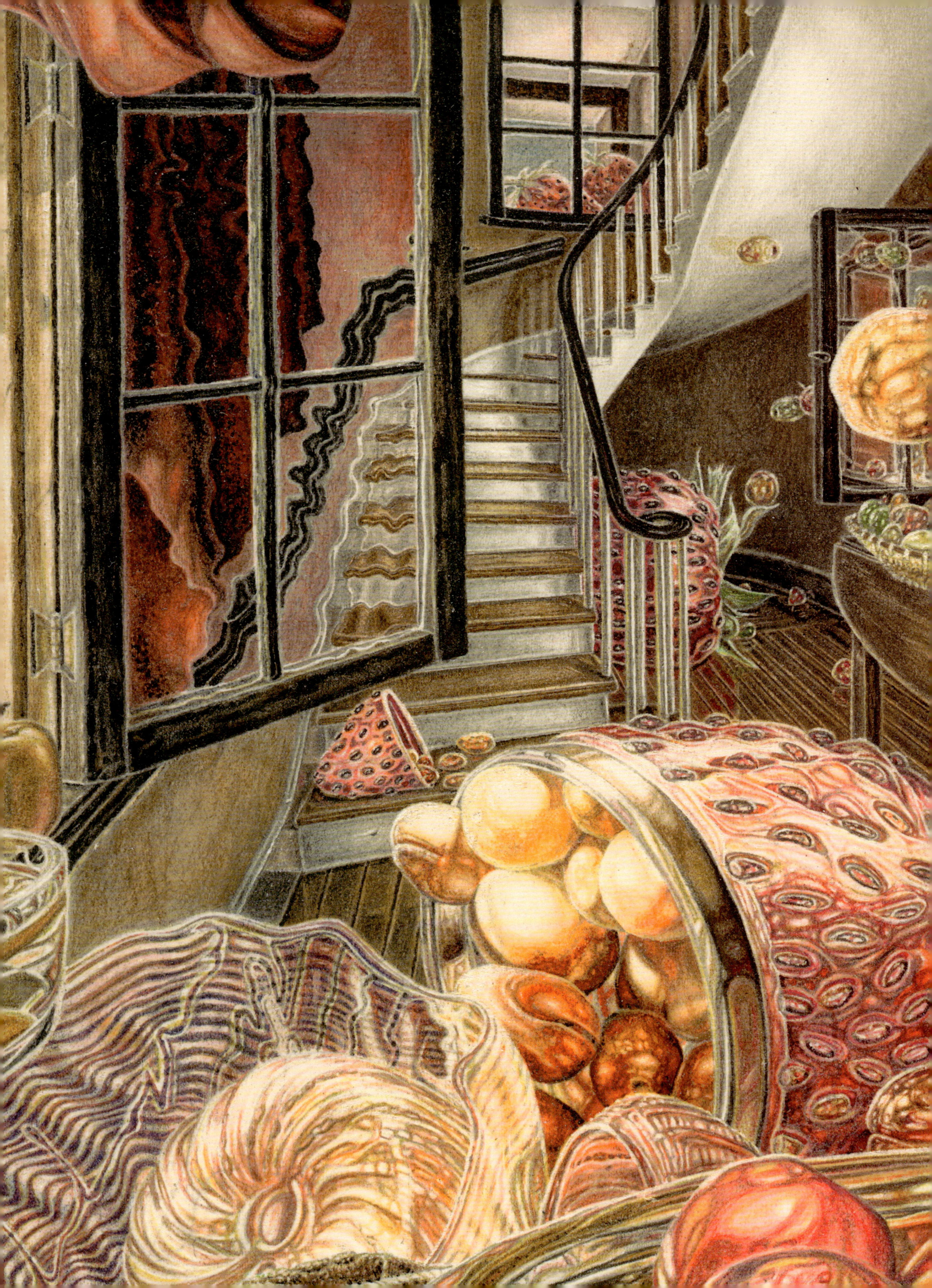

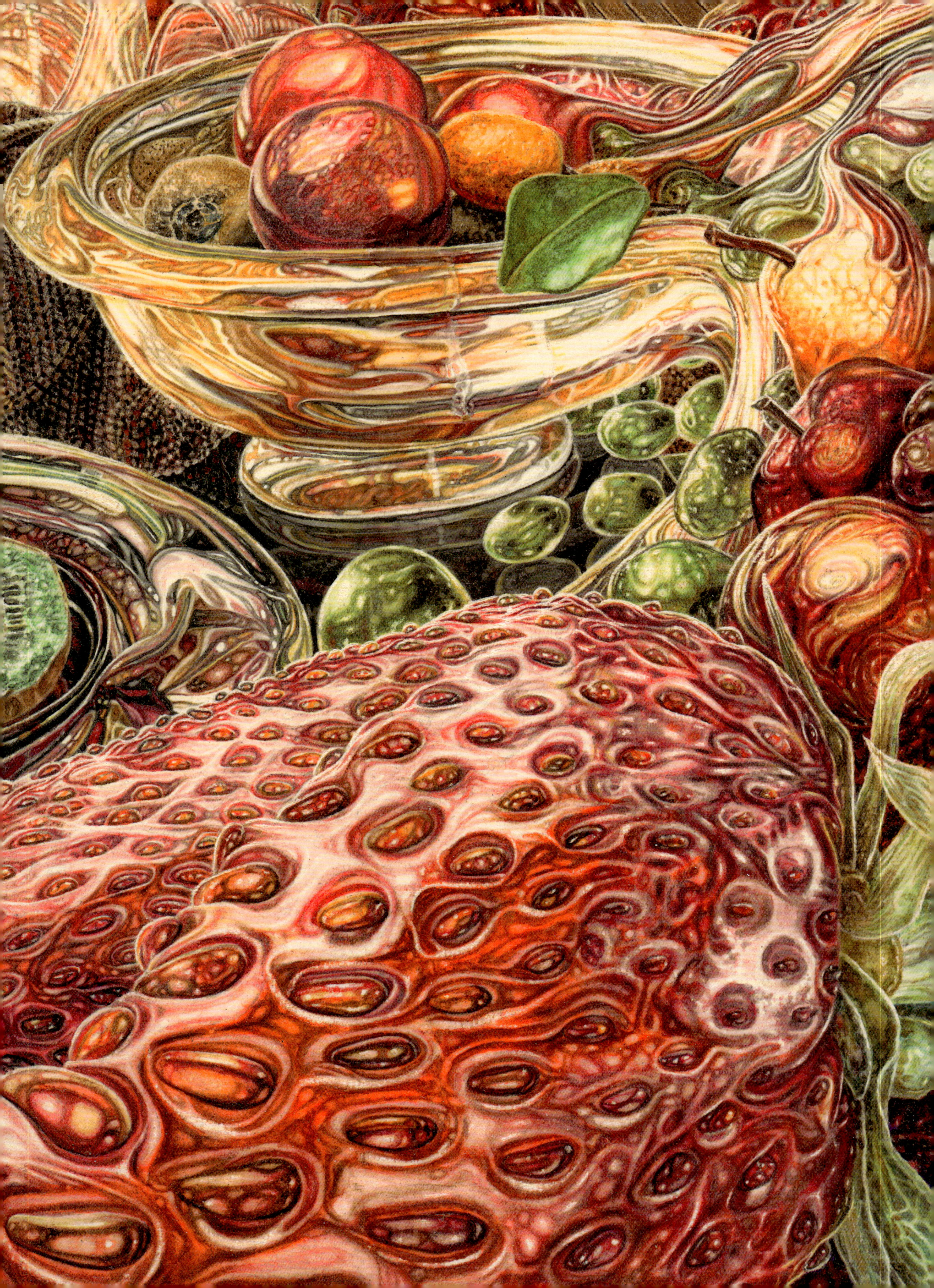

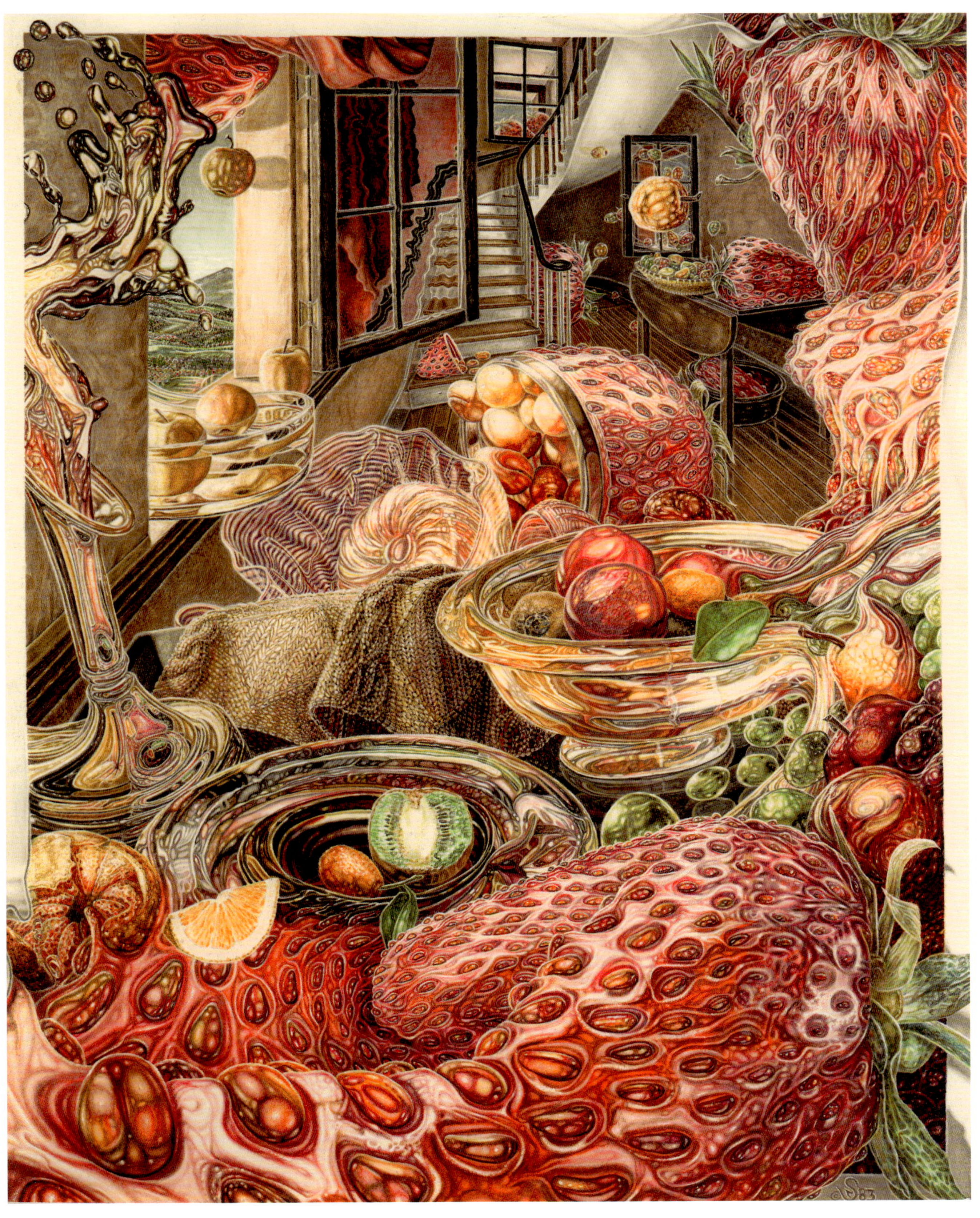

AT THE PERIPHERY of vision lives melt.
What vibrates there will steal
the very air from your lungs. You may
fear what you see if it is not you—

it is all you. Phosphenes giddy
in electrum brightness, metal forms,
plates and beakers bounce and spin sight,
in a clear bright light that is also you.

Apples magnetize with polished skin
like black pearls. The small metamorphosis
of every cleansed moment. A sphere
reflected in a dish mirroring a room—

mirroring a room that is not the same.
In the funhouse seen from the corner
of your eye, iridescence erases the
blackboard of still unmoving routine.

To be born again in magic, pilgrim,
you must learn to forget the trick.
When objects are gifts, remove
the wrapping and bow, read the card—

and receive the presence. The toy
in any joy is to receive the fresh
giggle of a new miracle. See how
we laugh and melt in the light.

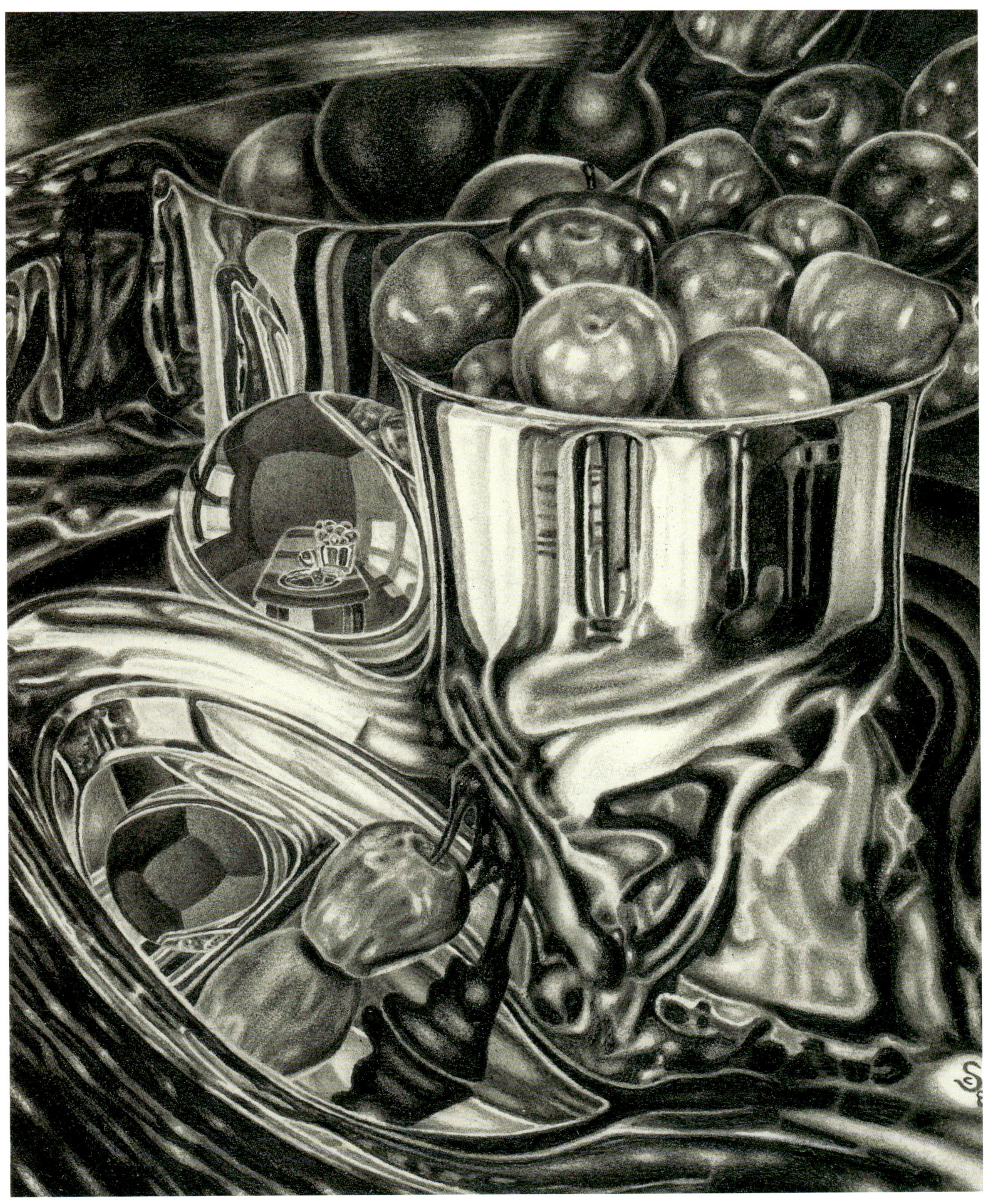

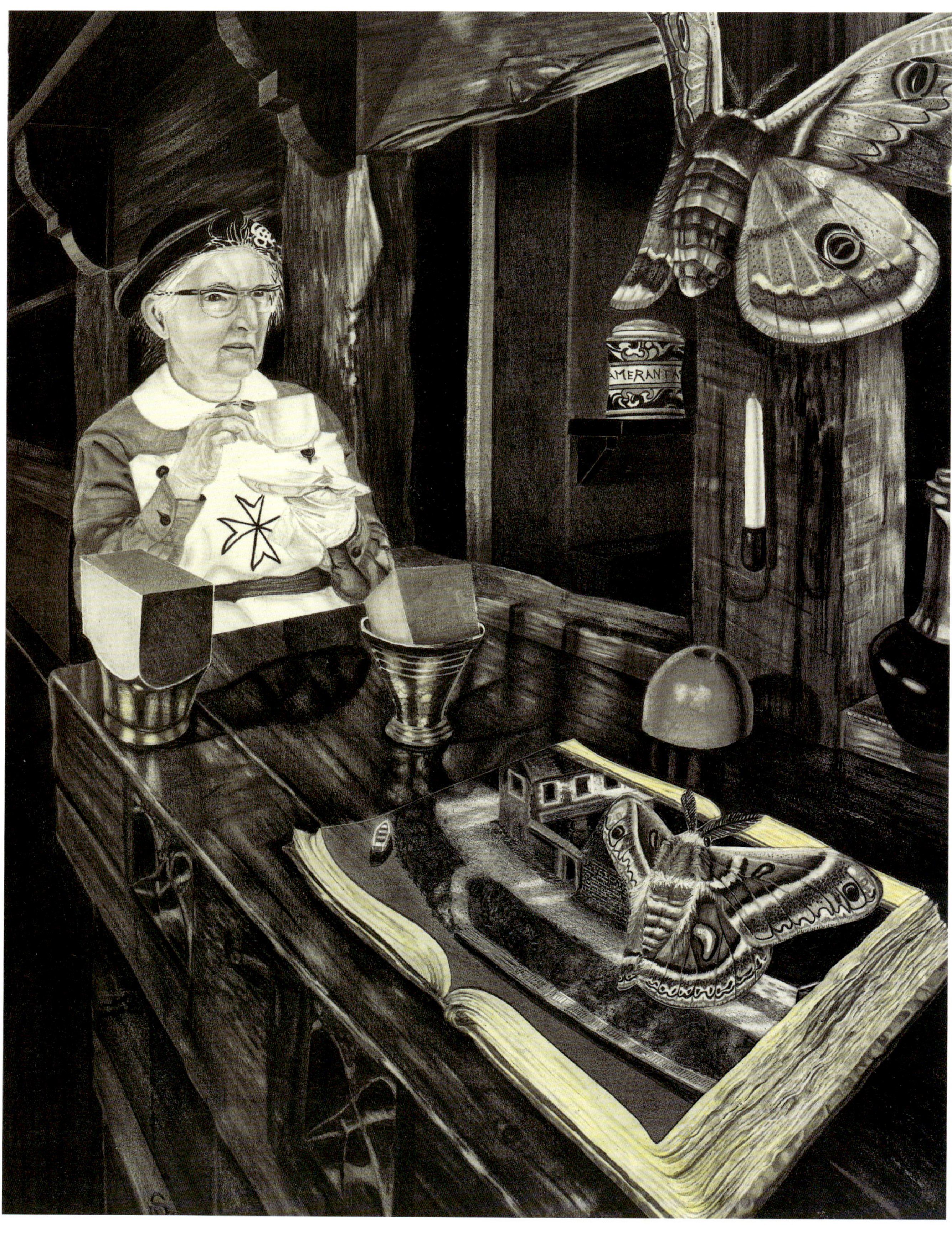

GREAT GRANDMOTHER Agnes had sipped
tea from a porcelain Bavarian cup
for seventy-five of her ninety-six years.

Thousands of repeated moments
in that mahogany-lined room,
where a warmth of wood and a comfort

of possessions had become so imprinted
in the afternoon ritual of tea, at some point
they ceased to have actual existence.

The extraordinary was not allowed
to be seen in Grammy's hermetic cave,
indeed couldn't be recognized or traced.

The family bible opens to a page of scripture
and the miracle it contains. The flight of fancy
is as without substance as thin air.

For Agnes the quiet lullaby of being an adult
lived her. Daydreams and the fiction
of childhood as distant as a star.

But the miraculous is without pity;
it spreads its mothen flutter back
to memory, even as Agnes sips.

If only delight were not so ephemeral
or sadness so precise and habit so without
movement. But when a splendid precision

etches the recall of a perfect day on the river
with that matchless first love, or even that first
singular, sip of tea drank in this room

lifetimes ago, then great grandmother sparkles
with a quiet light and seems to recall a silken
presence flying from her book into her sleep.

A PURITY of darkness drives the wind
as the first arc in a covenant of rain forms.
Air crawls through cloud corkscrewing.
Up rises Archimedes dust; conic sections
of force plow the earth; objects are free
of their long torturous debt to gravity.

The spiral in a chambered nautilus,
the helix of our most essential self,
the spiral sunflowering toward a star,
the hurricane's vast all hollowing eye.
Blackness is sucking the calm from light
spinning up the countryside, downing hope,

drowning its outer skirt in horizontal spray.
In its magnificent dervish, lives are lifted,
houses are stolen from their routine,
the Wicked Witch of Wind gaining power
cackles her hail across glass and the skin of trees.
Dorothy is here and Toto too.

What will you do when you are lifted?
Your dead will not be with you, morning
may never come and mourning is futile.
You are the center of your own eternity.
No one can save your unraveling face.
The mad carousel of joy and fear has come.

Uprisen in the vortex, past and future mix
in one grand and glorious circularity.
You are beside yourself and all your masks
have spun and sugared in the candied
floss of an endless emptied moment. You,
the carnival of the instant soul, sweetened, ready.

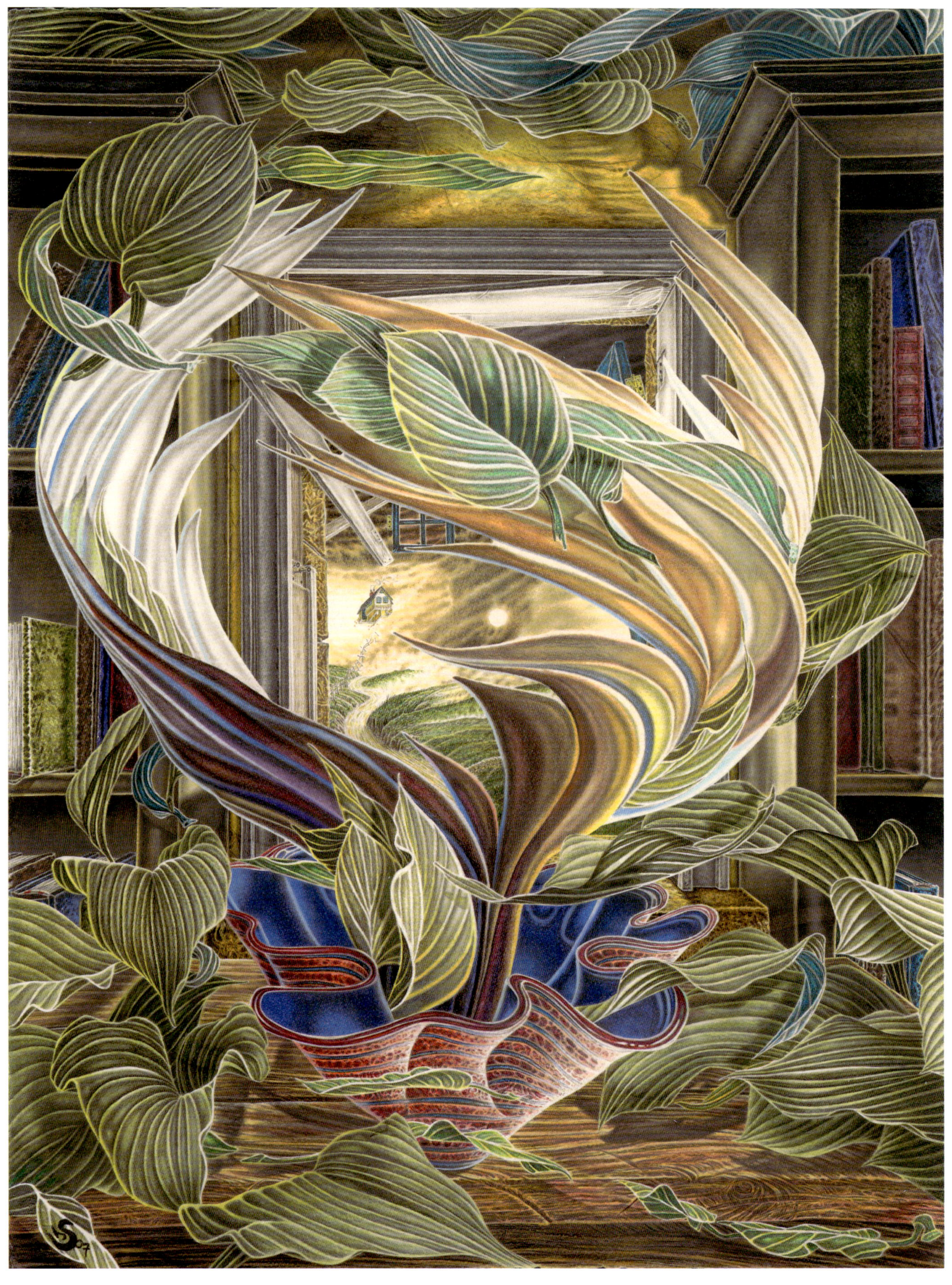

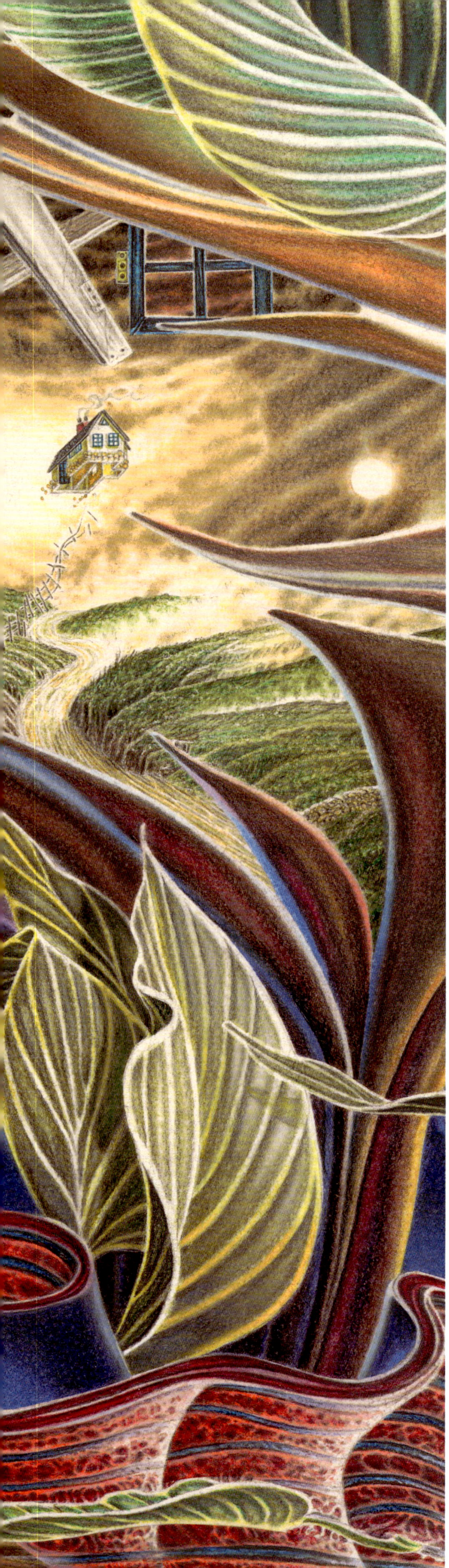

You may be set down without a blemish
or your molecules glittered across a dewy meadow.
Your bones may be found etched by sand,
you may chant your cantrips in the empty ground
or be driven through a trees enduring age. Anything
can happen to you now and everything will.

At last a surety of brightness opens the night
and the lost security of stillness reigns again.
Nothing can last and all things endure.
The house is on its foundation; butterflies hang
their parchment in the air like kites; sight
has failed but the vision has cleared.

The window out of yourself is the window in.
A huge weather knots its way beyond the frame
grasping the casements and splintering wood.
The window a permeable membrane between worlds
an open valve that bloods the earth and the eyes
for when you look out at storm, it will look back.

The room I'm in is also a-spin moving contraposto.
Yet safety seems always in rooms, lockable doors,
with windows that close and the whisper of books,
the silence that can be invented and preserved.
Everything rages but not in here. In a room
my identity does not become so emptied of me.

But we were not made for safety –
the maelstrom forms under our skin.
Leaves are flying, ceramic twists like taffy,
glass bowls drift into waves,
things shift and shatter, twist and settle
into a new life entirely changed.

When we think we are safe, a storm gives us
access to terror. All the primal mythogenesis
roaring through our teeth and bowels
conjuring up the entire friable, fragile
history of everything still stored
completely in our chest. Let it rain.

If I'm writing this or painting that
I'm not yet overtaken, I'm dancing out
redemption through my dread.
White death and black earth, white light
and black space, write life and deny
all the irksome and inevitable peace.

Let it storm and let it be gargantuan.
Take me up into a tumult of days, flay me
in cold green springs, goose-bump my comfort,
make me sting, make me sing in alpenglow.
At the top of the world, let me fall again
and again, but not be one of the fallen. 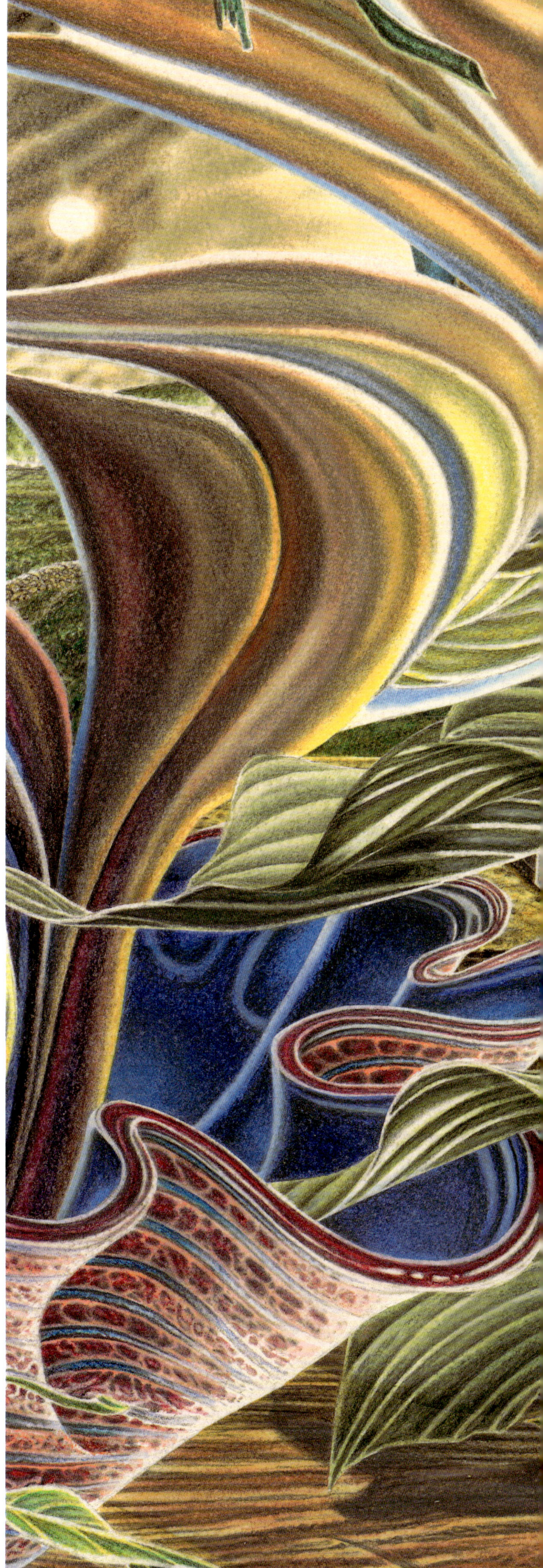

ANIMATE

I. WE HAVE ALWAYS lived
singly in many worlds;
the asymmetrical and
        messy complexity of life,
        the unyielding hard
        geometry of the workaday,
and the mediation of both
through the inference of art.

II. Sentience defies the gravity of death.
Art defines the transience of time.
Matter weeps from the blind eye of space.

III. We have no option
but to defy ourselves.
Where we have come from
is not where we are
nor where we are going.
The only choice
we have to make is to be alive.
The only recognition we need
is our whole name
written out and wholly made.

IV. Geometry forms the base
and the invading disruption
in a polished silver bowl,
swarmed by what could be
anti-gravitational grapes, be-
dewed. The visual opulence
of burnished metal, wet fruit,
and dry pyritohedrons may show
or at least suggest the essential
lovely incompatibility of worlds.
Juxtaposition is where the jazz is.

V. Become a grape with me
in the punch drunk
bowl of cherries
life is just a.

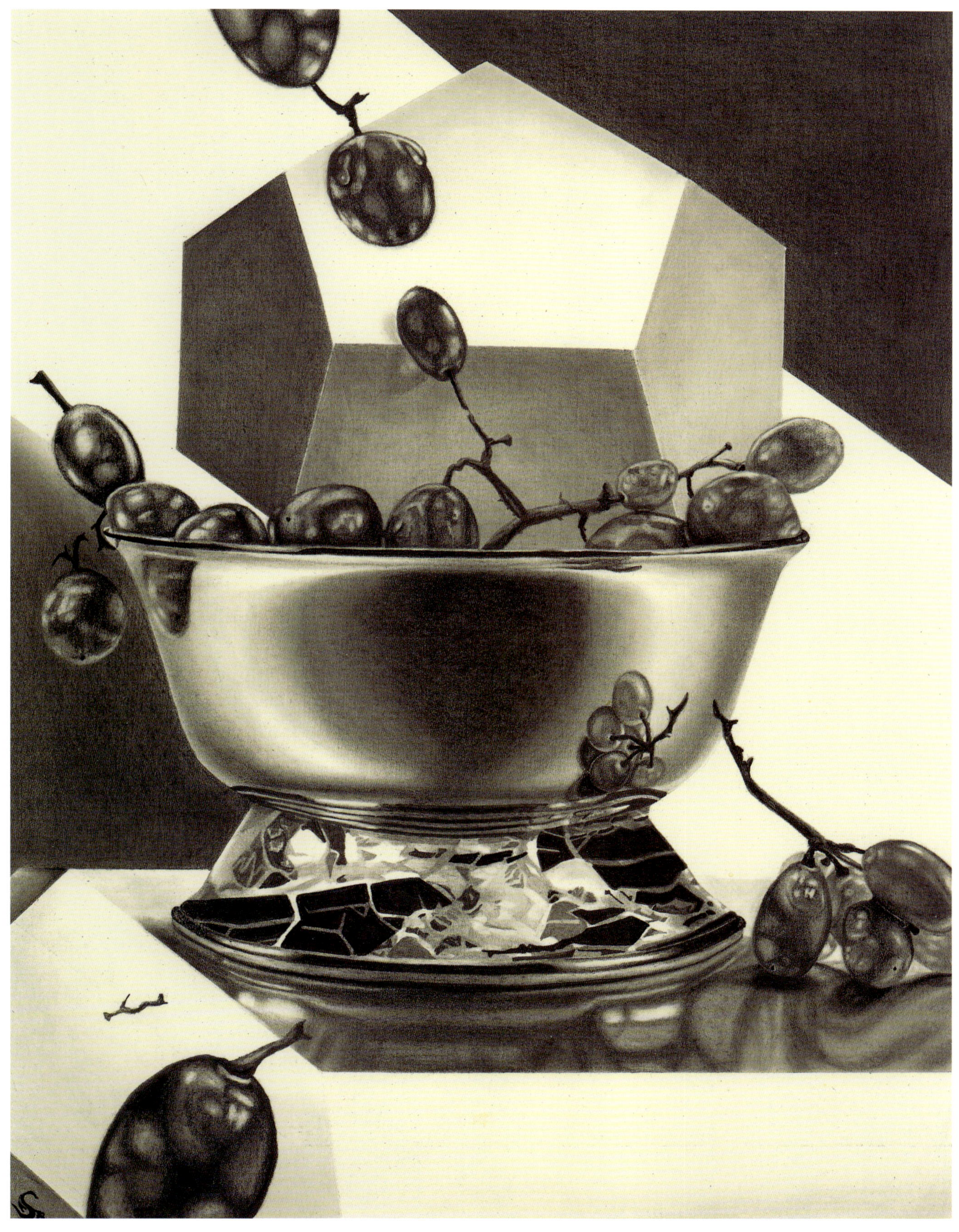

HE CLUTCHES them to her breast like a child.
She holds them in her hand like a tool.
They static her hair as they nimbus her head.

Dodecahedrons, octagons, cubic tetra-
hexahedrons, cubes, the monoclinic
and the twinned, the doubly terminated

and forms so complex their terrifying
dark gravity would disturb the hard -
earned lightness of a saint.

The young girl winsome with possibility
is in love with black magic.
She knows these tricks will work;

there are an unlimited number
of rabbits in all these black hats;
she abracadabras even in her sleep.

Every philter known and opened,
caressed and loved will reveal
a small hint of the infinite.

The narcotic of knowledge
has always been the most addictive;
remember the young girl in her garden.

Necromancy changes us forever;
there is no return to innocence;
 a spell of power is a grammar in time.

Every age develops its playthings.
We come to love the toys we are given
and in their dark symmetry there is

true beauty, as well as, a real terror.
She stands in her young perfection;
forever is in play around her, CHOOSE.

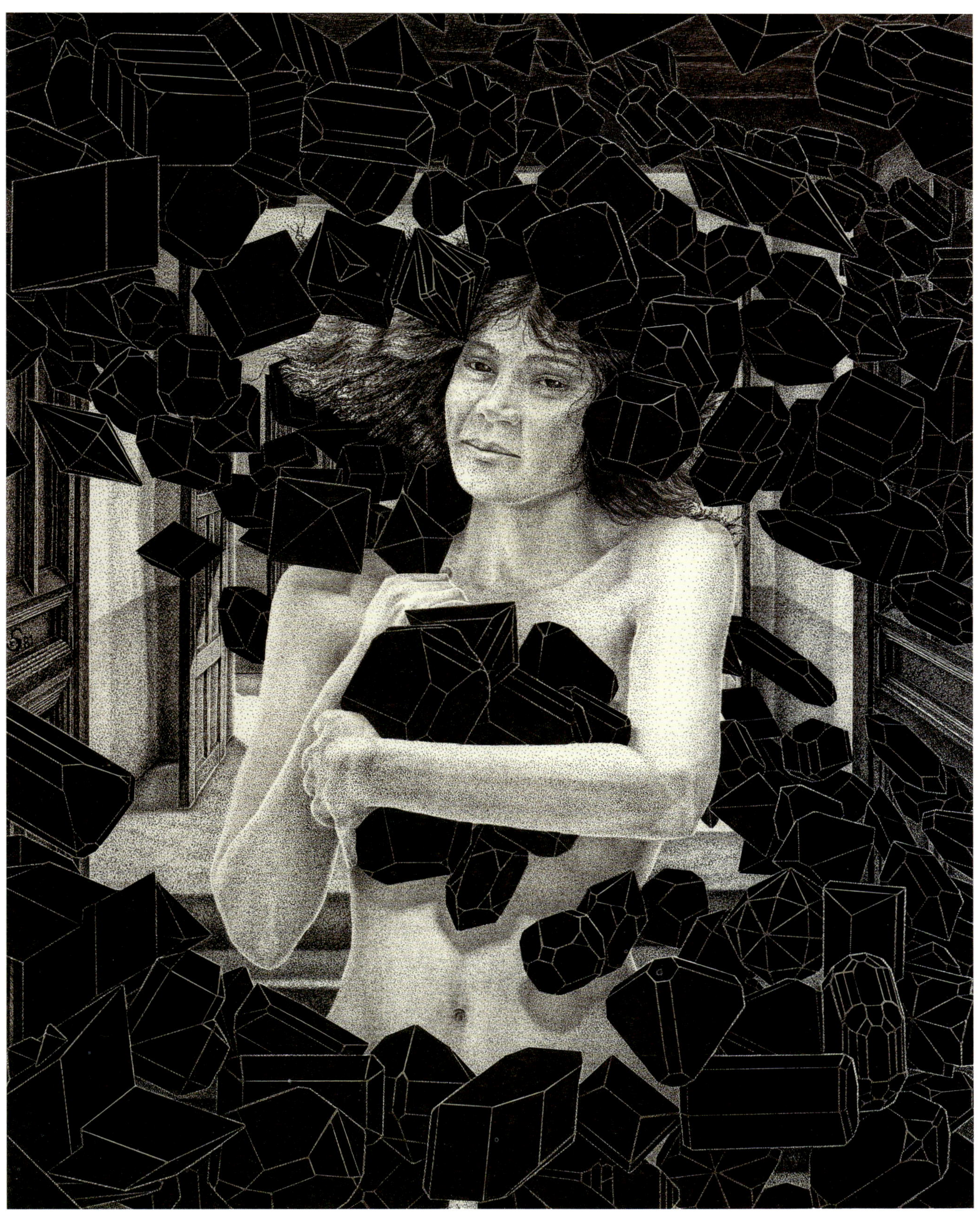

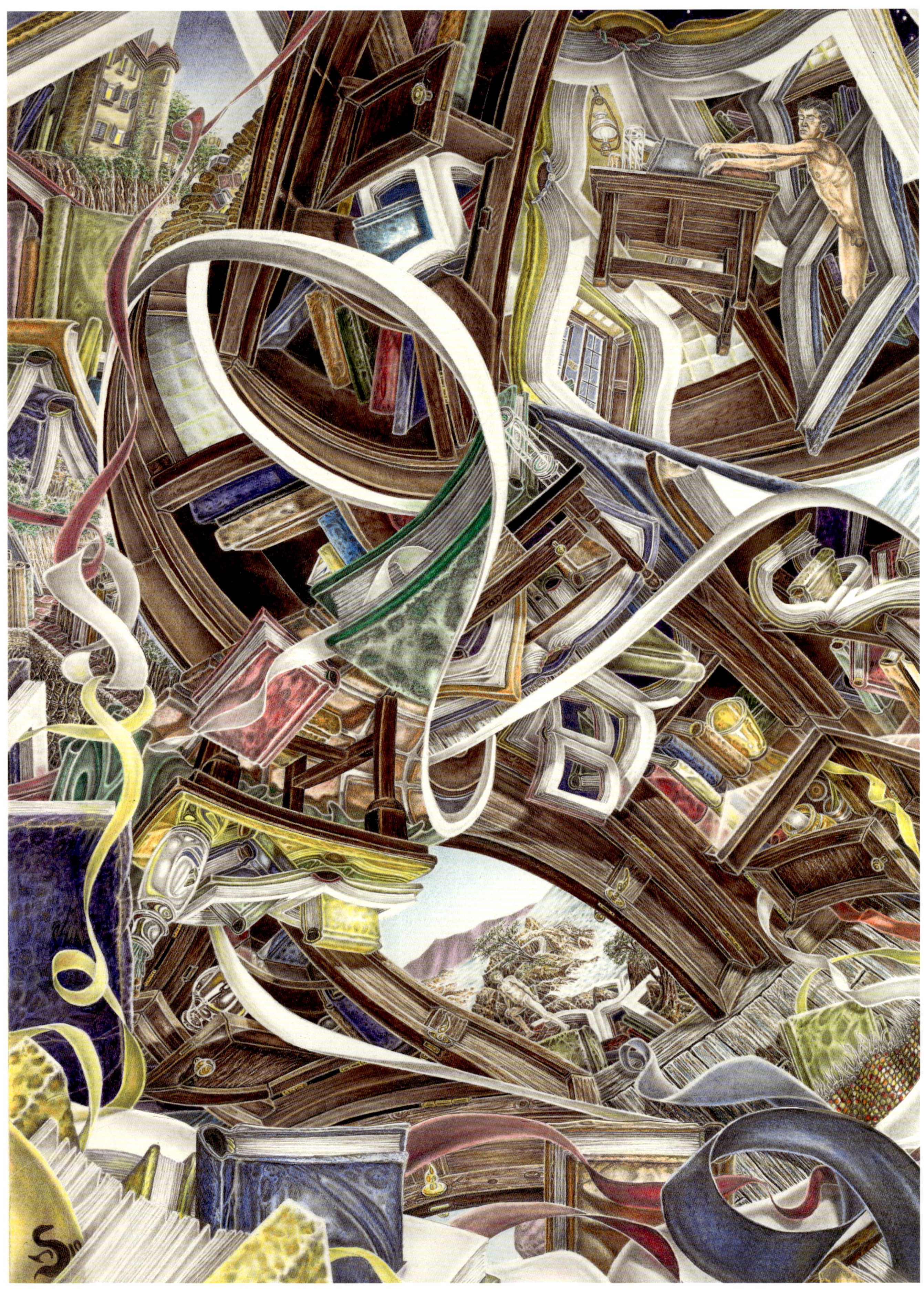

THE LIBRARY
AT BABYLON

S A CHILD I had a Fort Knox
of Little Golden Books
stacked like ingots
in the oversize closet I slept in.

The bottling works below rattled
of Orange Crush and Ginger Ale,
its halls of glass like a cascade of ice
but warm in my bed my books kept me safe.

Books like people
are never singular, they are plural.
Open any volume
and more volume will emerge.

Reference after reference opening out,
opening in distorting space,
comporting lives
to sit still and travel.

Libraries like mobius strips
are one surface that keeps
coming back to itself;
among books nothing ends.

Conventional reality
can only be maintained
if the books are hidden
and are never opened.

Sorcerers would lock their books;
the librams of lovers were
singed around the edges;
botany texts barked till closed,

histories could not help
converting to portmanteaus;
every kind of book
has a silent language

and libraries must
never be entered at night —
their whispering
can drive one mad.

In the scriptoriums
of the great monasteries
where the books
were illuminated, the words

of many of the murmuring dead
must not be read. The words
dance in power and when finished
must be hidden in the dark fissures

of the library's mind. The librarian
is priest and jailer. Books must never
be allowed to escape because
as everyone knows, they fly—

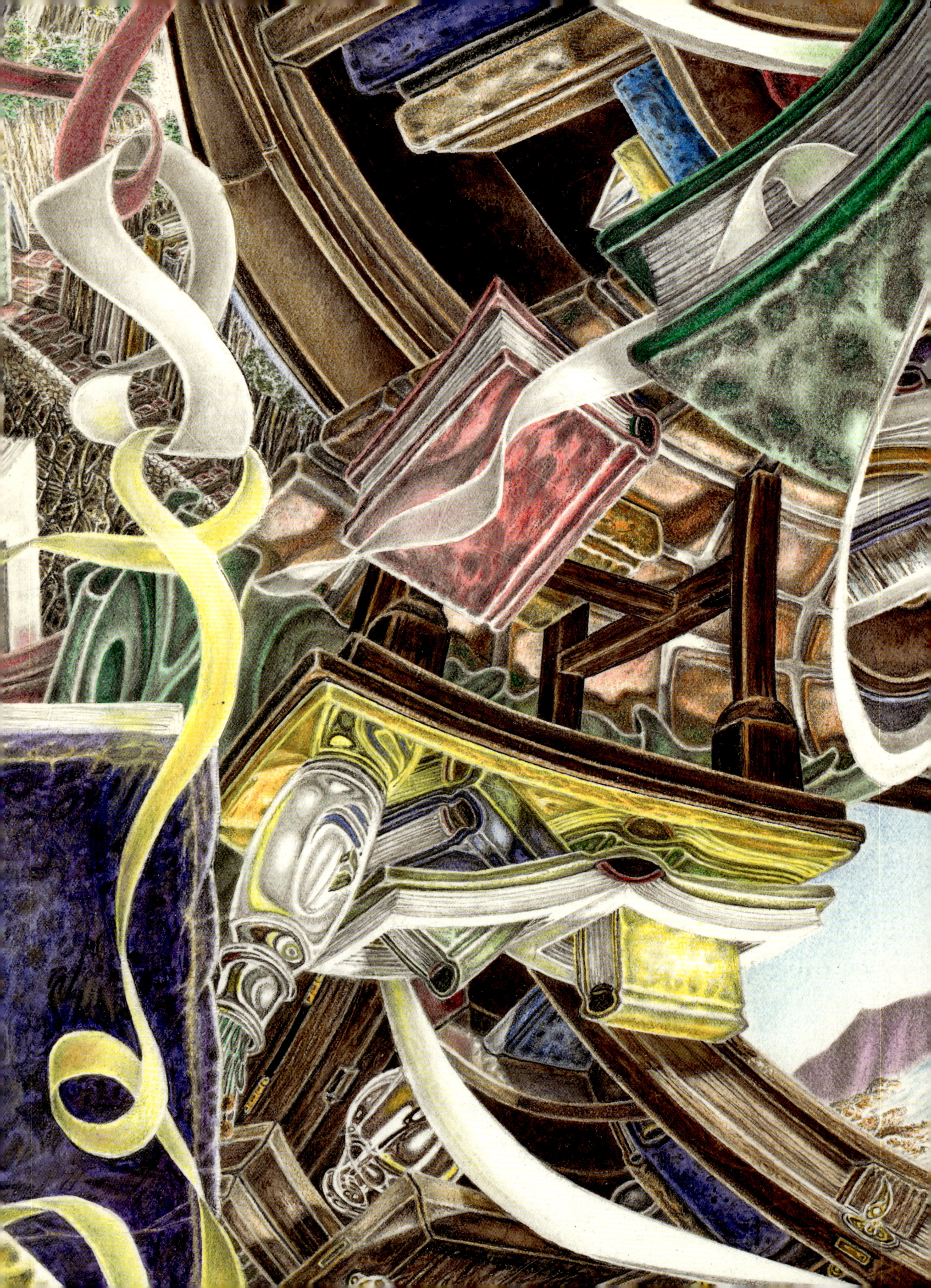

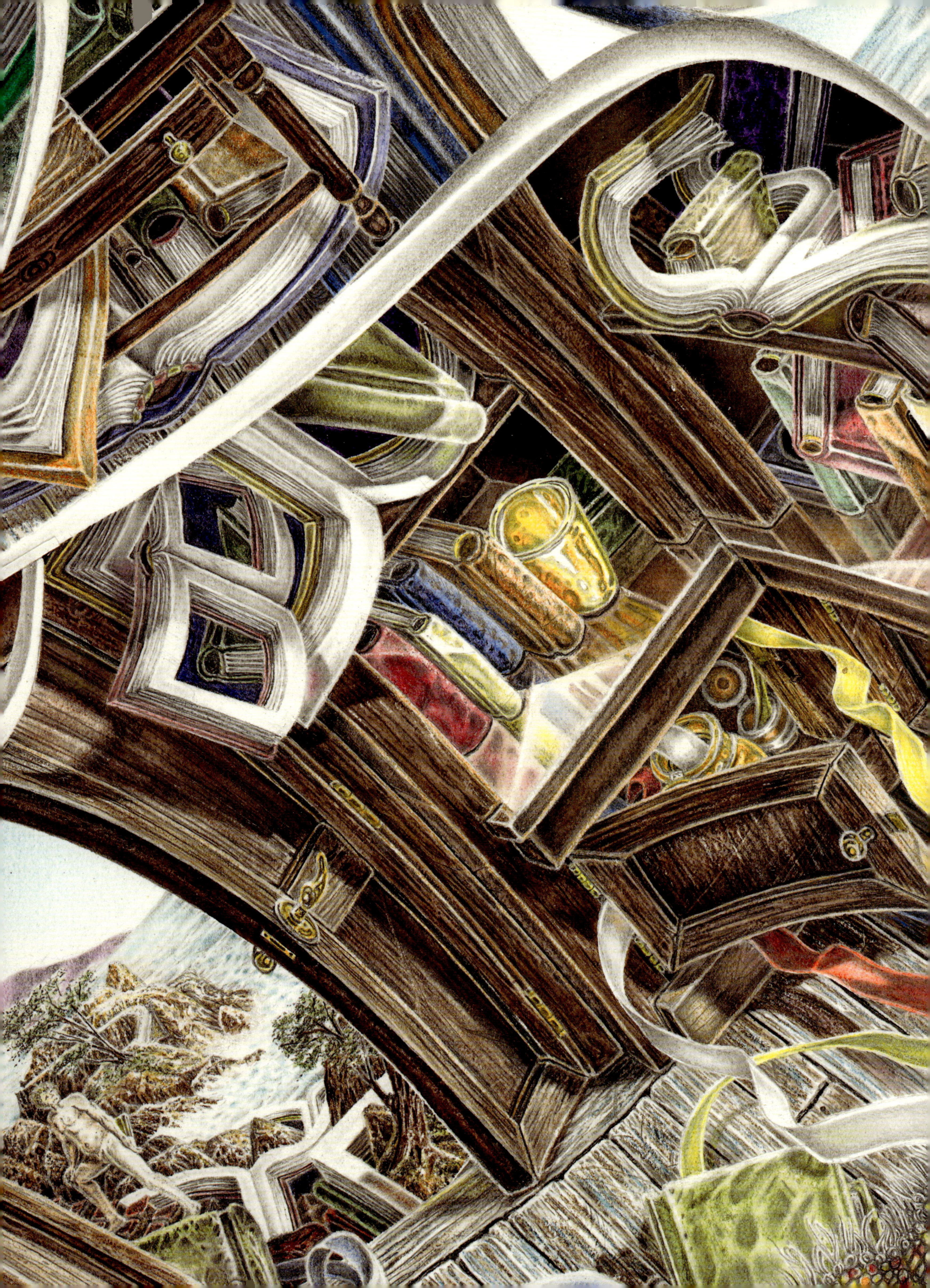

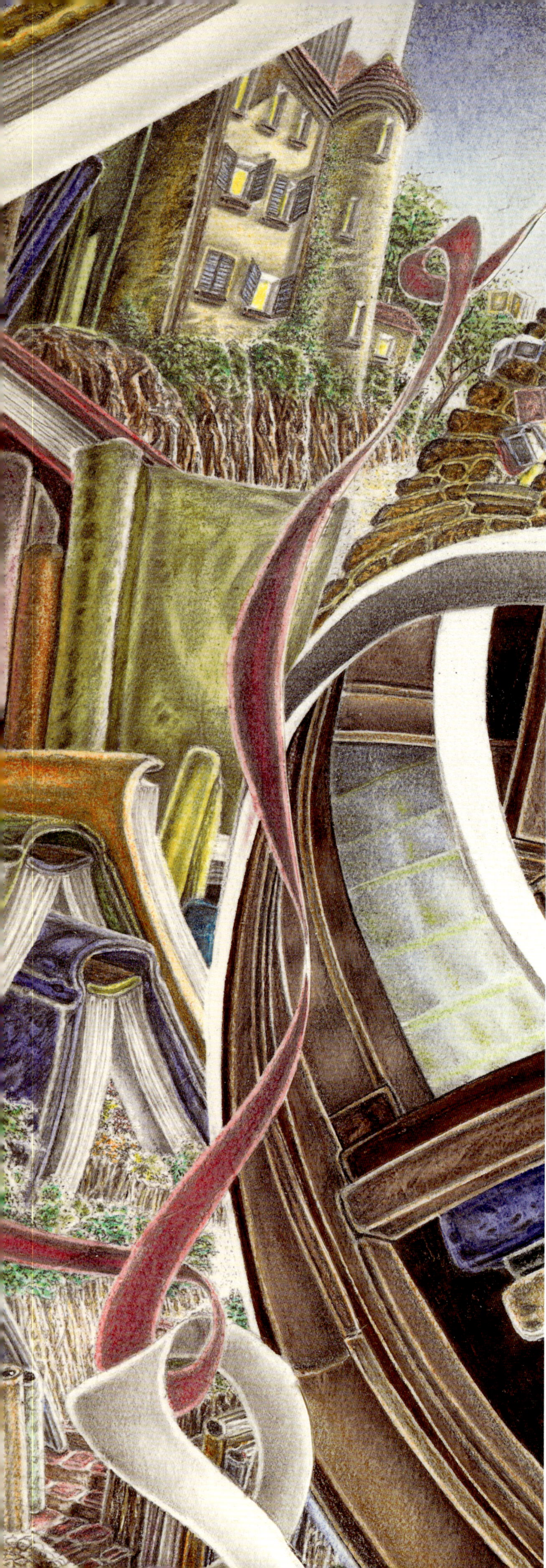

reinvent space and feed on each other.
Like the merciless predators they are,
as we wait to be consumed by them,
from time to time they will spit us out;

as if we are indigestible wracks
of bone, who mar their pages with
our garrulous hands and our
lack of gratitude.

Yet they need us, for without them
resurrection is a metaphor
and without us
death is final.

As a boy, Emerson spoke to me
in the avuncular charm
of perfected tweediness;
I never doubted

I was hearing him speak.
And if you're reading this… well
so what is the post-Einsteinian
sanctuary of books?

Books of course
are not information —
they are informed souls
and live beyond mere facts.

To grow up without their
learned ways and tactile charm
is to be friendless
in the world of knowledge.

Like the Book Of Kells
their illuminated past
is the humanity
of our unilluminated future. §

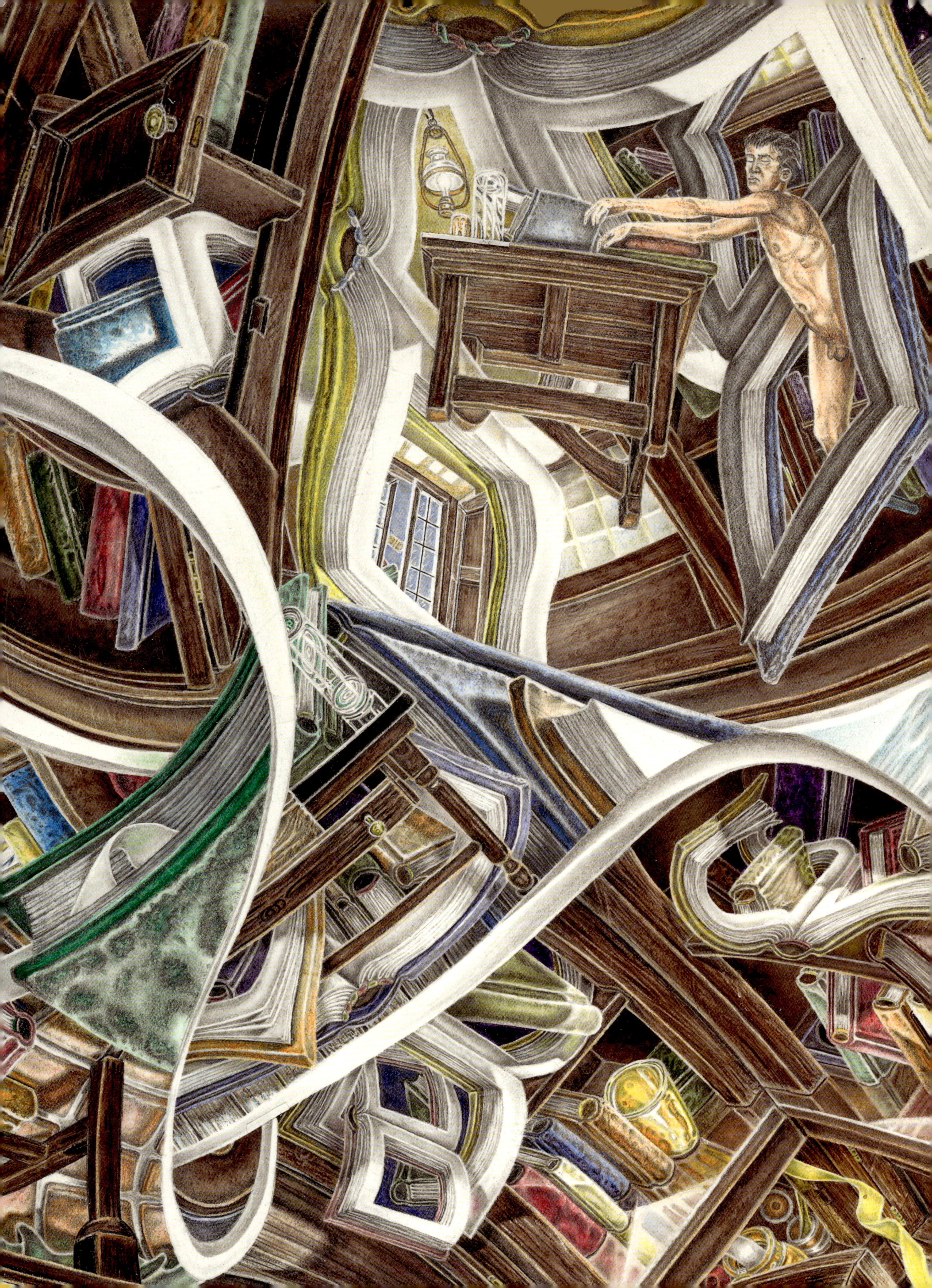

H

OW MUCH of any work of art is jazz.
You search for that perfect Gershwin tune
and happily begin the improvisation.
How much of any work of art is fugal.

That motif appears, and like Bach
the Goldberg Variations flow out effortlessly.
Metamorphosis insists! Wood
to window frame and back again, porcelain

to tablecloth and the roundelay reverses;
fruit is bronzed and patinated; bread
is leavened and marbled and as Heraclitus
murmured, all things change, flow.

Stillness is the hope of old men
that pray the stillness of death
doesn't find them too soon.
Of course even death isn't still.

In a world of cyclotrons, cloning,
computers and endless entertainment
only what moves can be seen at all.
However even if things hop and jitter

if the formal balance is just right
as things blur and caracole, careen
and dervish there will seem to be
the illusion of a quiet center.

Don't give up your meditation;
be as unmoved as you like —
just remember leaves dance and cells divide. . .

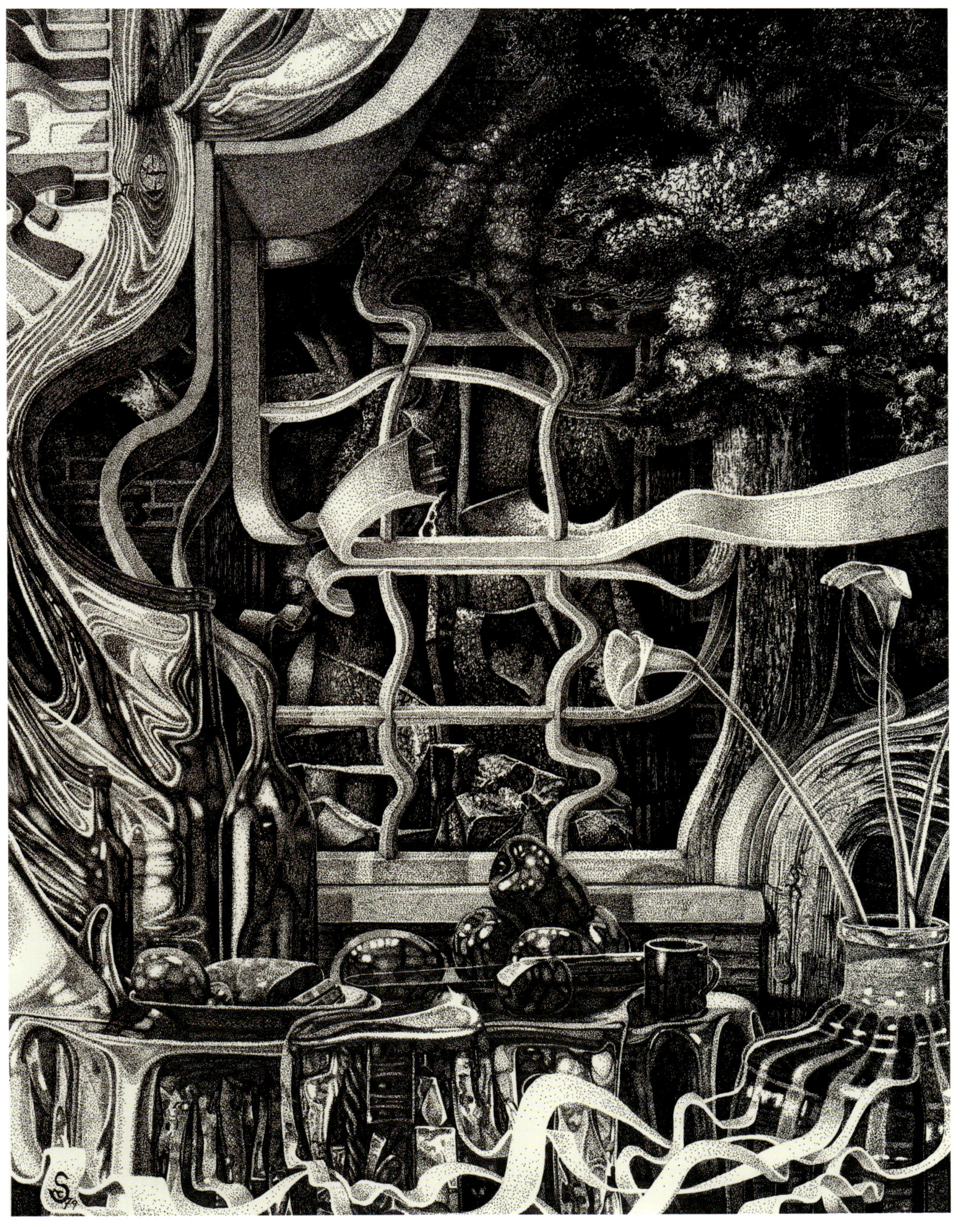

I THE LIP sticks true blue just as fudgsicles
used to when the shiver we were
wore heavy treads into Jensen's Ice Cream Store.

The eye sings as Jensen flings cosmetic scoops
of gamboled green, pistachio, oh the Click
of Butter Brickle, the Brick of Rocky Road,

the Lick of Lemon tarting and jawbreakering
up and away, a charade into puberty changing
nothing save perhaps the size of appetite.

I was sweetened quite young in a taffy stretch
of sallow manhood. Amid the amazements
of play, I attended, in my mind, Carnival

and Mardi Gras, lived the Circus, concealed
in powders and paint for pinking my ashen cheek.
I learned to wear ceremonial masks and the dye

berried my skin in a ritual stain, like a deeply
tribal lipstick smear. I was prepared for make-
believe, I could make up my face from scratch.

II. In the mirror the mask of our classically
aging faces wrinkle to strong Doric Columns
that hold up the temple of our identity.

Under the rub of rouge and herbal smoke
the balms of Gilead giddy-up across
our canyons of flesh. Young, for a brief bruise

and when and then the embalmer arrives
and brushes our cheek one last time
sweet mourning comes upon us as sunset.

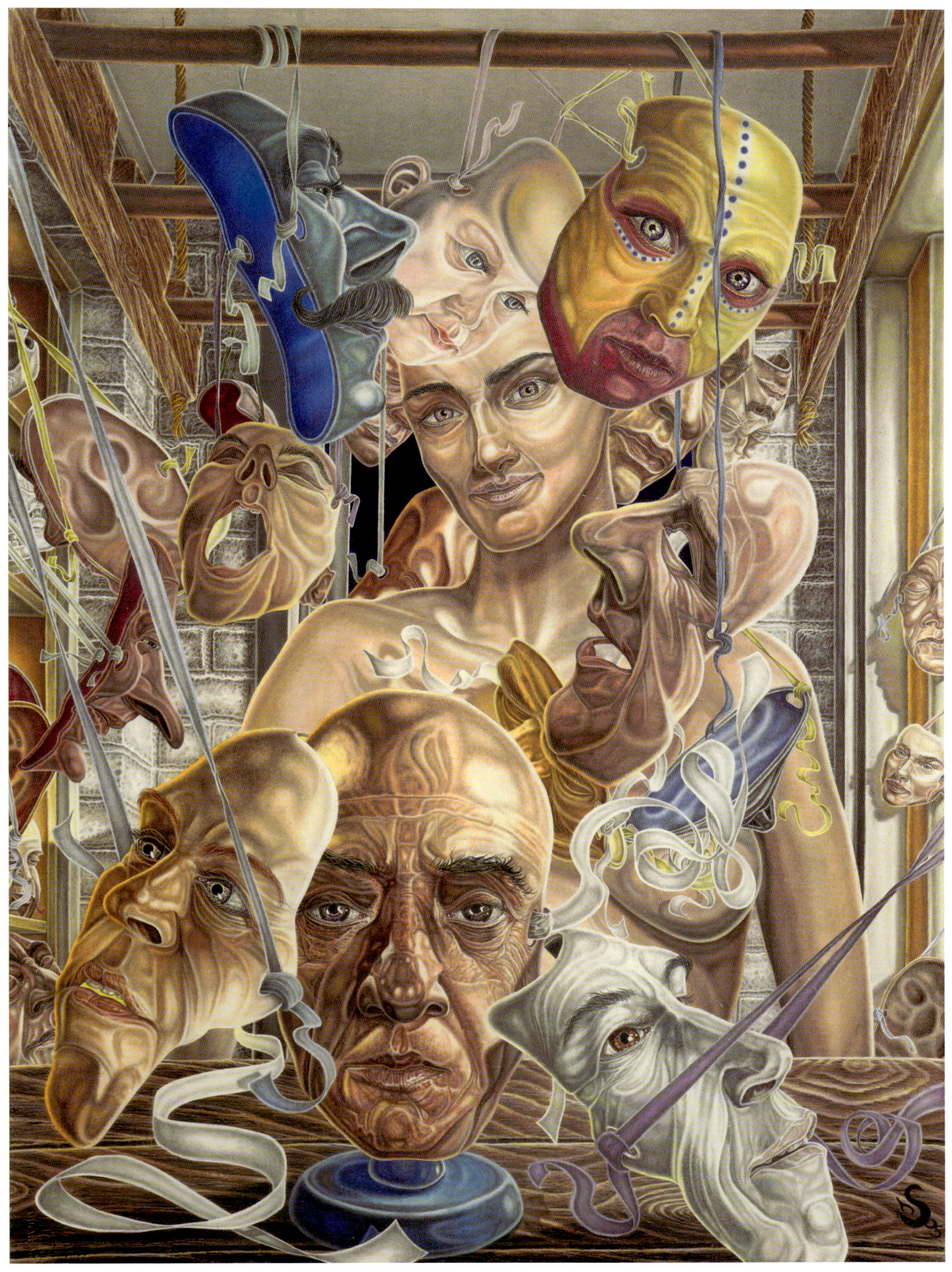

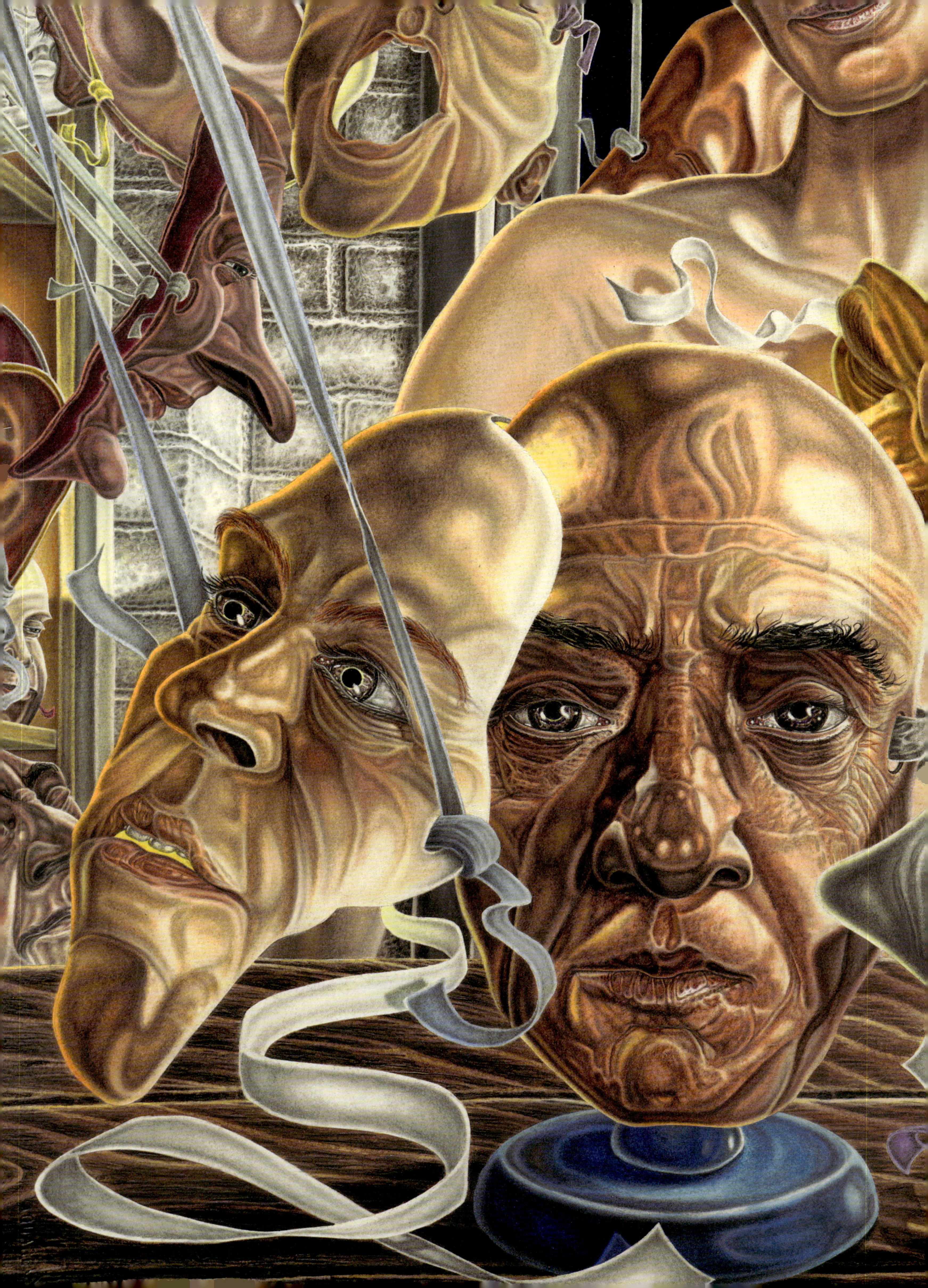

III. Changing disguises with each millennia
     dread-locked in the fatigue of everlasting life
     Jehovah sits powdering up a shiny nose.

     In a boudoir of starlight, polishing his teeth
     God gazes in the mirror of the flattering moon
     with the girlish crush of a virgin at prom.

     Awaiting the blind date of our obedience,
     forgetting we stood Him up in a garden
     fumbling one apple into crow's-feet.

     One pair out of Eden and into heavy labor,
     yoked to the moment, we learn to mask ourselves
     in God, just as God masks Himself in eternity.

     Masquerade at every level, into or out of costume,
     in progress or regress, the sincere guess of belief
     evokes the harlequin, the rest is theatre.

IV. I've been addressing and redressing myself
     making up my whole life from many parts.
     I am plural and piecemeal from the past.

     I am a Sumerian bald as a fresh egg.
     An Egyptian blacking my eye with kohl.
     A cannibal boiling heads in cinnabar.

     An Aborigine white-chalked, mudding my arm.
     Again the Bantu, scarring breasts in ringlets of blood.
     Perhaps a bone-thin starlet with store-bought boobs.

     I am the paint of war and wantonness,
     the hag behind the spell, the witch of the word,
     the mask behind the mask behind…

     The make-do and doing under the artist's brush.
     How I hunger to wake up free of persona,
     made up as the whole of creation. ʂ

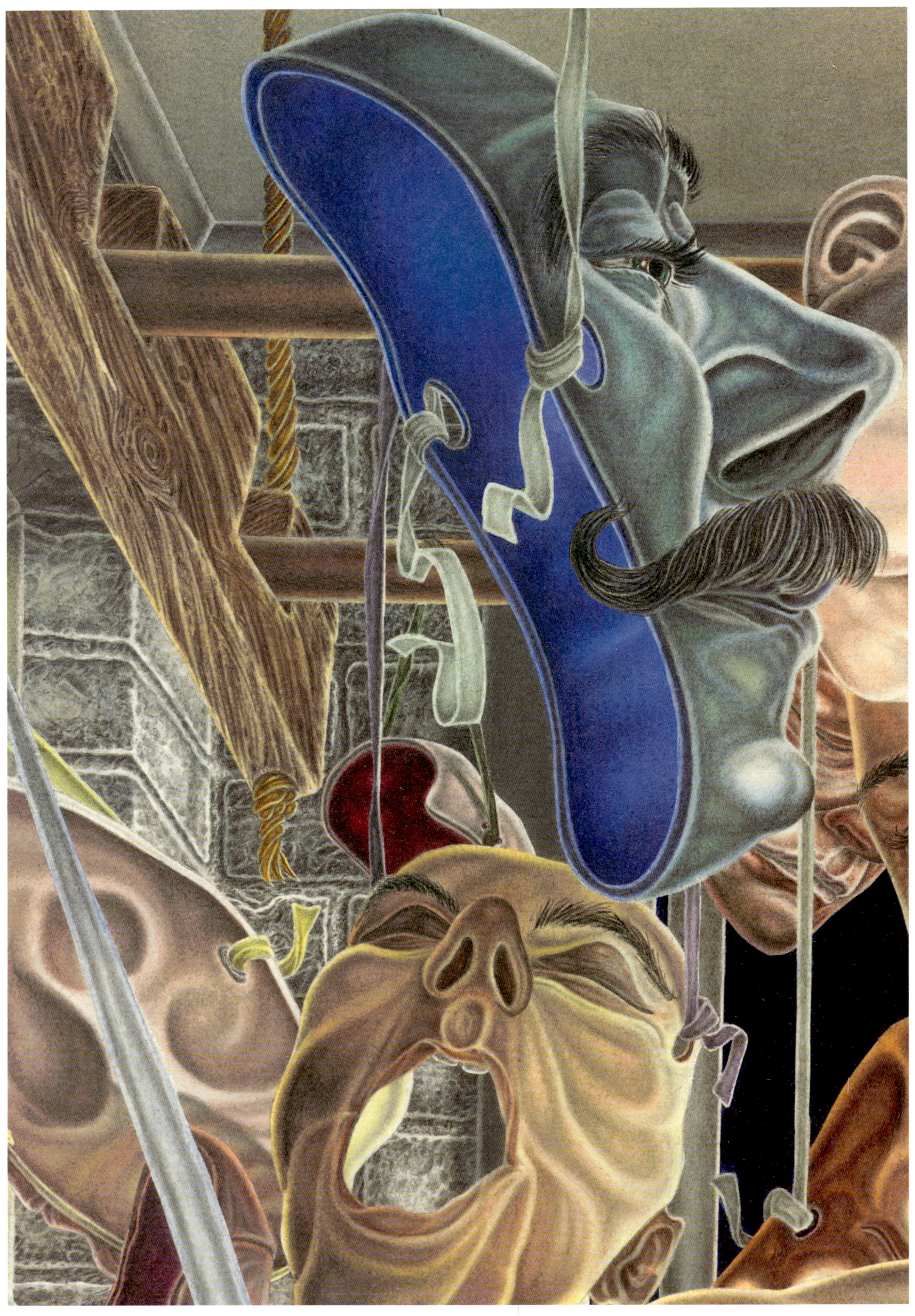

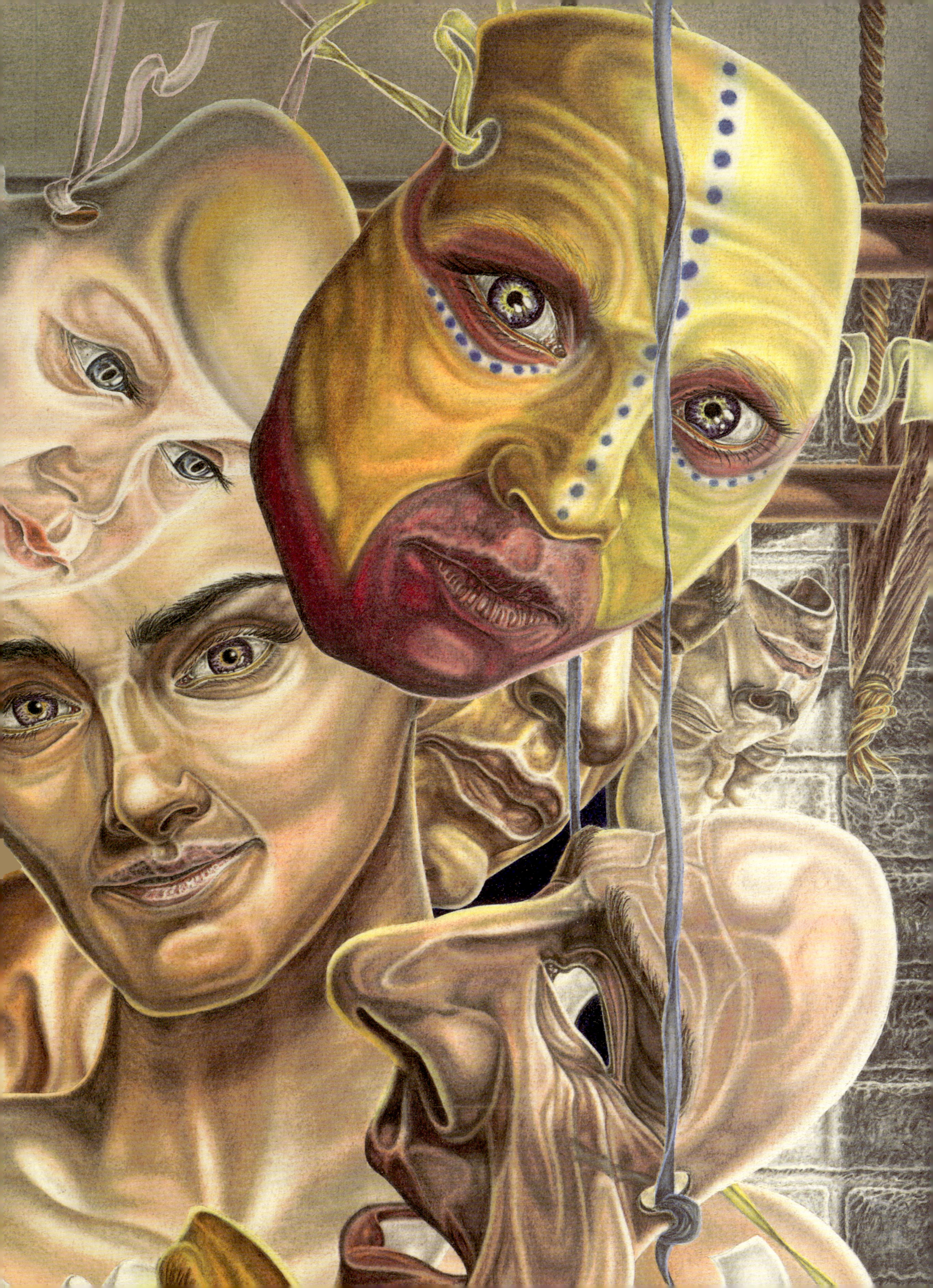

O F COURSE, smoke is the perfect
fractal environment; within its
confines, anything is possible.

No distortion of reality is out of
bounds, but curiously the distortions
of reality are not permitted.

In vain, you will search
for the small comforts
and conformities of the symmetrical.

Our bilaterally balanced bodies hunger
for order in nature, and desperately
try to manage it in ourselves.

A twirling breath of air,
a sneeze-up or a cough
makes a plume of smoke Rococo.

Tunnels, spins, spider-web's lace-
a circumlocutional net across
what we think an object should be.

When a forest isn't burning or a city
being razed or a gas oven being lit
or an argument being fogged,

smoke is a fey-thin something
we tend to ignore; it's after all
so dreadfully hard to look at.

Our mind easily assembles the objects
around us; catalogues, uses, defines,
hierarchically shames to obedience,

categorizes and of course names
but an object in smoke cannot be named –
it exists like the Cheshire Cat.

Perhaps smoke brings us to the place
where symbolically we cannot see our
selves. Even partially erased is avoided.

Within a realm of uncertainty
or discontinuity, what after all
can be even partially grasped?

Take a translucent bowl, for instance,
a vessel of considerable visual distortion
but it holds oranges, and so therefore

we tend not to look too closely at it,
for it's within the purview of the everyday.
To see smoke you must be entranced.

If candles and matches have a God —
it is probably smoke. And what a God
it is: infinite mutability always unpredictable —

and changing everything that enters it.
And if smoke has a God, it is probably a mirror
that shows it the unrecognizable infinite.

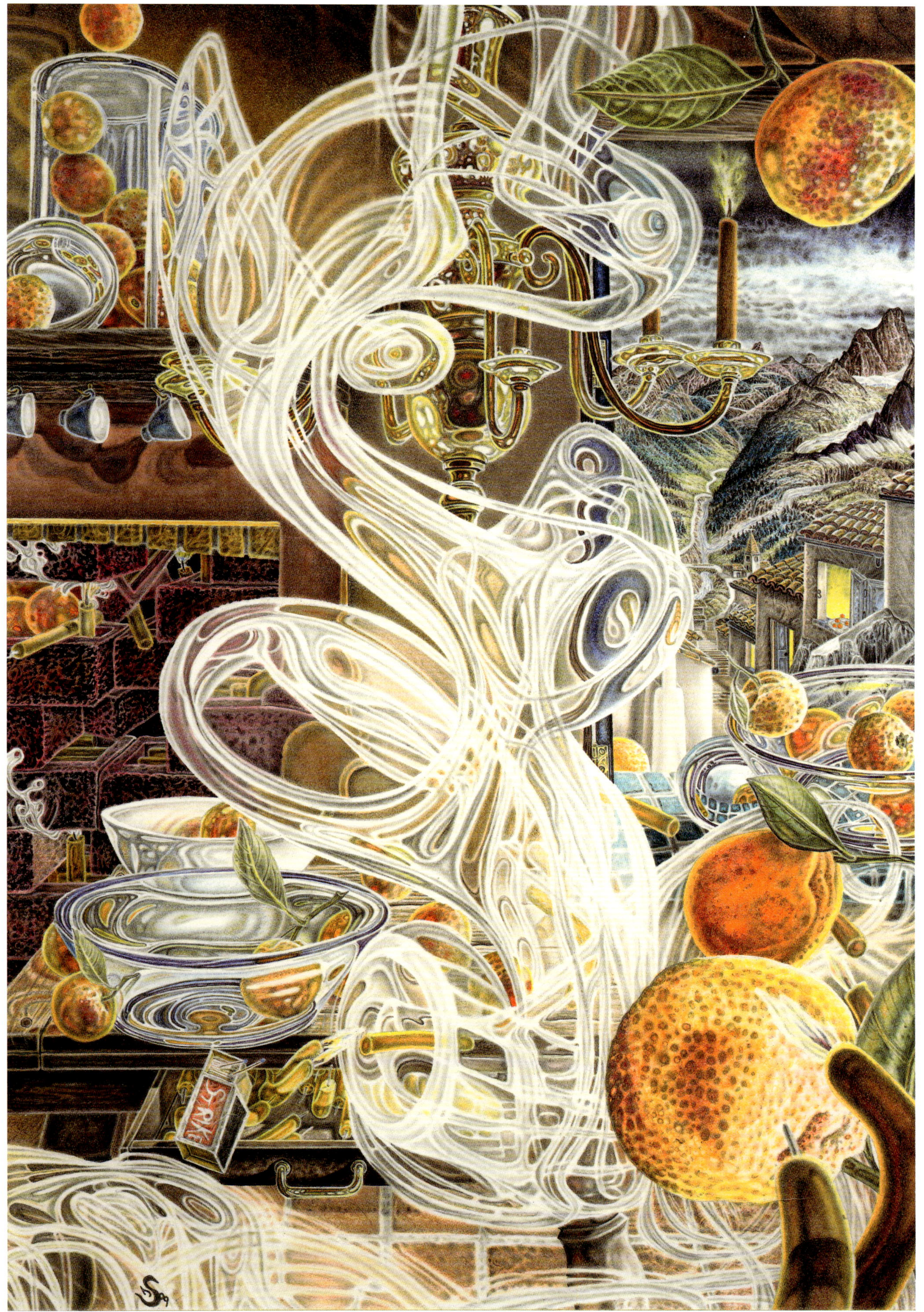

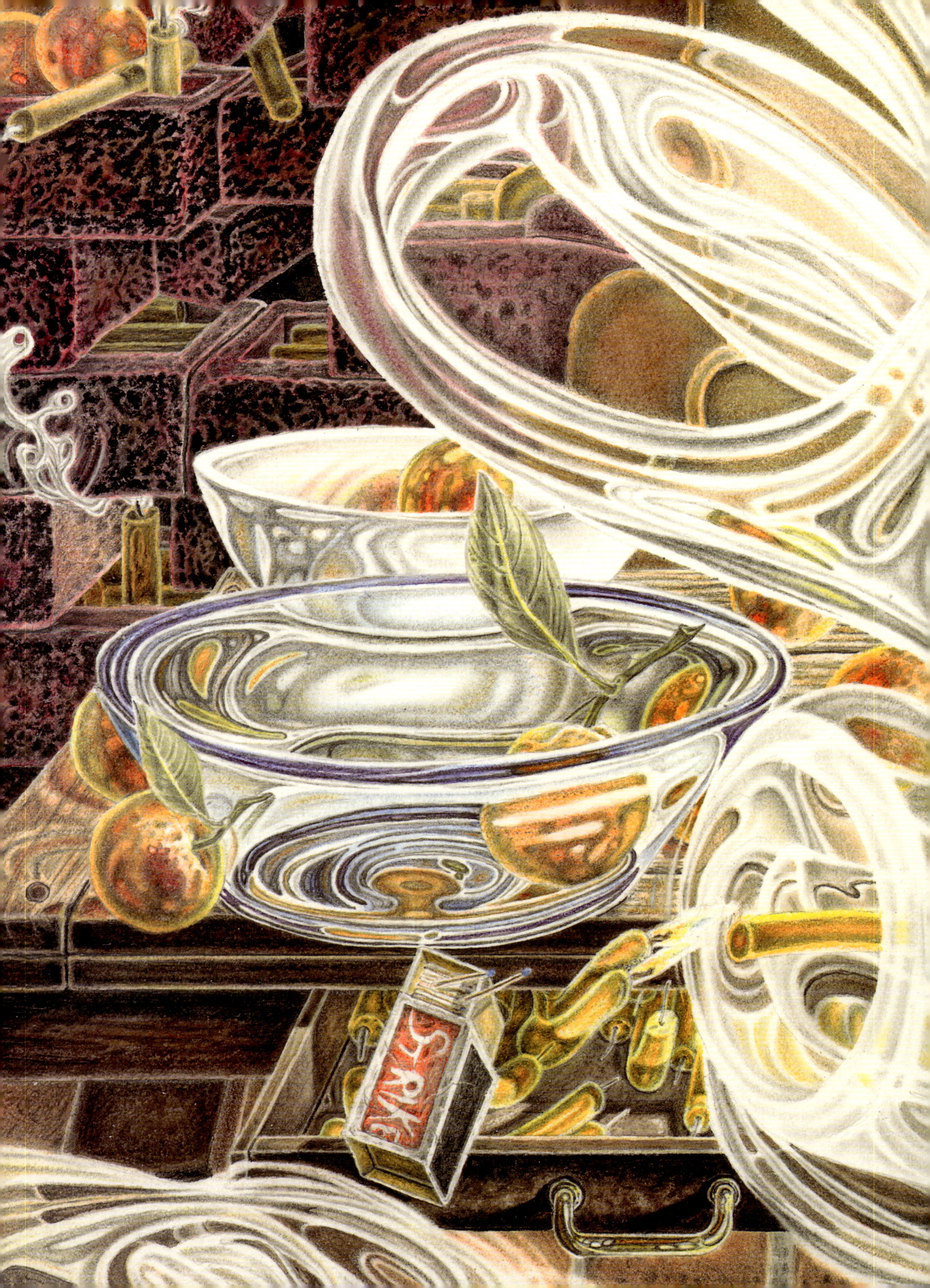
STRIKE

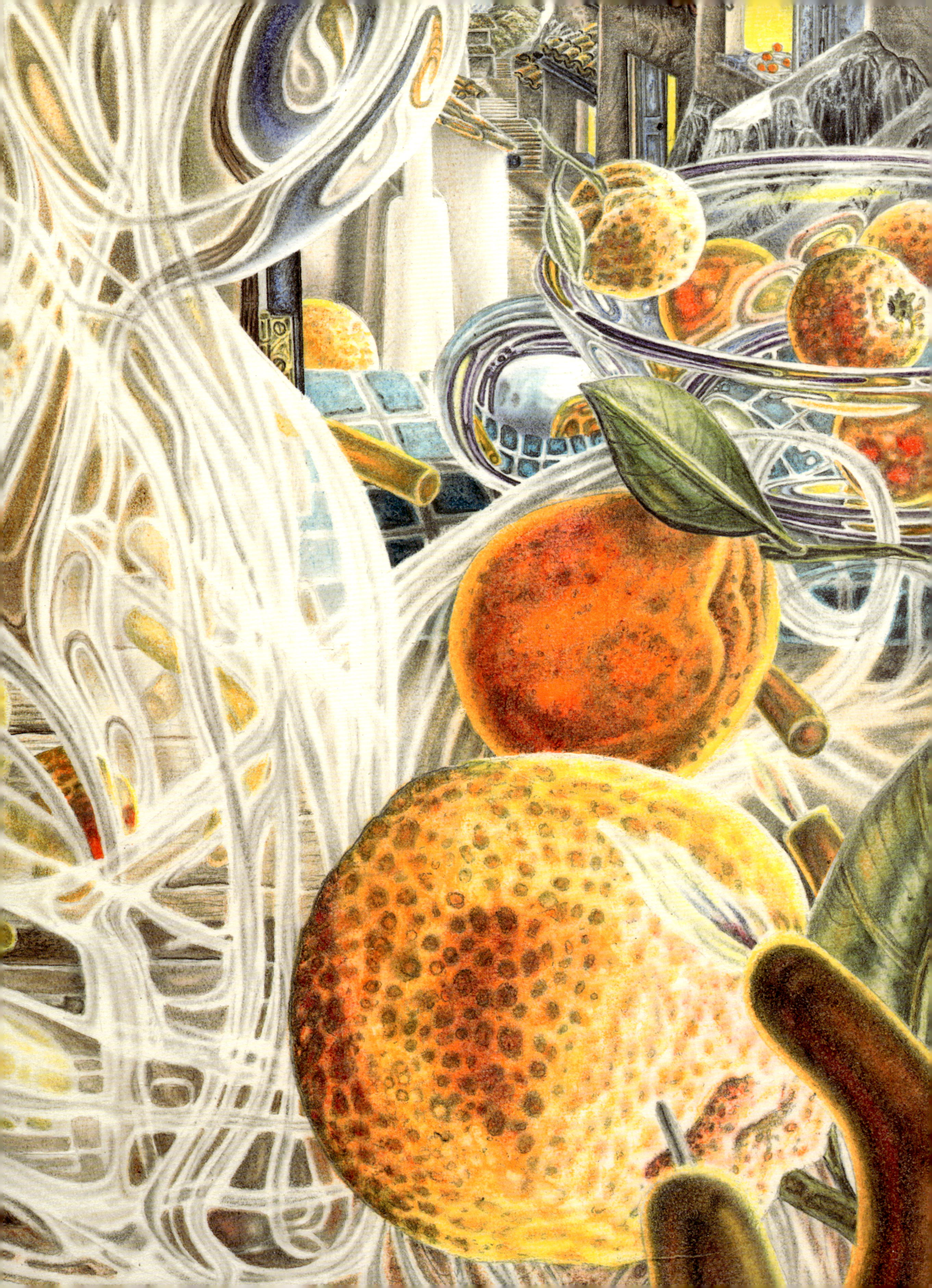

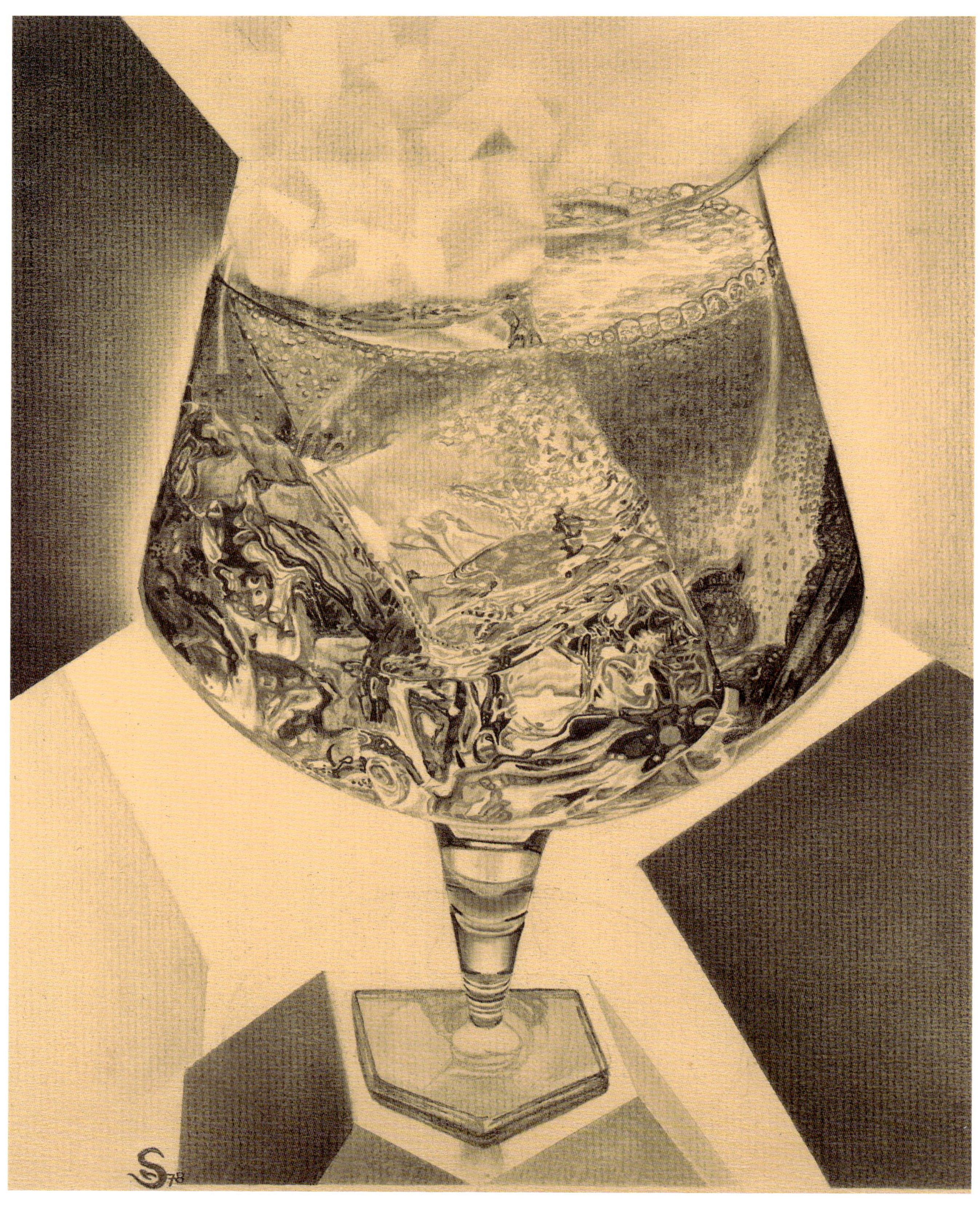

WHEN YOU fall into your first mixed drink, you'll know what I mean. Oh I don't mean predictable inebriation, no, what I mean is, what ice cubes in water become.

The curvaceousness of ice in liquid is comparable to the Parthenon Frieze. If you believe this an understatement, of course you're right. This incomparable tipping point between

real and abstract is the whole politic of 20th century art. Anything out of or with skewed content is abstract. Once we've tamed an object with a name, it's real.

But the feel and real look of it may be something else. Da Vinci said if you want to see unlimited landscapes, observe the patterns in a peeling wall. Reality is the crutch we hang our terror on.

There's a real danger in really seeing an object you may never find your way back to naming — or worse, words may begin to connote rather than denote, and civilization will rewind and start anew.

But all you need do to end this irksome reverie is take a few sips, pay the bill, and go home. The genius of civilized life is that you never have to look intensely enough to give up reality. §

EGGS

CRACK an egg.
Mandatory men with the squeaky voices
        of grammarians invented rules to account for
        Shakespeare's language. He didn't give a fig.

Crack.
What are the rules for carving Pentelic marble
into a perfect Venus. My guess is Praxateles
knew all of them and couldn't care less.

Crack.
What gave Beethoven the right to all that
chromatic dissidence in the late quartets.
I don't know, let's dig him up and ask.

The Alchemist in Prague, the Scientist in Berlin
the Artist in Paris, the Farmer in Iowa
watering his corn in a most peculiar way—

the eggs of possibility sit nested in every soul.
To pull an egg off the shelf and turn it around
is to see Faberge', and to await the Romanovs.

An egg not only contains a world
but the life that will surround it.
Every act of imagination is egged on—

Crack.
In the artist's large hands,
the egg becomes an act,
and the act becomes an actor
the actor lays an egg, and you
can't make an omelet unless —

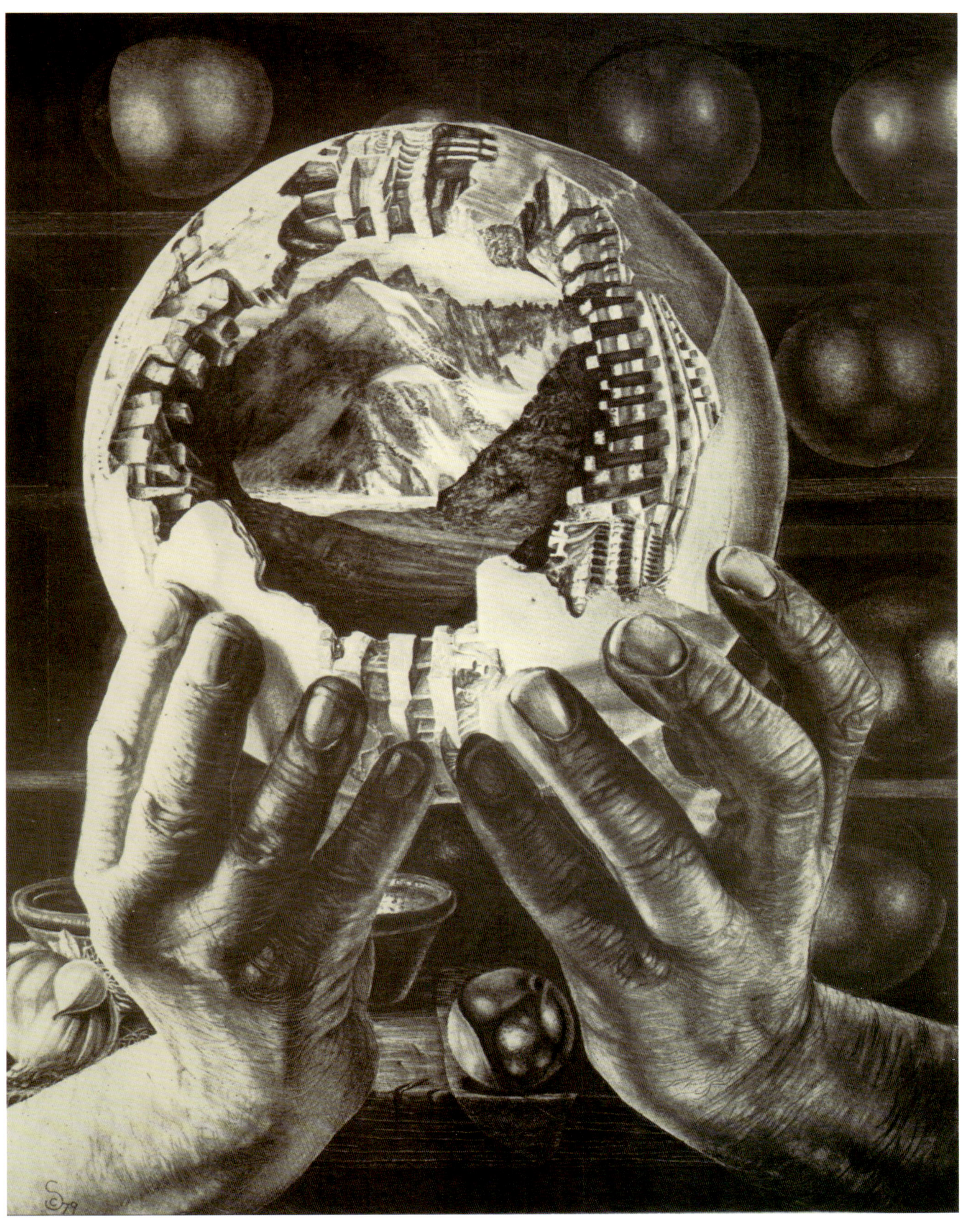

PERCHANCE TO DREAM

THE SEEDLING of my father's death grew
through the whole of my childhood.

He knew I must be carefully shielded
from danger and would set me in the library

with the biggest book he had upon my lap,
the capacious Janson's History Of World Art.

The first plate was a black and white photograph
of animals romping at the dawn of consciousness

Lascaux's primal nature twenty thousand years
before Christ. And the first color plate,

Holbein's portrait of the merchant, George Gisze.
Fur, metal, accuracy, depth, an astonishing

Tour De Force. From the very first I knew
art must be about energy and magic.

Near my father's bed was frequently a bowl
of pomegranates, the Greek symbol of resurrection.

Persephone had eaten nothing in Hades, and Demeter
had tearfully begged Zeus for her daughter's return.

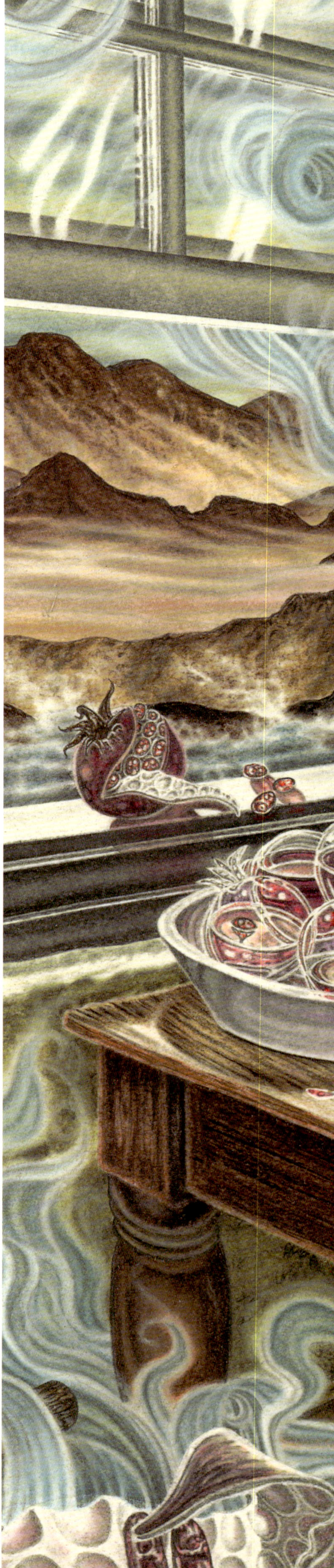

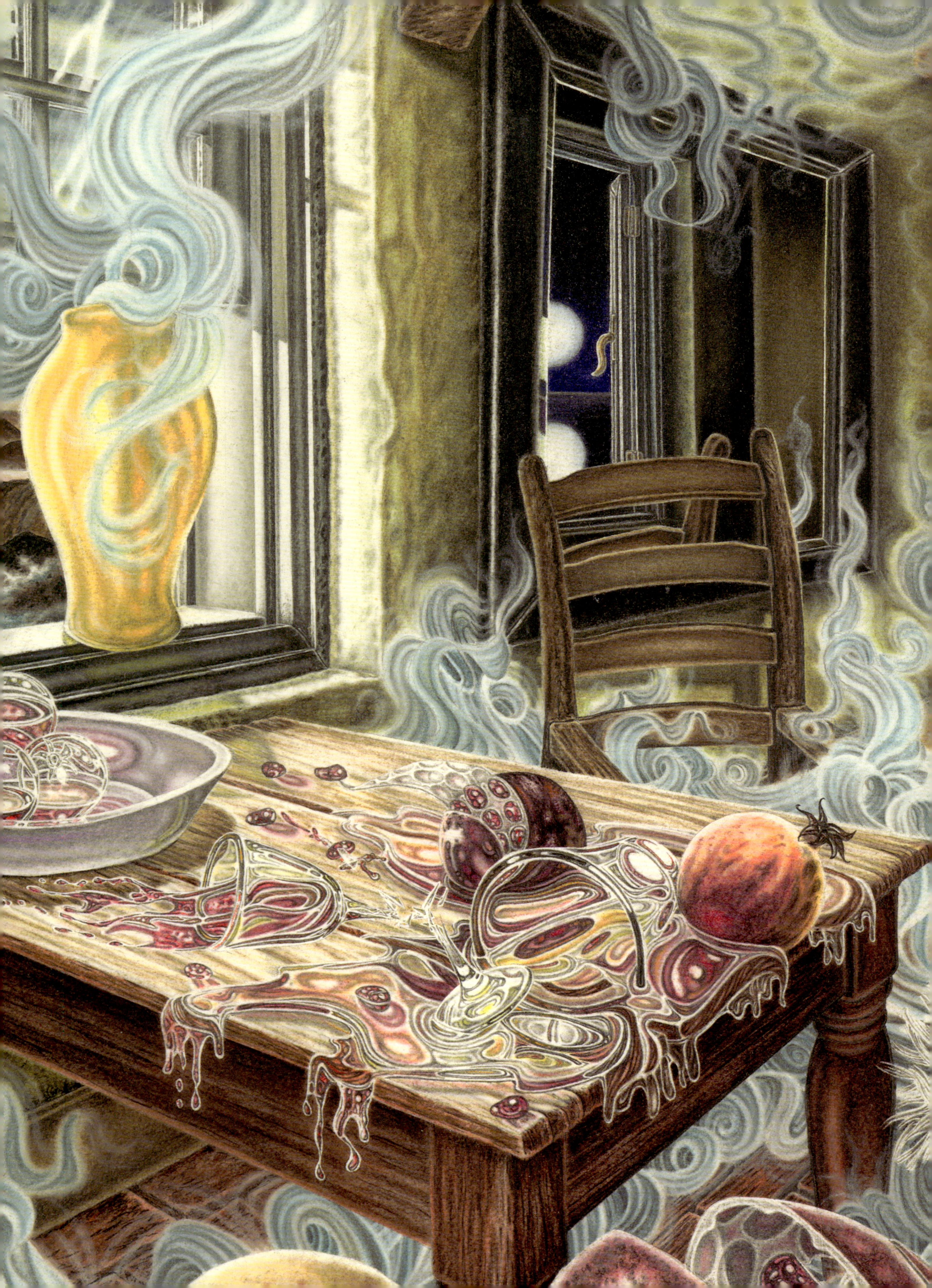

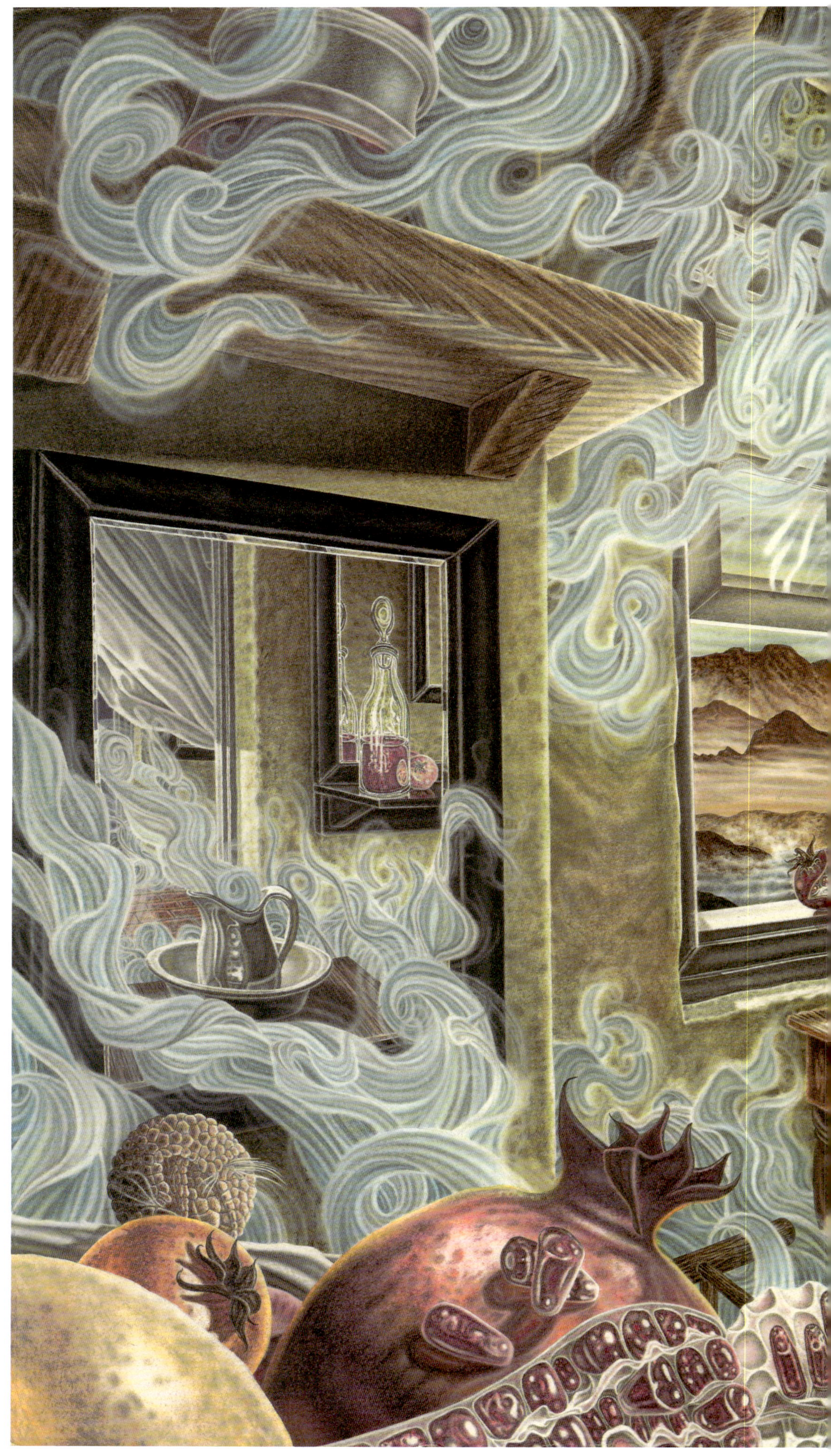

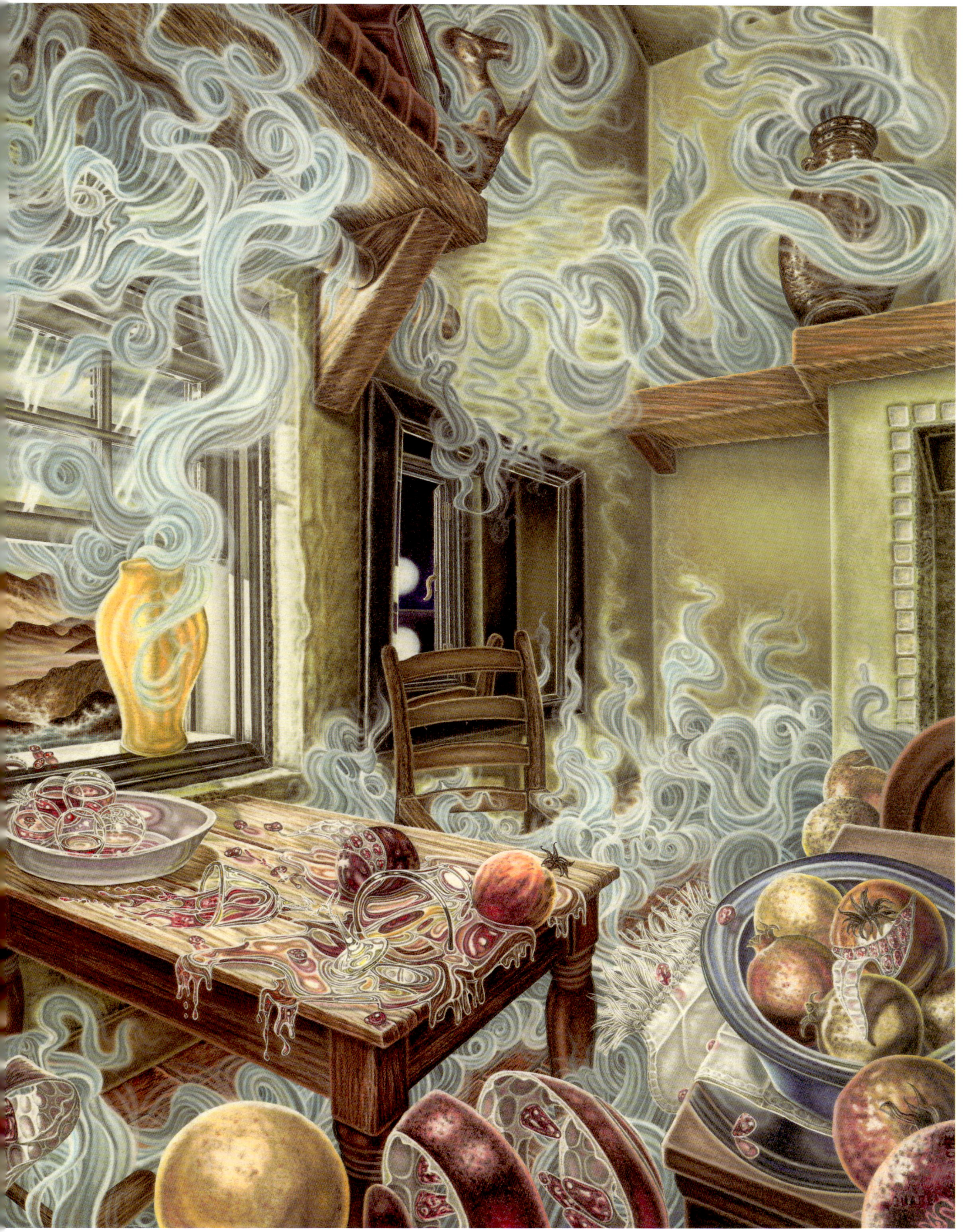

Alas, it was discovered she had eaten seven
pomegranate seeds, so for half the year she would live

underground like a shroud and the other half
circle poppies in her golden hair with her mother.

Dad was slowly moving underground but
still the pomegranates glowed red on his table.

The tart seeds in the mouth of the upstart hope,
yet live on the other side of the looking glass.

Wine glasses shatter and spill frozen in time.
Smoke is suspended in a quiet stasis—

and my father's hand beyond the frame
still reaches for the glowing fruit.

Perchance to dream of returning to the son
who waits, practicing magic and movement

in an aging childhood that still contains him,
making pictures that still contain me. §

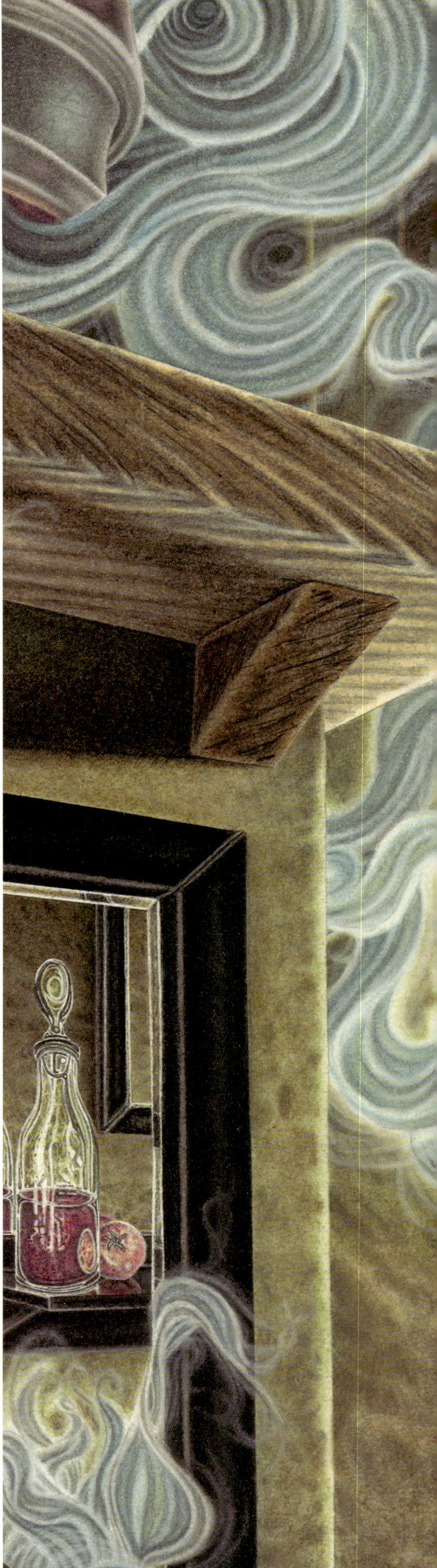

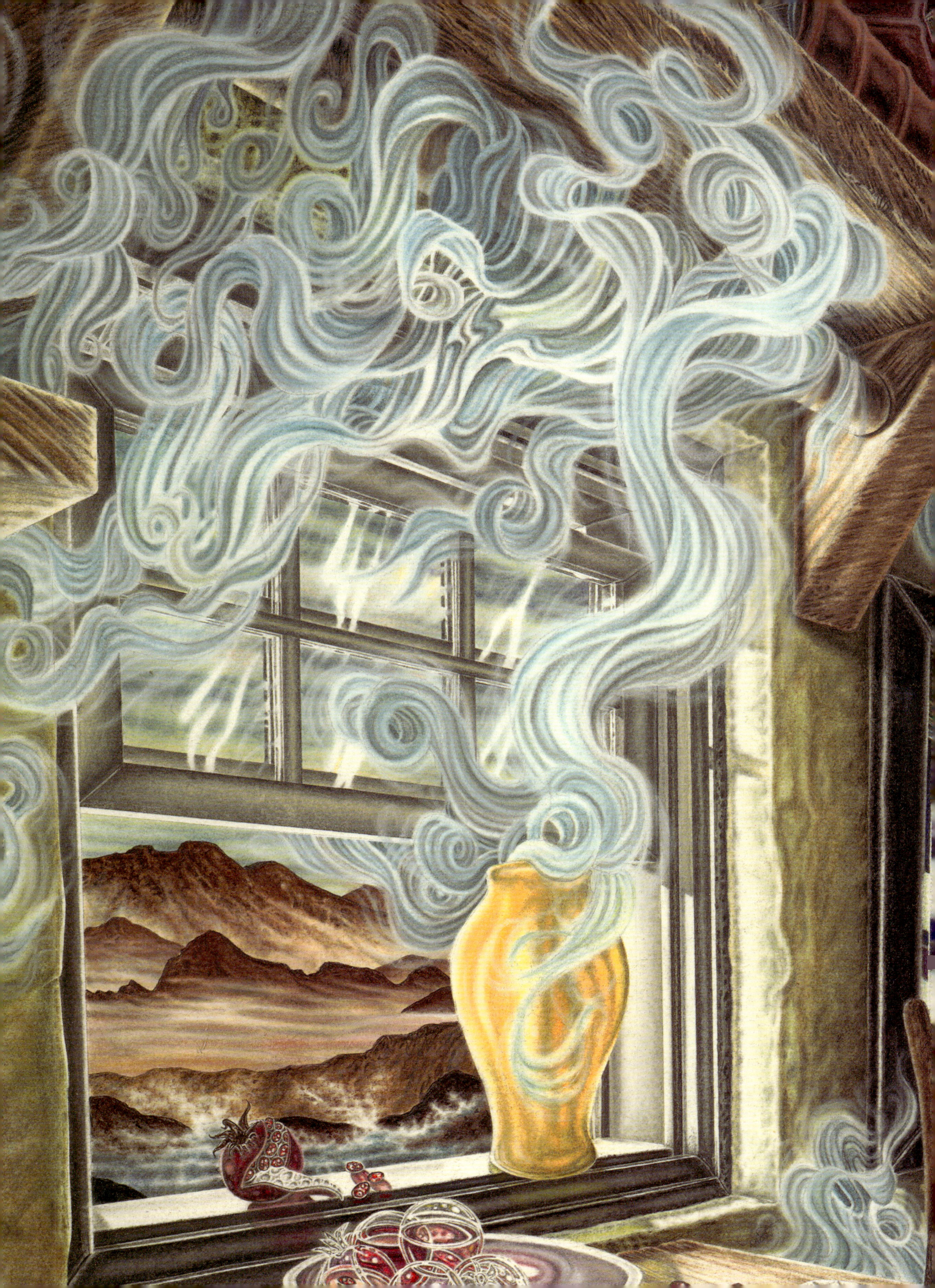

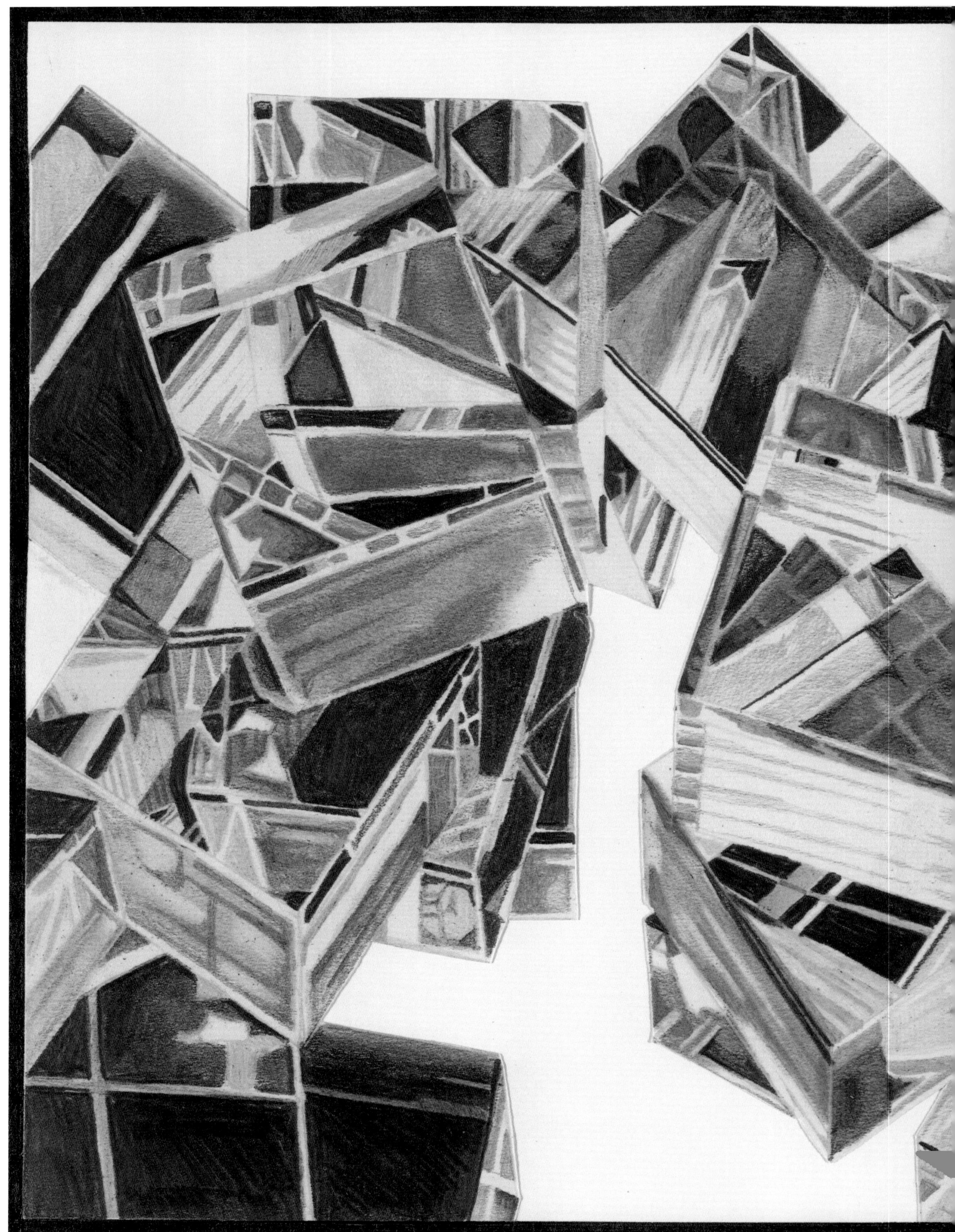

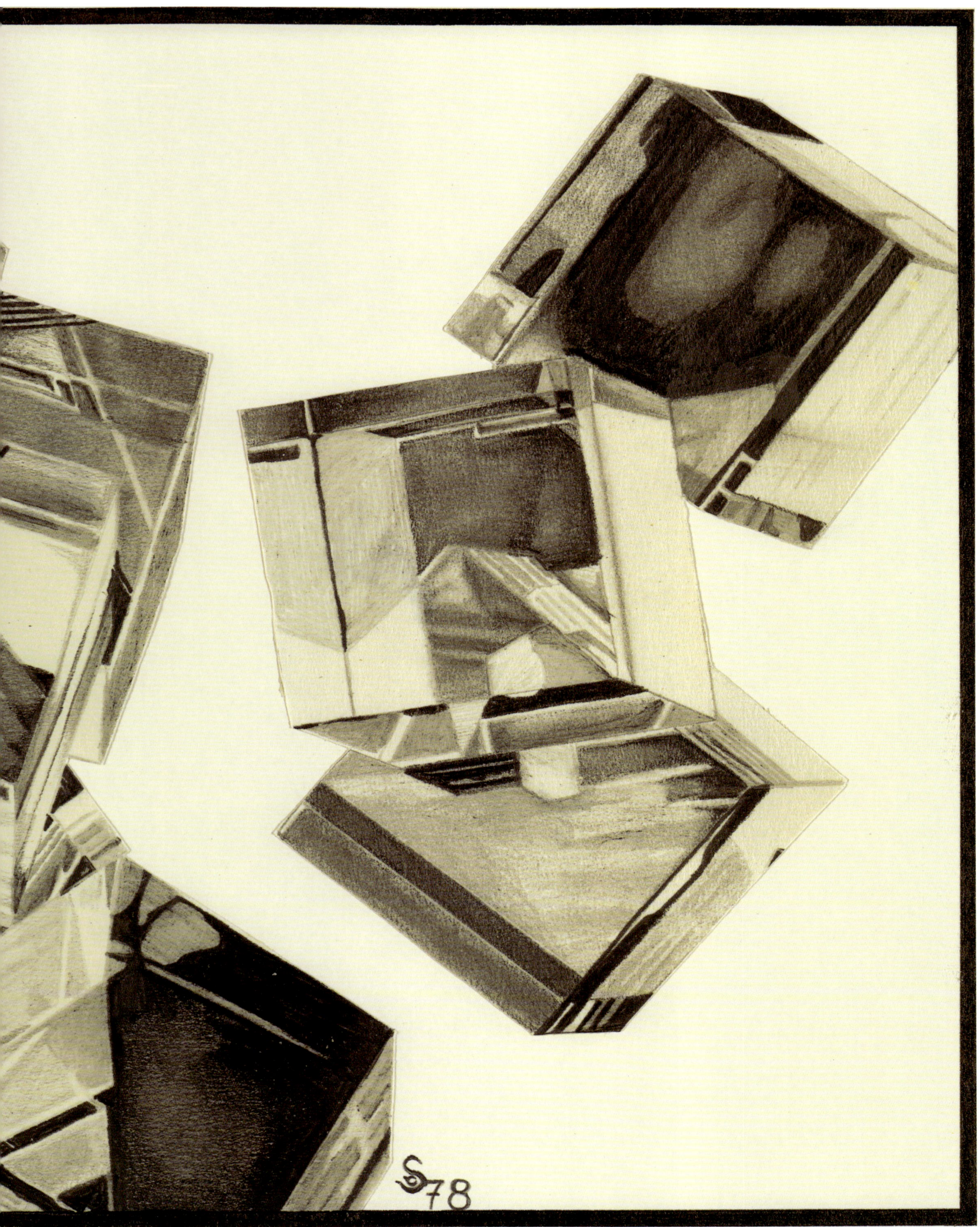

CUBES

GEOMETRIC ABSTRACTION based
on a series of stacked glass cubes.

As a boy I was a rock hound,
mineral hound more accurately.

Desperately wanted to be a mineralogist.
However the gods of math decreed otherwise,

my fascination remains. In these shapes,
I would daydream out cities of the interior.

Dana's Textbook Of Mineralogy
had so much to say about forms like these

but so little to say about wonder,
or being, lost in their prismatic inner life.

I reluctantly came to accept I had
the poet's temperament, not the scientist's.

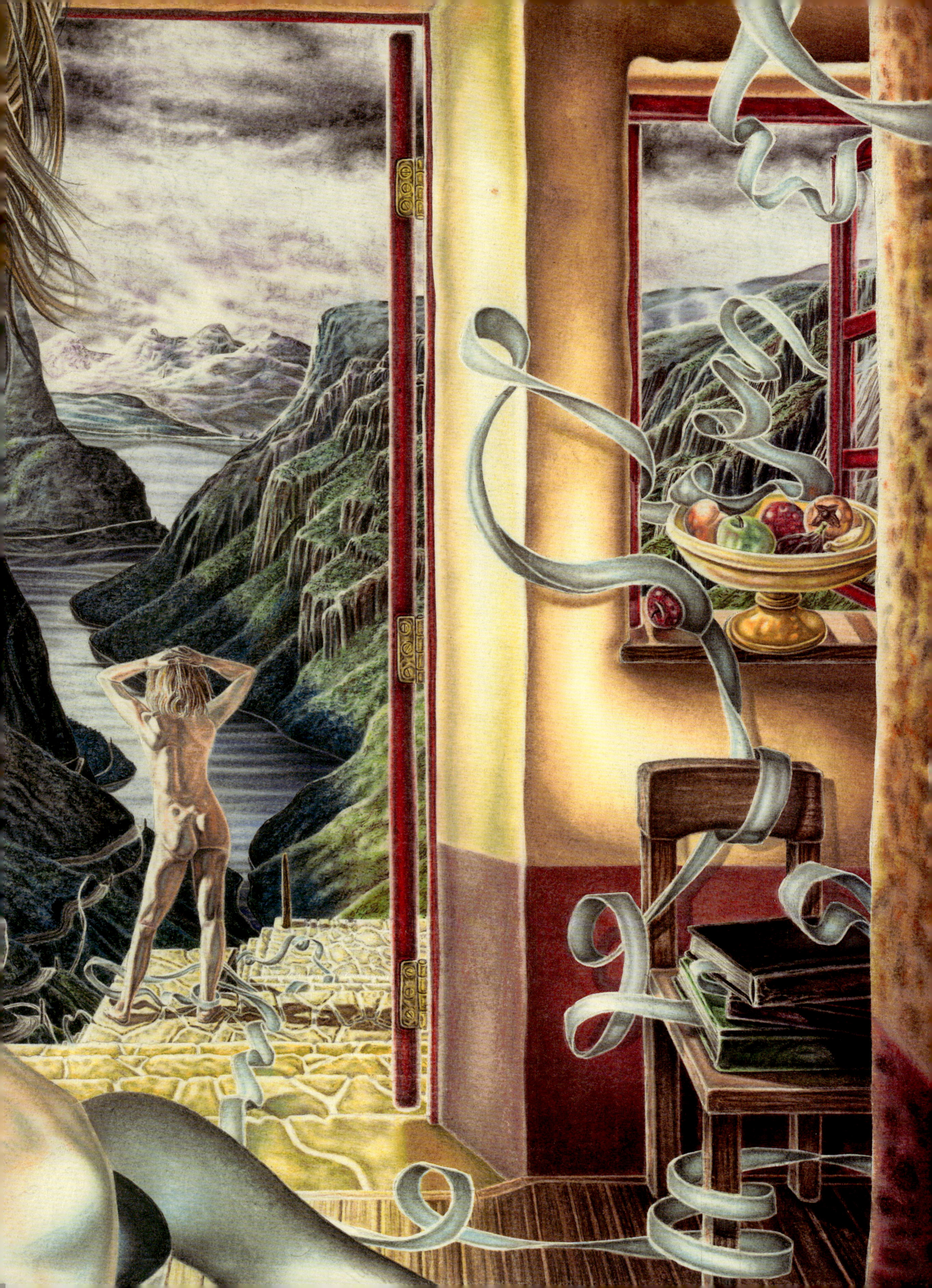

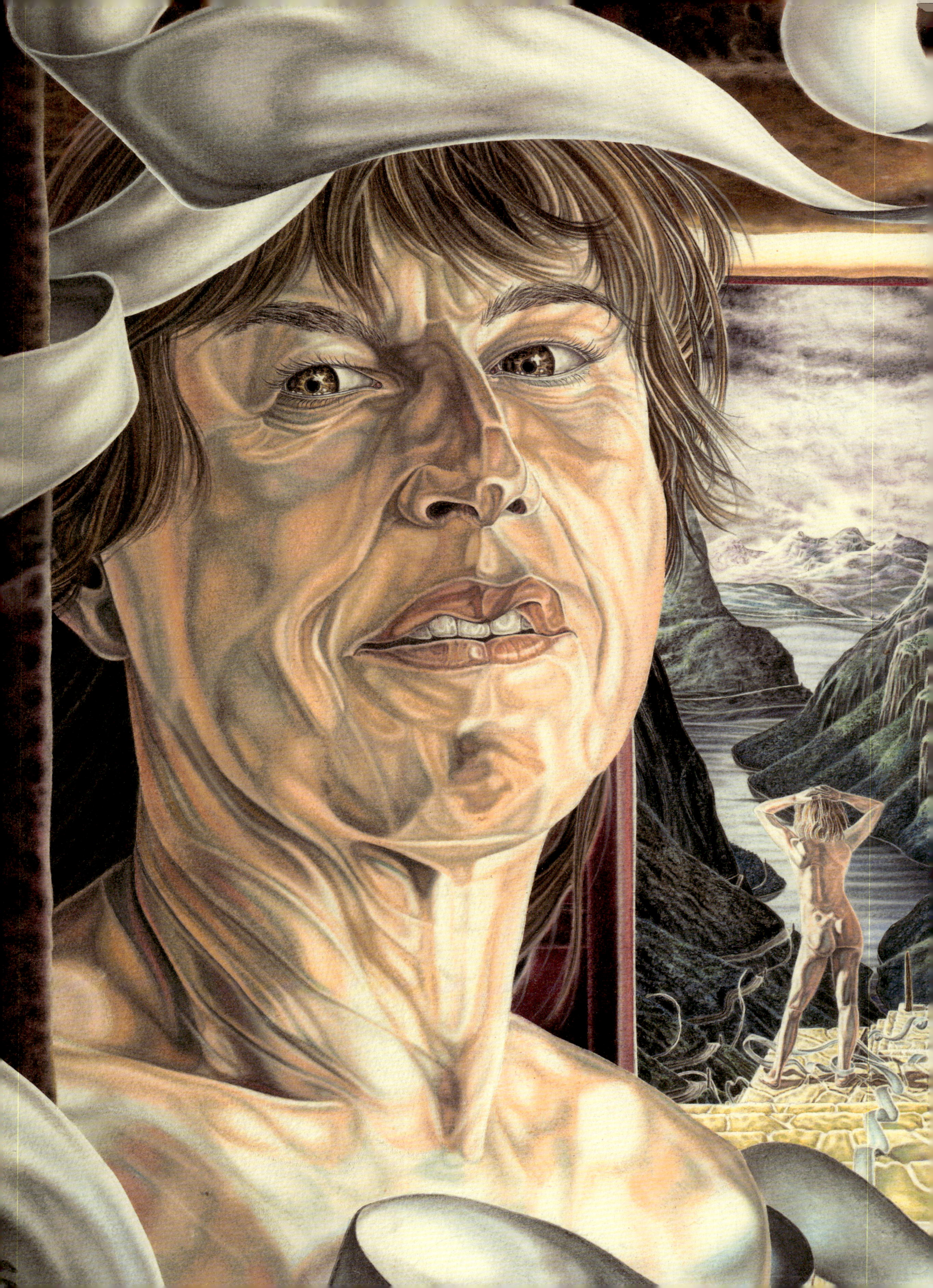

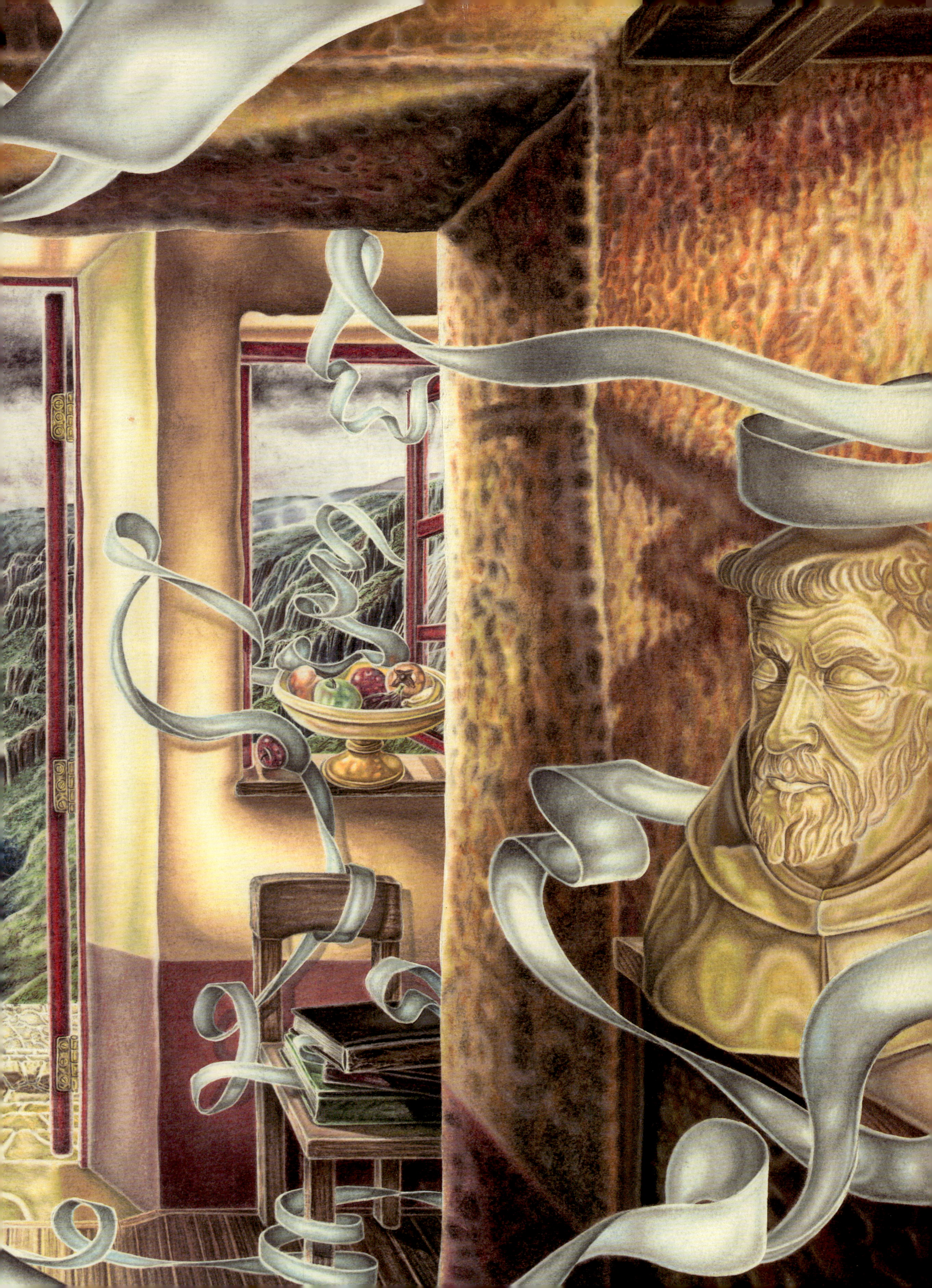

THE ROMANTICS had mislaid God
and went searching for the Divine.

They searched the highest alp
and trod the mossiest forest.

They looked in cathedrals
and the marginalia of arcane books

that had grown so old, mold
had forgotten to grow on them.

But the deep, great abiding hollow
they tried to fill — was in the soul.

It wasn't merely the lament, *"Quo Vadis",*
where am I going, but, what will I find

if I get there? An anxious temporality ran
like an enduring fever through the mind.

If all these delicious new landscapes
and attenuating verses were to have

meaning, didn't they need extension?
The infinite mind in the finite body.

Yet also the narrow hope in the wide miracle.
Tuberculosis may have been the Poet's Disease

but eternal longing was the spiritual one.
And so Keats and Shelley and Wordsworth

looked into the earthly divine. Like Emerson
or Whitman, they knew eternal longing

could be addressed in nature's presence.
If only a key could be found. Alabaster

monks had meditated, sensualists fornicated,
innocence had tried sin; Stoic and Epicurean

grasped at a middle path. But only the Romantics
had been smitten without any hope of redemption.

To this day the foul prospect of narrow death
can only be countered by the fair aspect of nature's light.

God, Nature, The Infinite, Cosmos, Logos are all
spelled the same. Their differing histories have been

blinds to block unity, stitched to enduring identity.
Unity at the cost of name. Buddha without

the budding earth, and a specific hand, and a specific
life to know it, is what the Romantics did not want.

Of course, the Romantics became Symbolists,
Surrealists, Fantasists, Painters of Fairie,

Writers of Myth. Where else could they go?
And naturally, they were diminished by realists,

who longed for nothing they couldn't acquire
by power, or buy with money. All the old creeds

were reborn and trivialized. They didn't, after all
interfere with the current of cash or the aphrodisiac

of force. Romantics went underground, fantasy
became comic and comic became manic but—

the eternal longing still lives our deepest
dreams of renewal. As Blake had it —

wash the windows of perception and see
new-minted, the world, like Christ.

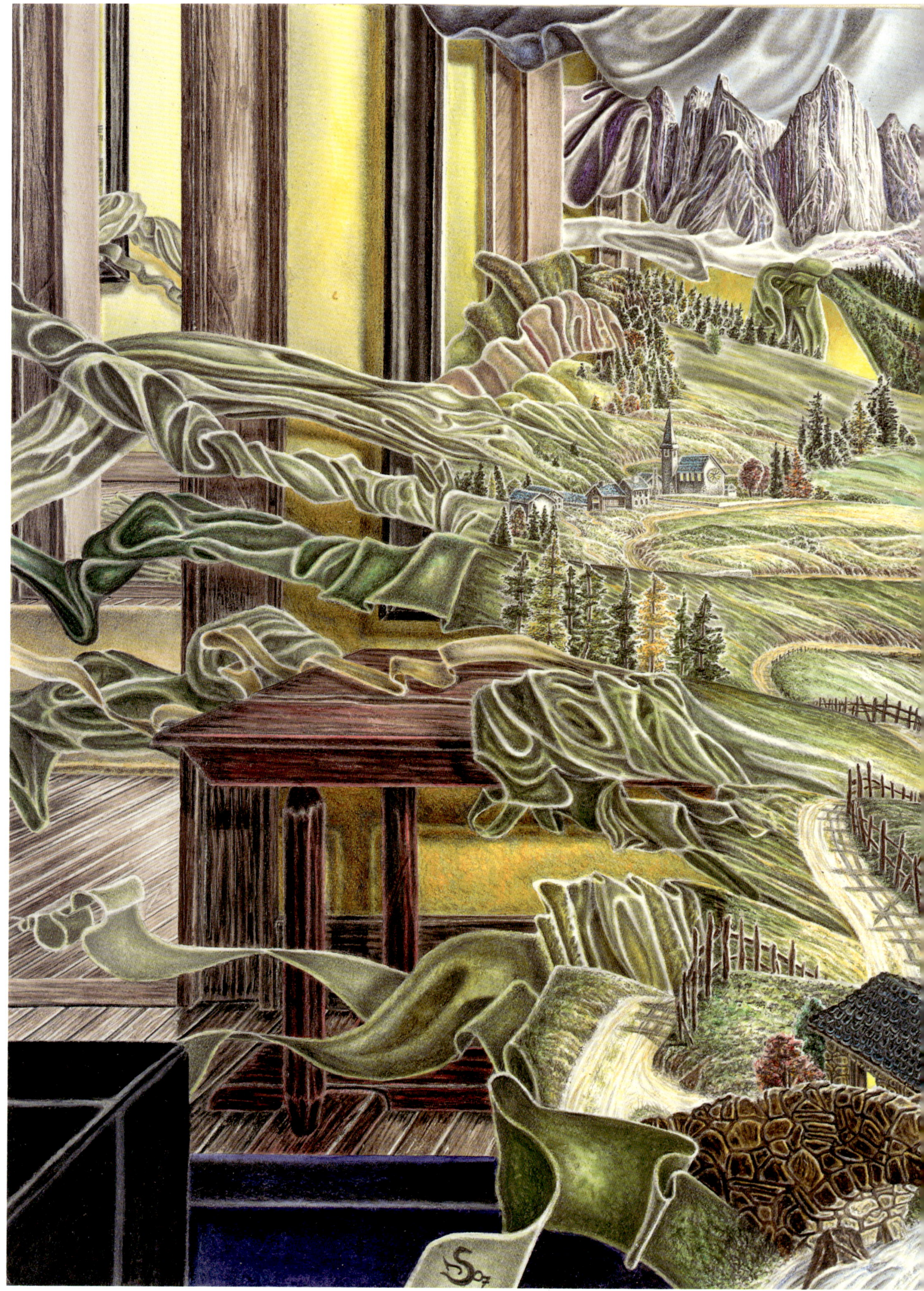

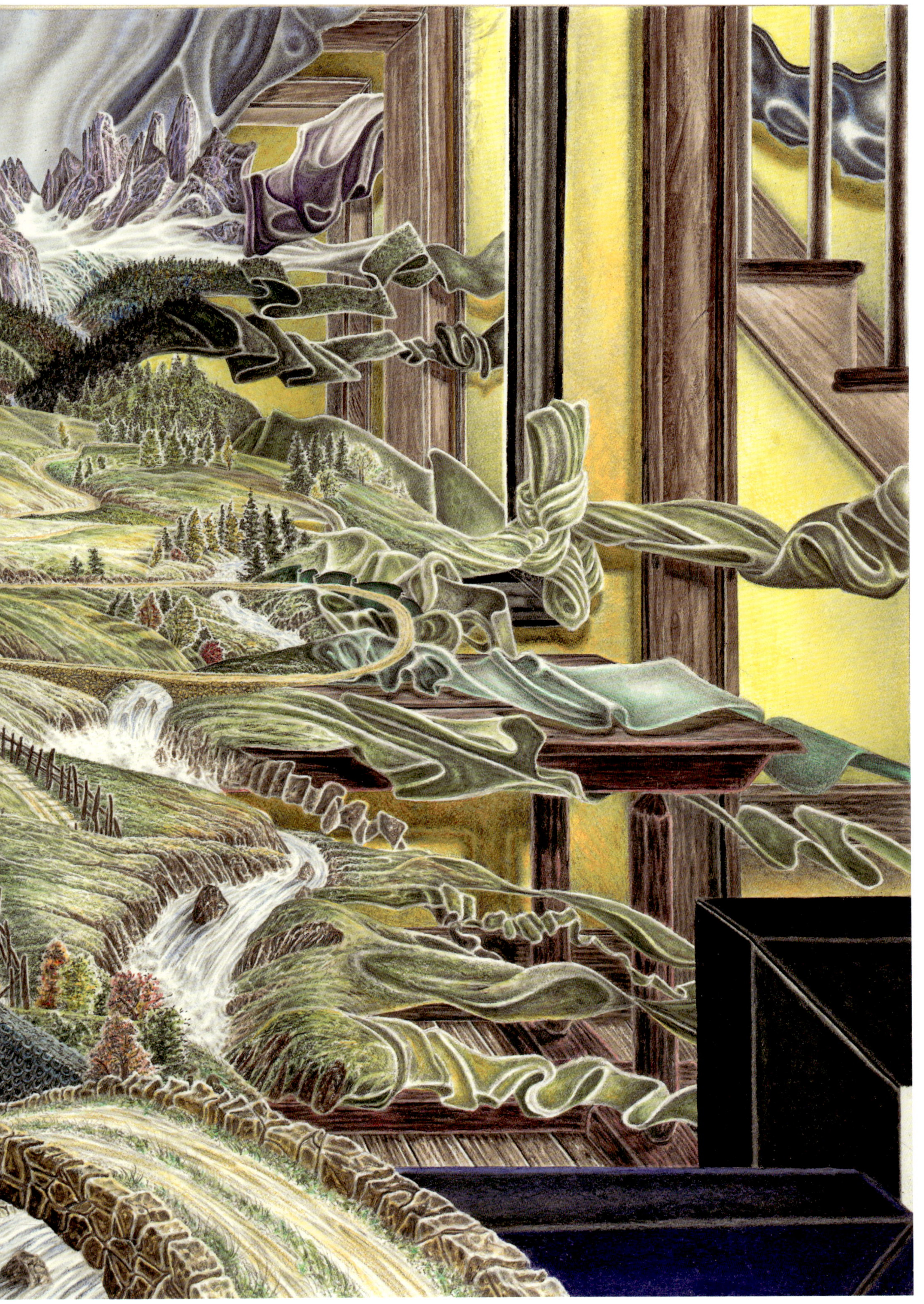

I. EMERGENCE

I FRAME THE PICTURES I make of myself.
     The frame captures a set of boundaries
     but the picture extends without limit.

I write light upon the text of earth
brush letters that formalize mystery. I don't
know what I seek, I know how to search.

A clot and culling in the name of art, alone
pushed and pushing into a when and waiting,
bought by and buying paper and brushes alone,

for anyplace you start begins it. Grayness lifts, the
dim dull fatigue in a room's routine lightens,
somehow something sparkles, waits to be born.

II. Wouldn't I love a magic mirror, for there
I can find everything I'm workadaying away from.
The imaginings I cannot yet imagine are there.

The mirror suspended in a room, which within becomes
all rooms. To deliquesce myself into its liquid skin
through chambers and doors and attics of jet.

And worlds emerge to meet me as well —
to romance the road within me again,
to river the eye in tears of joy.

Time runs backwards as well as hence.
I am not a duration, I am an emergence
before and after, from top to bottom.

Nothing in forever that counts
and numbers inside me can
draw me out into a single line.

Space whistles through me like a song
yet how can I catch the substance of this?
How can I sing the song I hear.

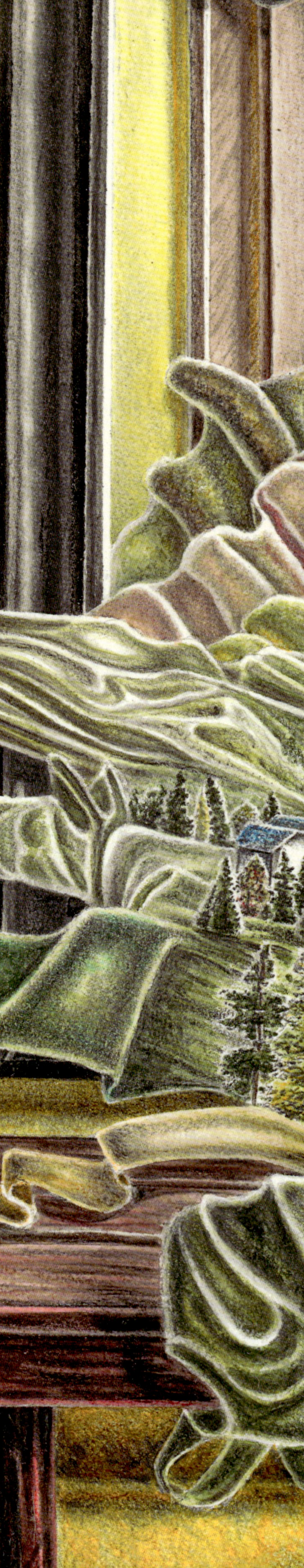

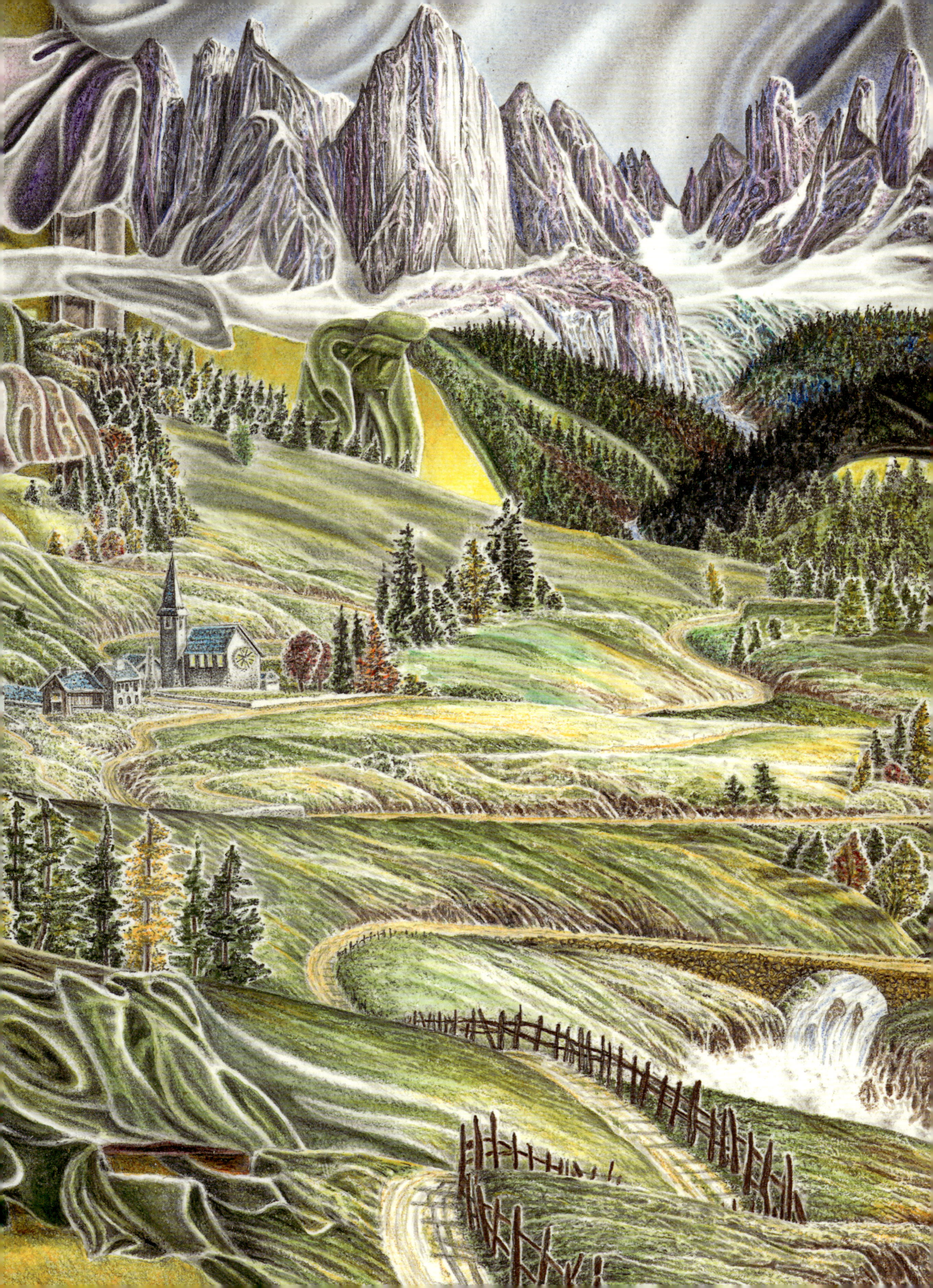

In a sense, we are a place where worlds collide
where histories are lived and eternities pass.
Like a summer day, we are in a sense of place.

Have you ever seen two worlds
in the same place at the same moment?
Have you never been two worlds

forcing reality to overlap — and two places
offering up a fork in the road and a choice —
how you will choose both and remember one?

At every joint in our reality
a choice must be made, yes or no,
back or forth, left or right.

And all these interlocking and complex
tessellations of choosing, compounded
by hours and days and lifetimes.

A staggering zoology of other lives lived,
different families, scholarships of different
and alien knowing, tears shed for other Gods.

Parallel chronologies without end
and in each more forks, more choices
and on and on endlessly.

And here we are, sad snails
following one line of memory
one line only, in the tapestry of us.

One thread only and yet this
is a blessing from God, really, to keep
from being shattered in wonder.

The Angel of Death arrives only
to take what we've remembered, but all
the multi-formalities of us continue to emerge. 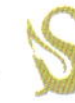

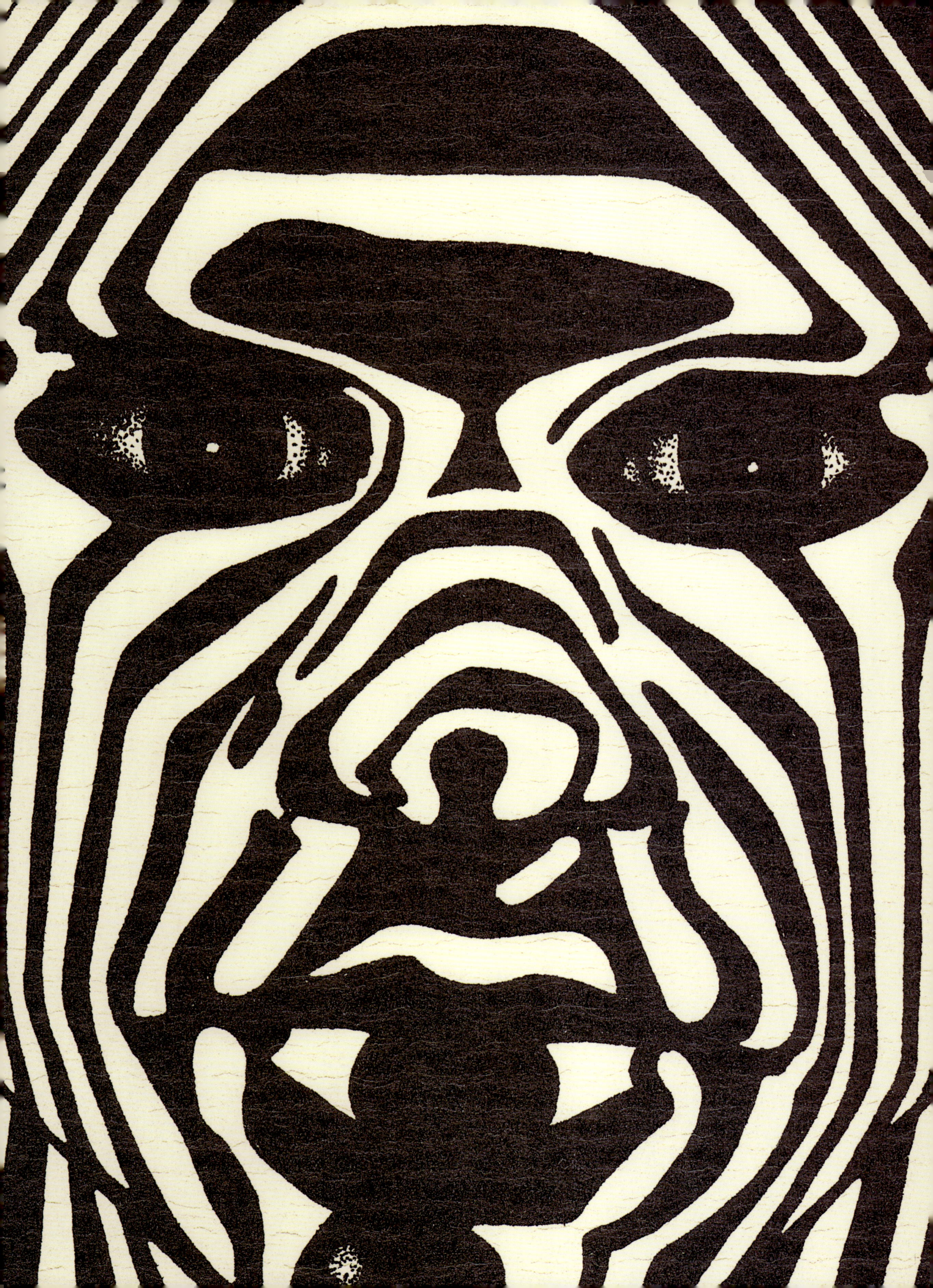

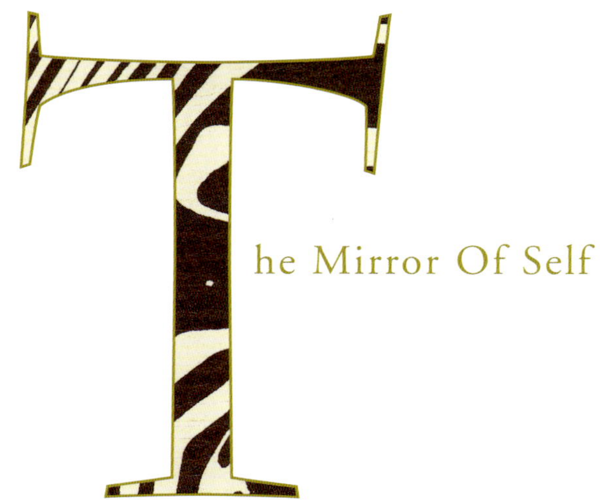

The Mirror Of Self

S T R I P E S

He looks into you because he knows
you cannot fully look into him.

Shadow forms an absolute for this man;
life is lived between the cracks.

If you torment your eyes to see only
the whiteness, the black man

cannot be seen, and if you observe
the blackness, where is the light?

Both together cannot be seen, only sensed,
reconstructed, a visual disconnect.

This legerdemain, is a duchy of trickery;
you cannot see a striped man complete.

And so you can never forget him.
Shadow spits its way between thought.

The workaday we on the street can easily
be seen and, hence, so hard to remember. 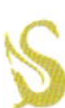

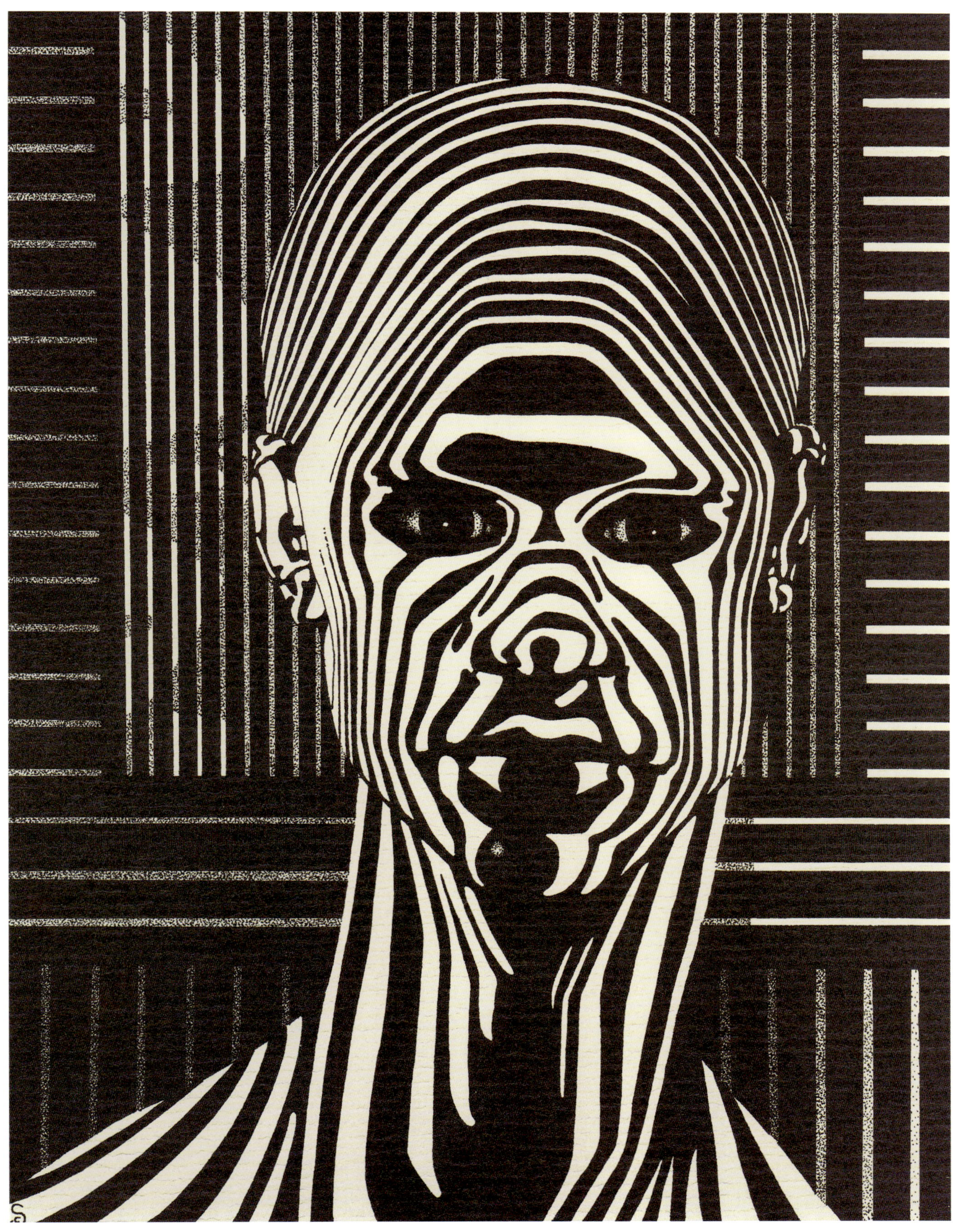

WE BACK INTO YOU by mistake.
The needle of your breath raises
the nap of our short-necked sleep.

We don't believe you're there, we
have felt the chill north wind before;
the ice in our nostrils has always passed.

What could you after all look like,
not the night sweat of children I suspect,
more an exquisite map without desire.

Your followers we would recognize
painted in the semblance of youth
speaking with the rasp of fallen leaves.

You have taught us to distrust reflections.
The mask we see is what you desire,
but we remember childhood and spring rain.

We know you don't come for us —
we come to you, walking backwards
toward the darkness of your special light.

When father disappeared, you painted him,
but he was too young to walk among us then —
but how he walks in memory now.

In your eyes there is no hunger, only
the quiet continuance of the entire race
and yet nothing can continue in you nor disappear.

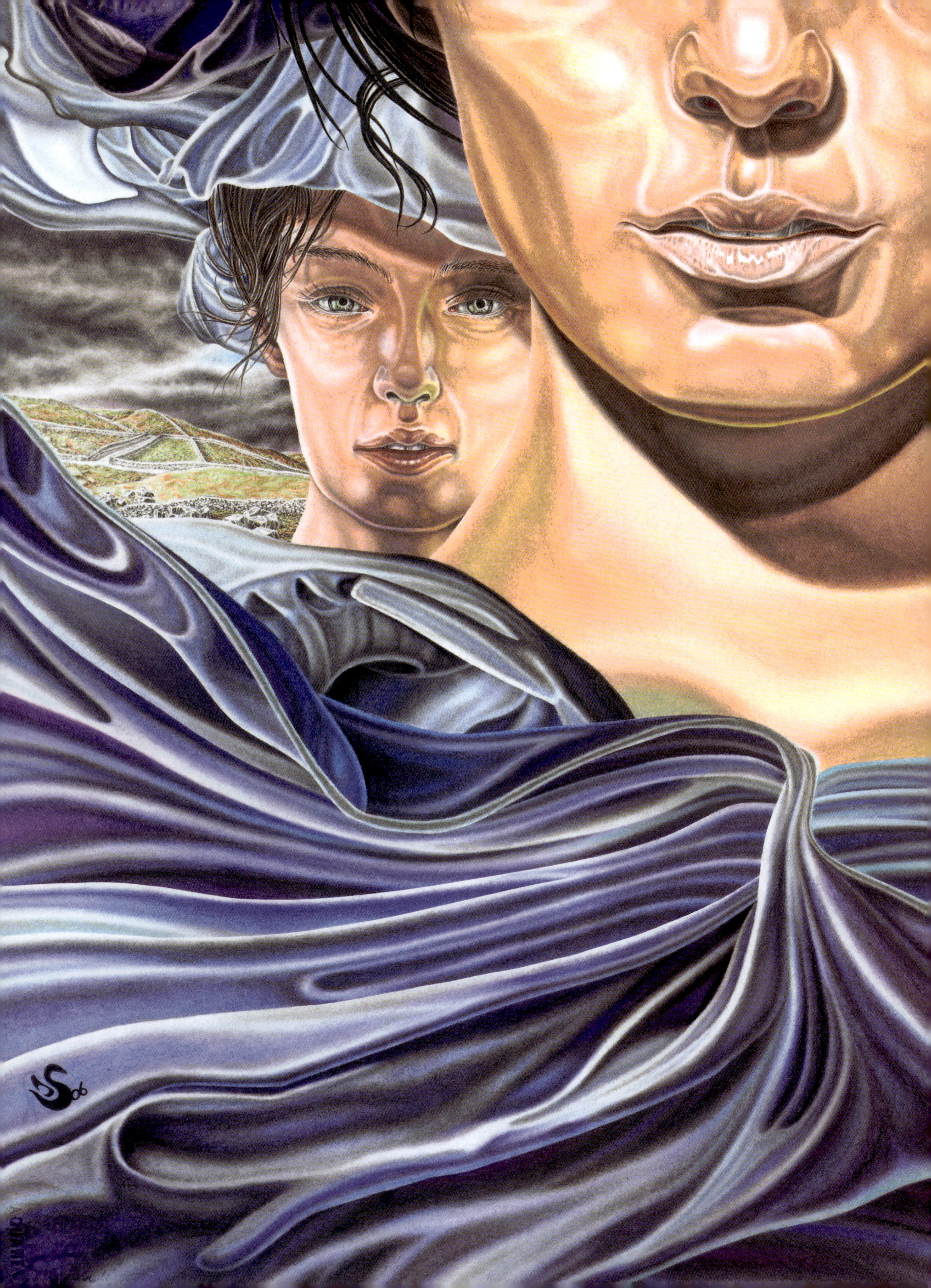

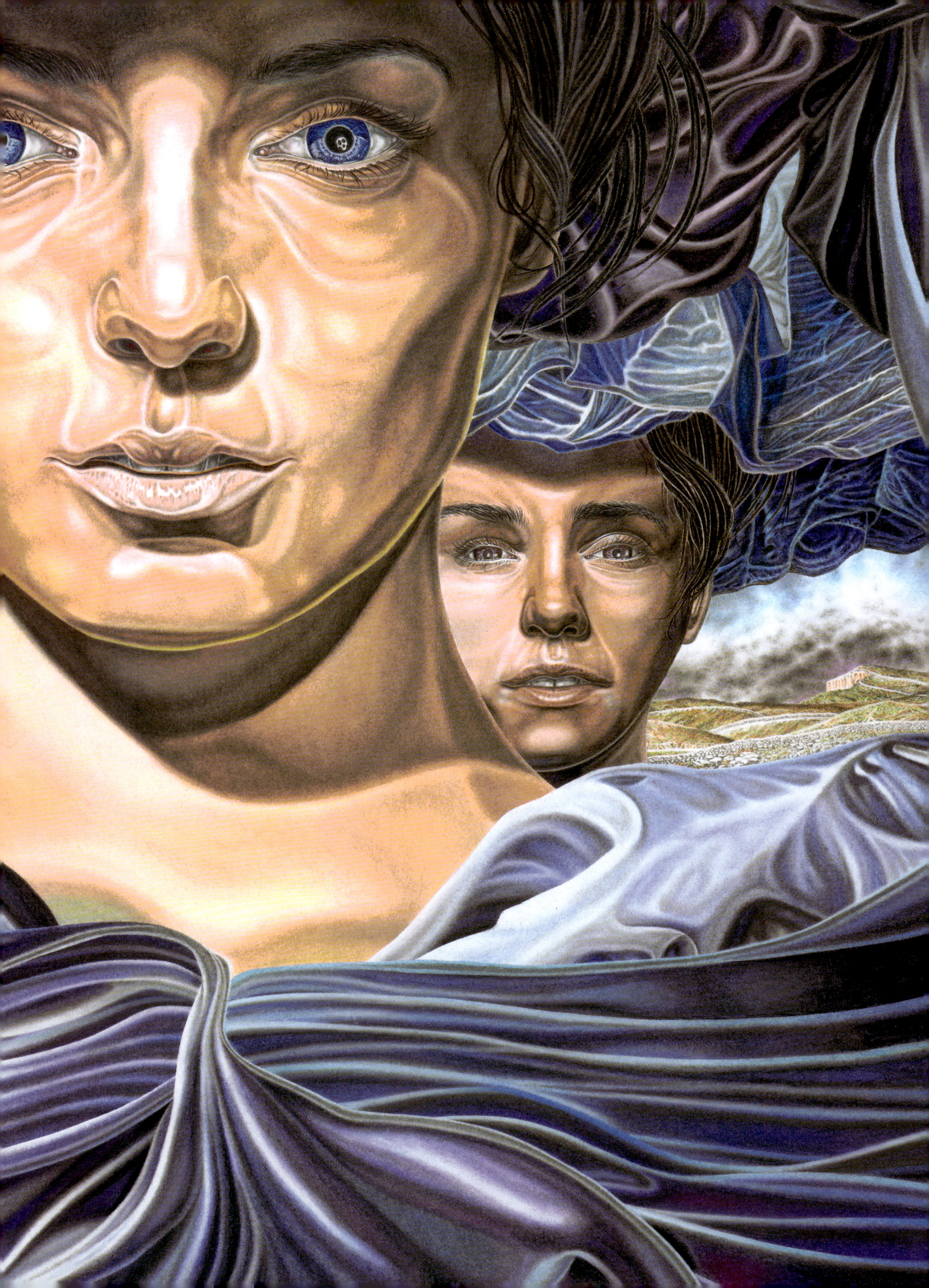

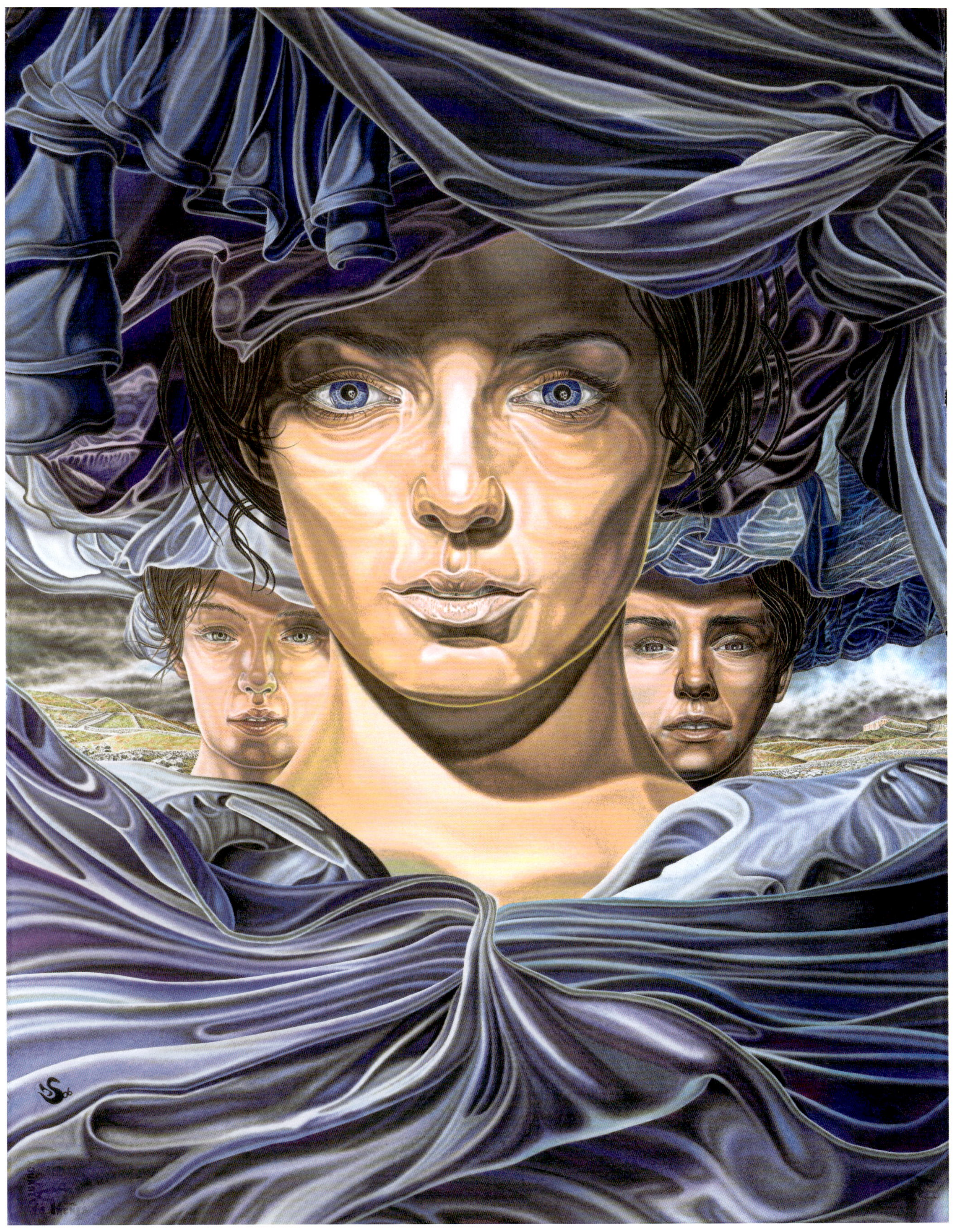

SELF PORTRAIT

WHEN WE LOOK at ourselves in the mirror
how does what looks back, see us?

Are we his more garish puppet, and when
he leaves the mirror's frame, what becomes of us?

Is he the we, that can become anything
we choose him to make of us?

In this trace of a possible past, I'm stamped
upon this page like the Shroud Of Turin.

I remember my double allowed me
to portray him as a young woman—I was

encouraged to correct my broken nose, it seems
I was either coming apart or coming together.

The eyes are more lustrous and have seen
more than mine, and have seen it clearer.

Do we ever know enough about ourselves
to draw ourselves out, especially on paper?

Behind my twin is absolute nullity. But that's
because he's only a drawing I've made, right?

And that, over half a lifetime ago; there is
no blackness behind me now, is there?

Would my double know I'd be saying that
and so allow me to transfer it to him?

Perhaps portraits are the martyrs of the self
that would or wouldn't be invented without them.

I'm still drugged by the prospect of seeing myself.
Trust me there's far more yet to come.

When you draw yourself out of the well
of nothingness, consider, this is so very unlike

a photograph, that moves silver, pixels
or emulsion with the speed of a heartbeat.

When you capture this instant fully in a photo
without the hand in time, you will be missing.

The moments of you pass through your hand to paper,
slowly a fiction builds, and when you're done, a day,

a month, a year later you have engineered a memory
with time, become yourself and passed into art. §

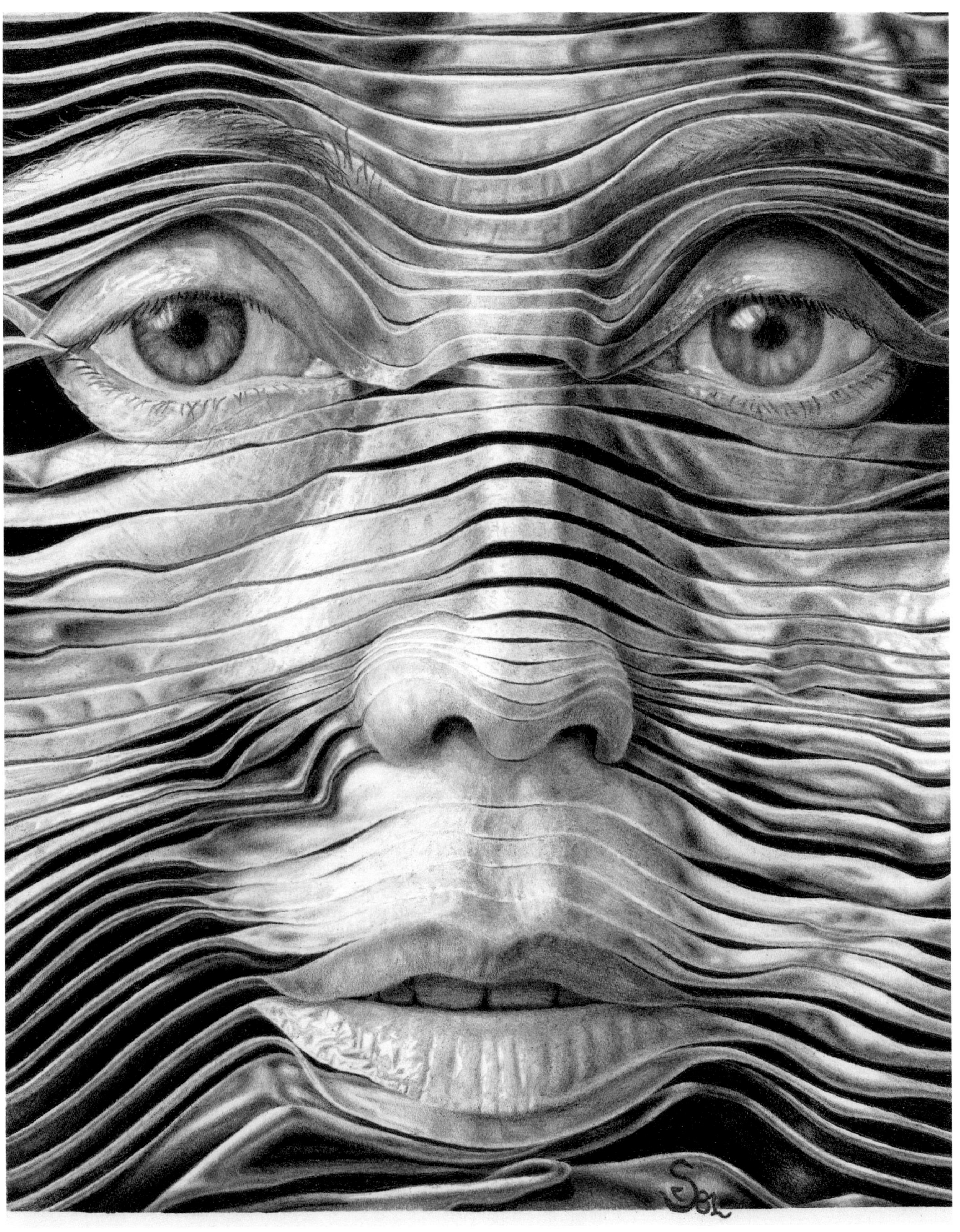

BOOKCASE

HE BOOKS WERE in the wild minds of the storytellers.
She probably started as the master design
stamped in the overmastering passion of first love
    and continued somewhere deeper than metaphor.

After the hydraulics of procreation had passed, she was
still there. She has been called so many names
in the history of our passing; Lilith, Aphrodite, Sif,
Astarte, Eve, she stays in the lost closets of our memory.

We can hear the voice but not the words.
Isthmuses of books have been written out,
many pretend she's just a woman, just a story,
just the mothering beginning to all our

pretensions of art. Yet we know full well
in her sacred womb are built palaces of light
and that all the cities of the world emerge from her.
But she is not about quickening alone—

Nature's allegories work for that. Somehow she became
the governing dream of home as well. The metal men
in the surface tension of war placed her on a pedestal
in the mud so they didn't have to look upon her.

Murder is so much more difficult if faced daily with
the sanctity of life. The fundamentals of her renewing art
diminish any impulse, save growth and self expression.
After all, in nature you eat what you kill.

Only the broken face needs the mask of power.
And so she is carefully buried, placed in bookcases
across the quiet libraries of noisy action.
But she has always known how to wait.

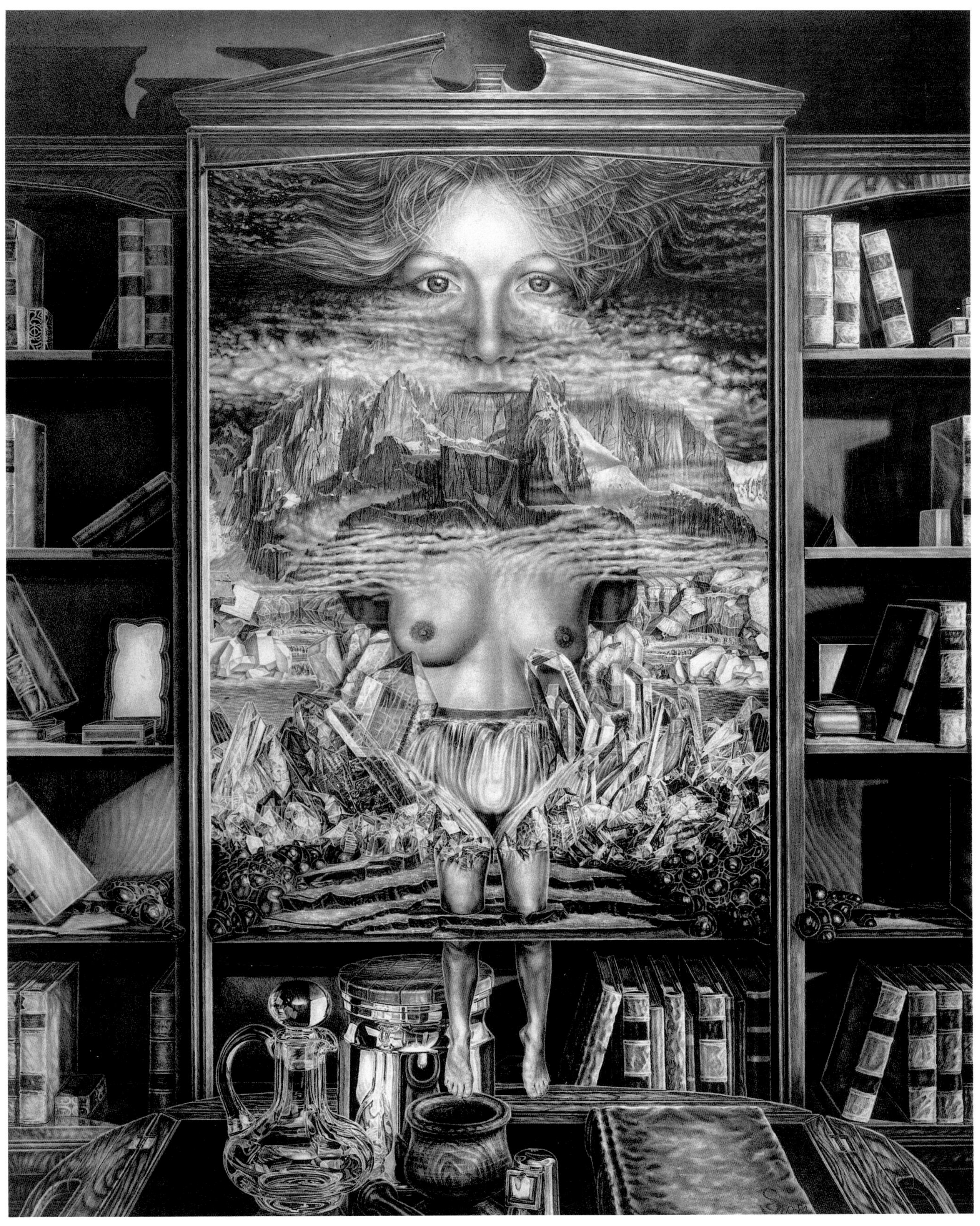

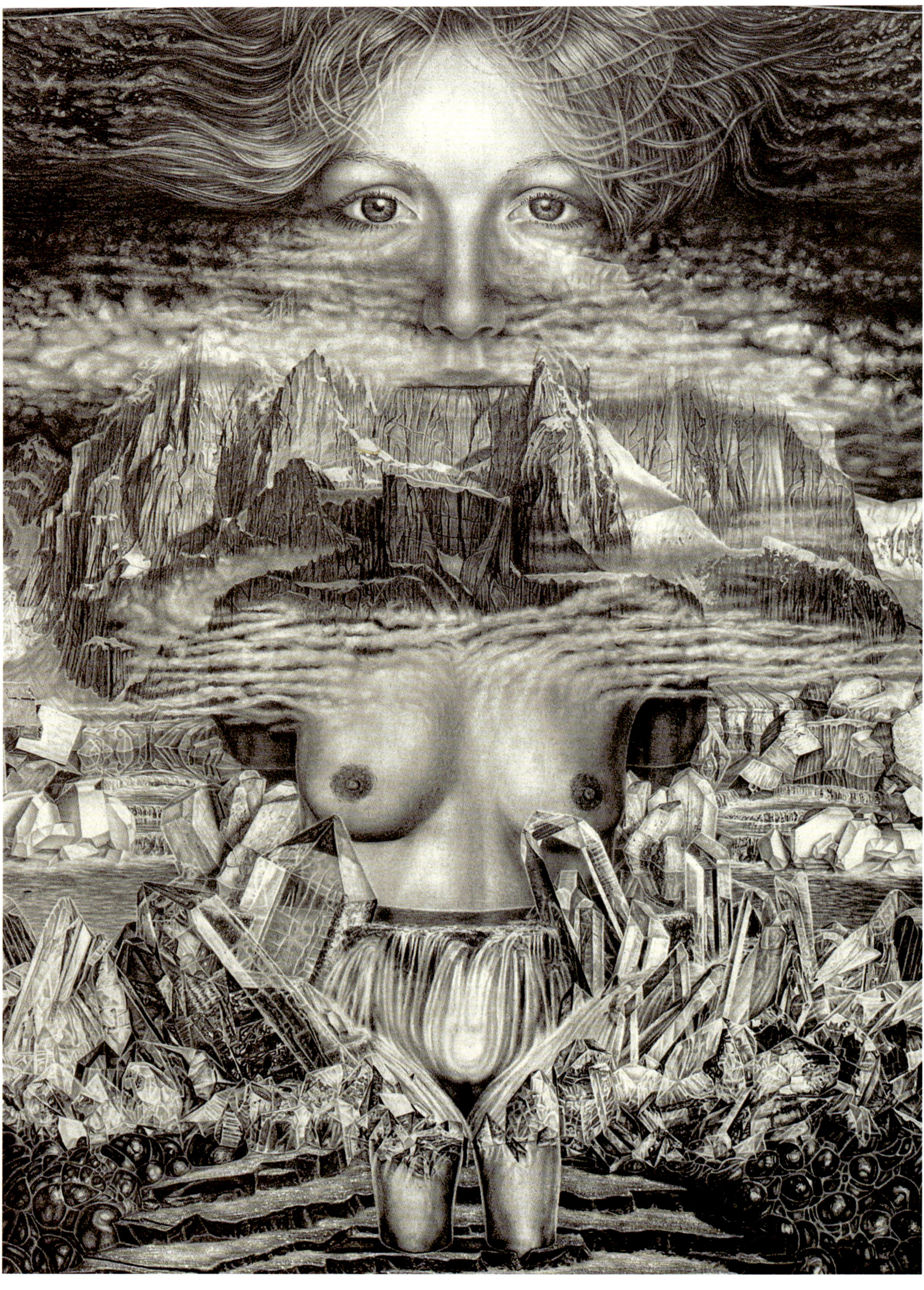

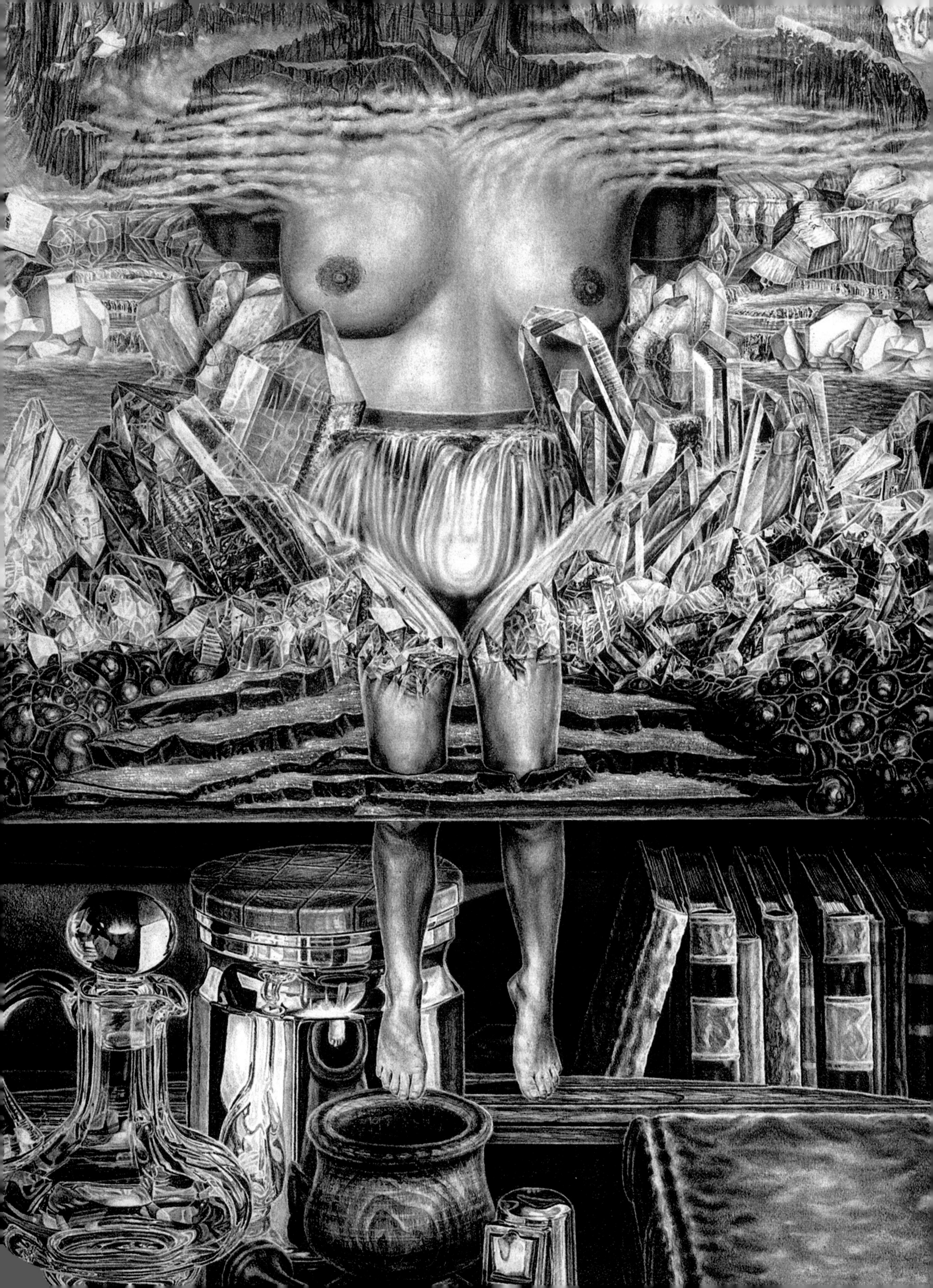

The dream of her can be seen in the cathedraled eye.
There she is mistress of first howls, progenitor
of passion and pity. Jeweled in the high places
above the clouds, bookcased within a thousand rooms —

she is safely bound until the world can remember
how to need her by needing itself less. If she is Nature
it is our nature to love her. And there may come a time
when good natures will prepare well-nurtured again.

Eden is first a garden, then a Venus, then a hope,
then a library, then a volume, finally within the ruffle
of pages, a promise of a garden again, and then
someday, she will again be, a promise in the blood.

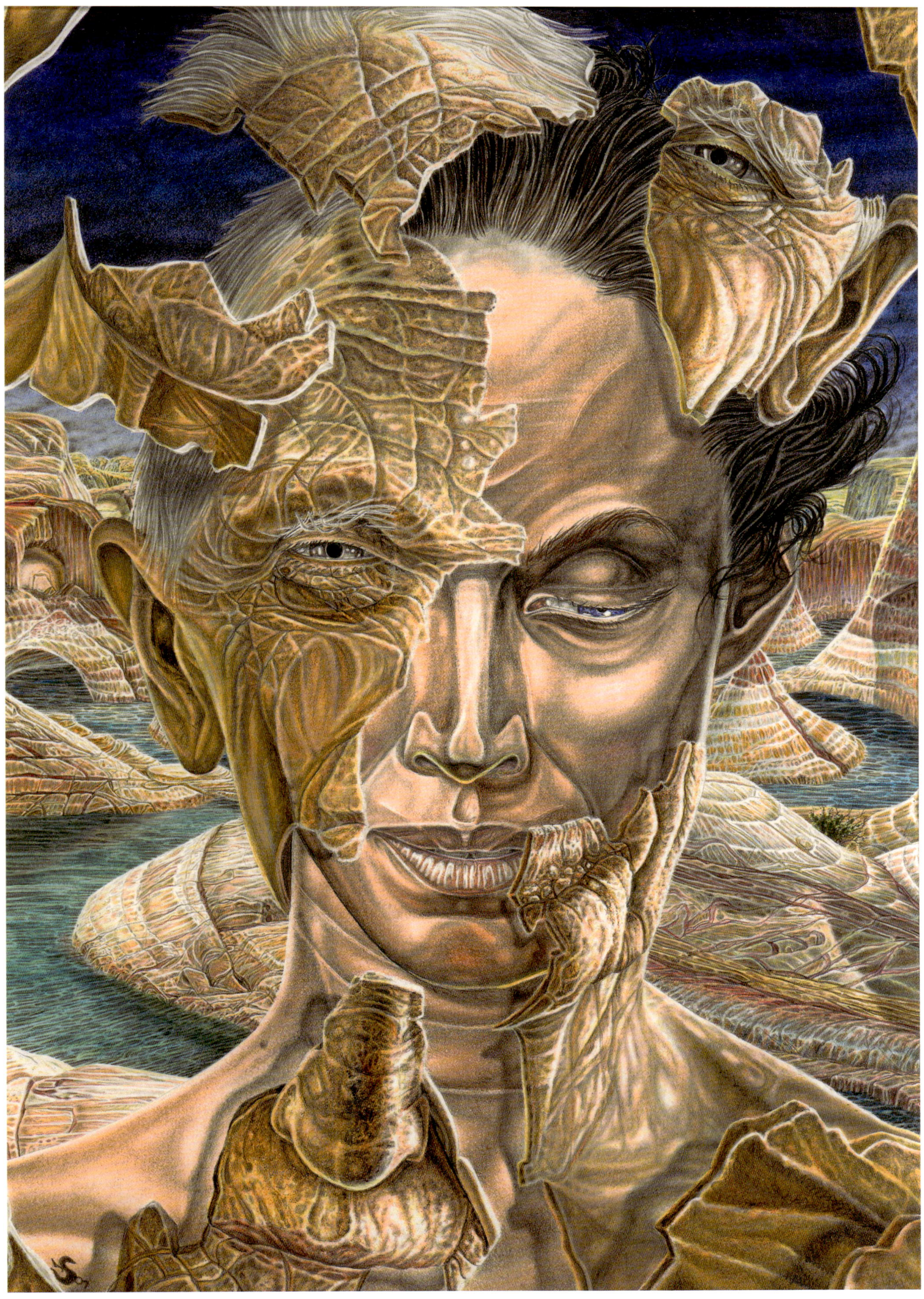

ADAM

I. Have you noted
a face is a geography.

The browed uplands
fissuring sleep from
the force of gravity.

Mining-up thought
in vents and faults
mind-creased from
a lifetime of effort.

Salt sweat runneling,
weathering hollows
down to ageless blued
pools of light, mirroring
lakes whose depths
touch back to the
beginning of sight.

The bridging bone
divide of breath
releasing the force
of interior life,
spinning the air,
dividing and clearing,
opening space.

The broken complex
erosion of speech.

Wind and waves
the percussion of rain
echoing out
from the cave of self
the place of naming.

Have you observed
a face is a destiny.

II. Within the mirror
in the deep loam of us
we see the earth
aware of itself,
an inexhaustible randomness
simplified to a natural
selection of choice.

The ego's brass
serving the living earth's
endless rhythms
the way a chisel serves rock.

For a brief moment
we are the whole world.

We infer, or state, histories,
allusion and myth,
the seductive alchemy of science.

Our stony appetite requires
metaphors of rock.

To keep from going mad
we must steel ourselves.

We become landscapes
pretend we are
the whole of space,
the furthest reaches
of stars, red shifting
beyond the possibility
of temporary poetics.

Geology, my dears,
begins and ends in us.

Our bones will work
themselves down through
the humor of soil,
burrowing beneath worms
and womanly heat.

Under pressure down
to a metamorphic finality,
a purity of compression.

Down to the earth's core
of fluid chemistry
that a synapse ago
arrived at our smile, down
to the unstable glittering
of the eternal now
unwatched by time.

If we can speculate forever,
in us and without us,
what plate tectonics
move us through ourselves
and what crystal lattice
becomes our mind
when the synapse stops.

III. Have you noted
fate is a geography.

What terrifies us now
is not that we are
temporary but that
we are eternal,
not that we are similar
but different from.

Have you noted
fate is a destiny. §

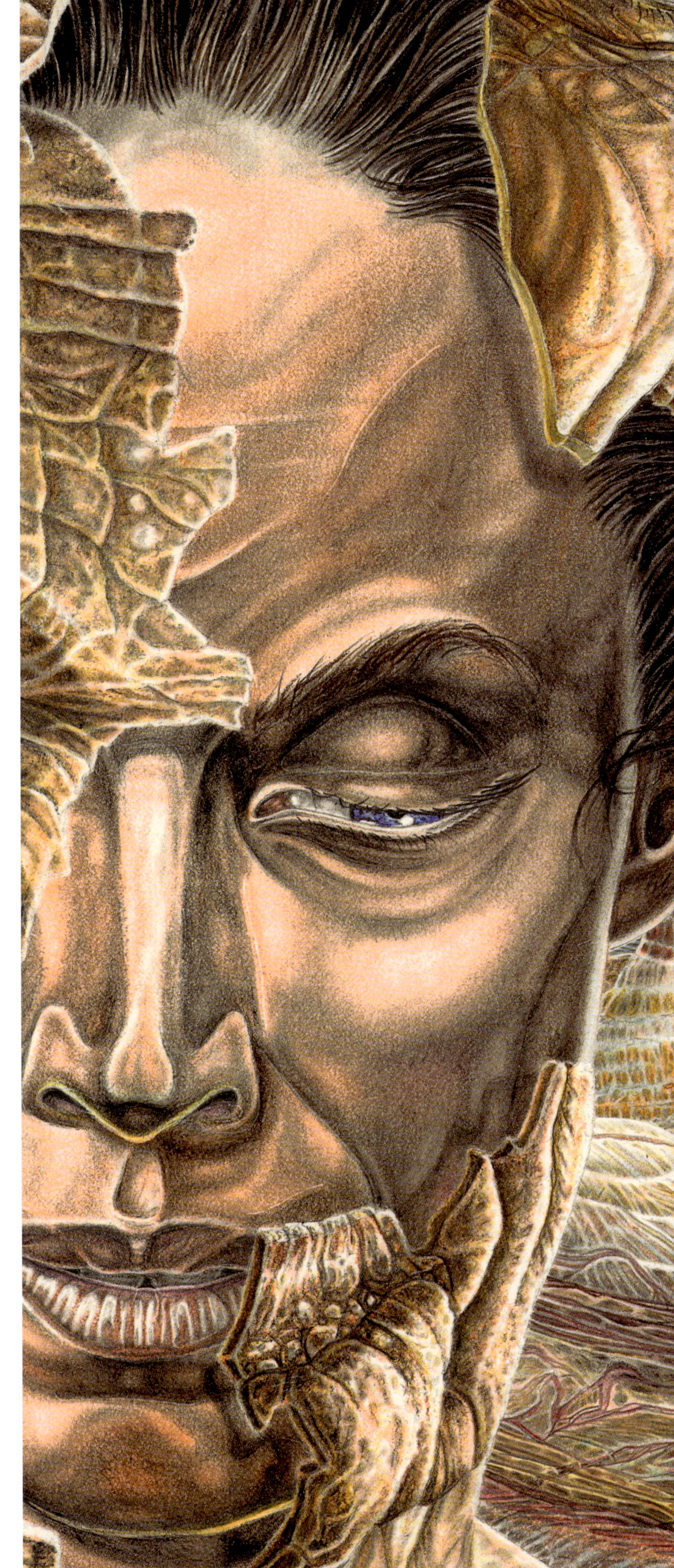

THE HIERATIC NATURE of divinity
has always been symmetrical.
The bilateral mystery we are
finds gods within human faces.

The real and abstract typography
of emblems still hides within our faces
the grand heraldry of our broad smile
a cool Mandala in our eyes.

The original way of securing beauty
in our brief spiral of days
was in the symmetry and flawless
balance of the eternal feminine.

This regularity has blown through time.
Egypt, Sumaria, Greece, all pursuing
a statued grace in the logical dialectic
of our numerically regular features.

And into this primary matrix, the energy
boiled in from the sun, and from the white
ghosting of the moon, and perfectly matched
the radius of the inner-eyes black star.

Lightning, helix-raw, in a pleural arc of fire
around those supremely modulated features
burns the mind back to first causes
and educates us toward the threshold of joy.

We can't stop being hexed by symmetry.
The attenuating circularity of ripples.
The sunflower's spiral-nebula of seeds.
Whorls fingerprinting the dust.

The refracting eloquence of crystals
hiding their axis points equidistant
in the chrysalis of their prismatic souls.
A numerology even in a hawk's wings.

A language of mathematics that formulates
the very symmetry of the earth itself. At some
Gnostic level, as we search our interior god,
the elegance of balance changes our breathing.

The twinned sex of food and fondness,
blessing and forming, our dualities
in the twin sockets of a skull's chalice
show the very nature of beauty's passing.

And still we gaze into the marbled frontality
of Aphrodite, or the blood-stained eye of Kali
and know beauty is knit into the very fabric
of what we desire. Beauty and terror are one.

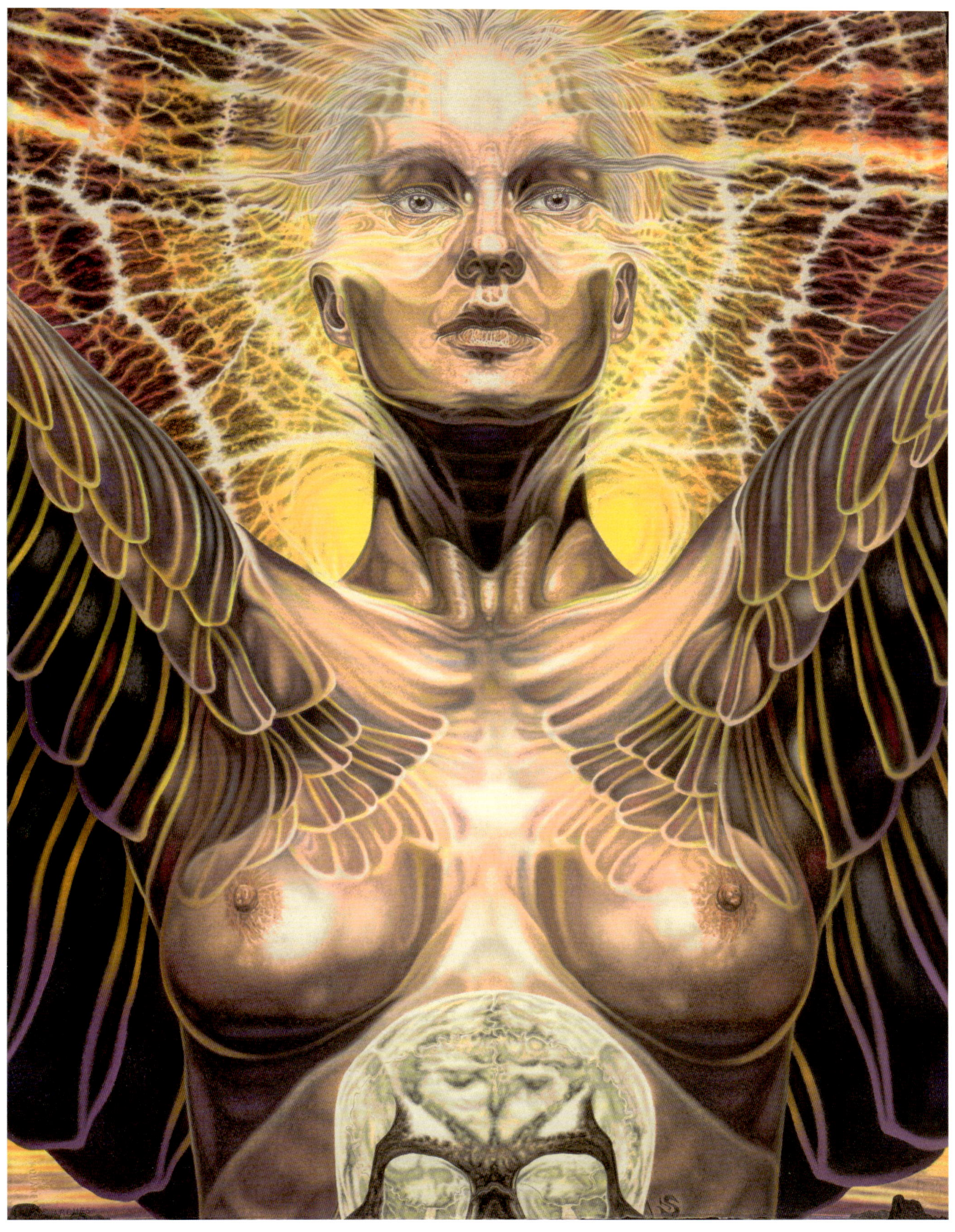

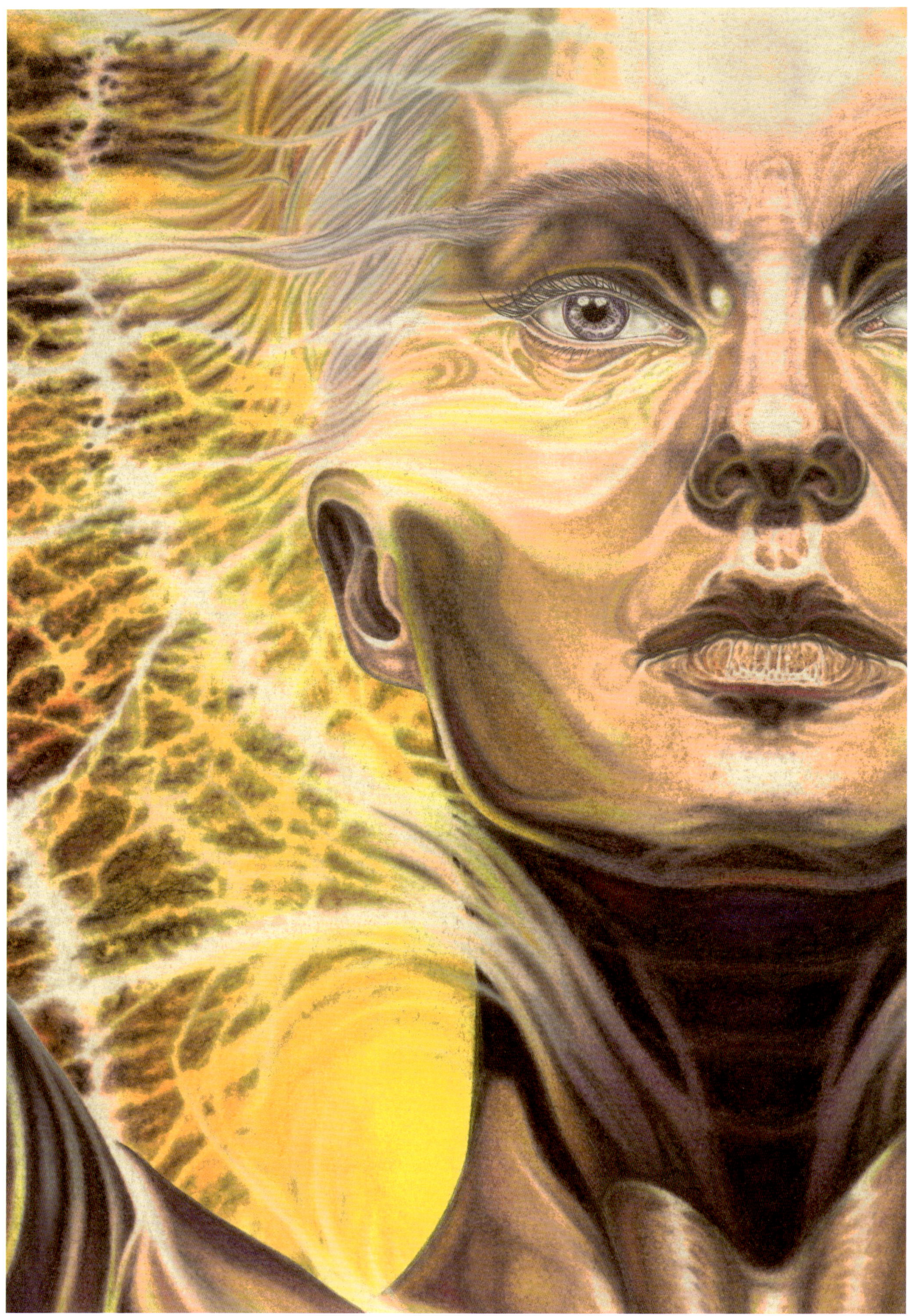

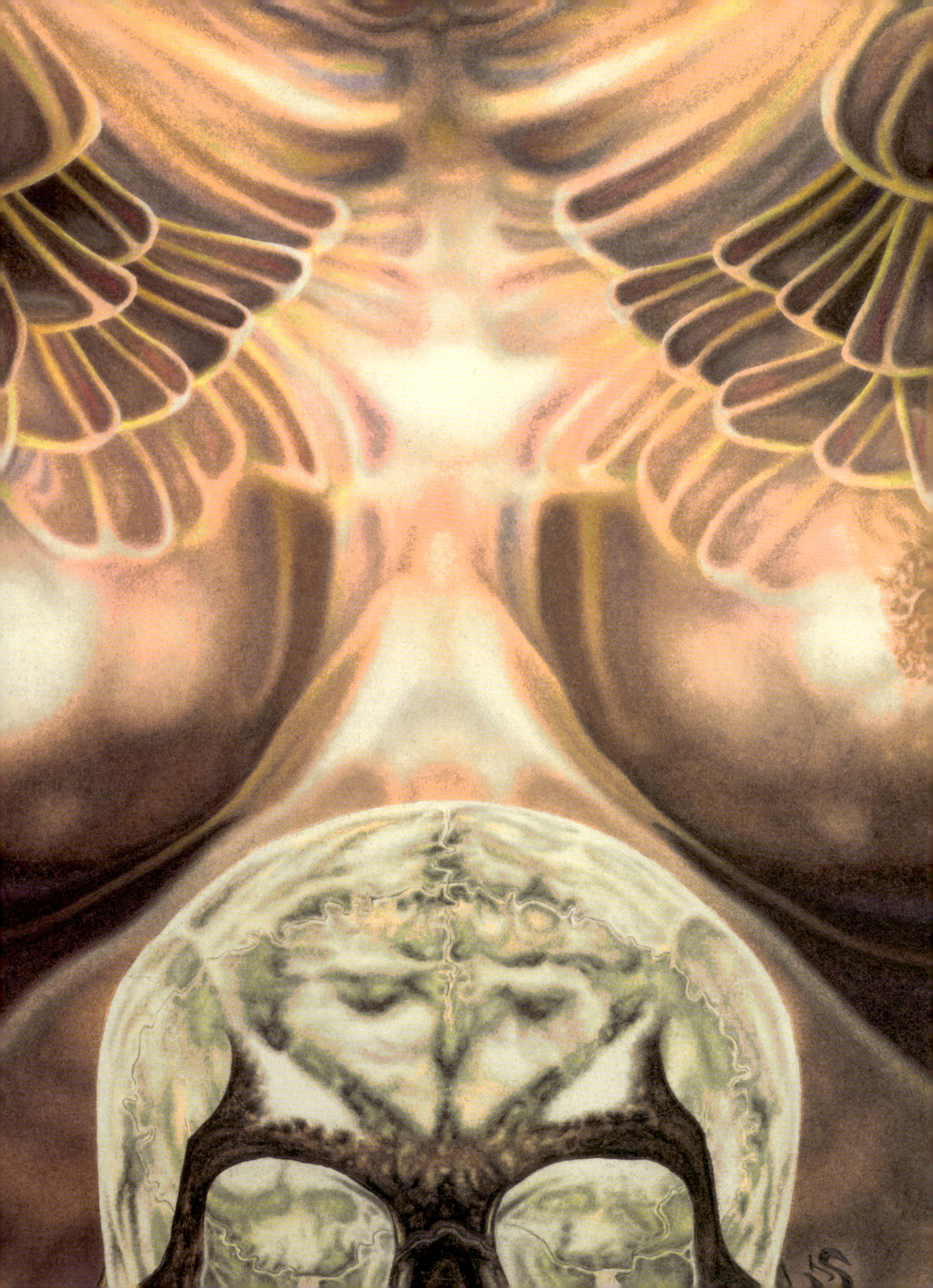

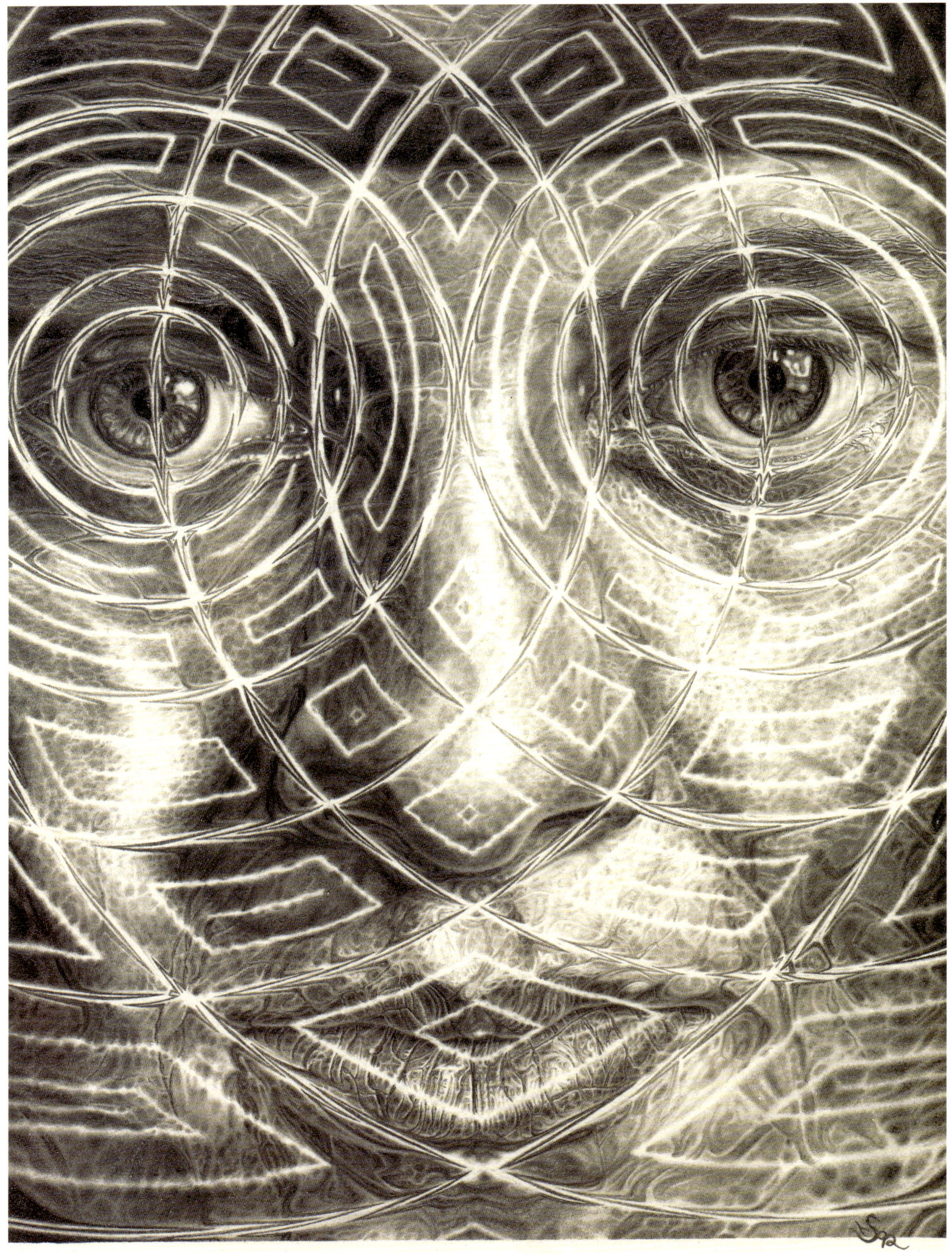

I THE SIMPLE drawing pencil.
Graphite is the most subtle
extension of the hand
that mind has been drawn from.

You can achieve gradations
 of tone inevitable as fate
or feathered, fine as smoke,
a simple tool to complexity.

If you have the inner force
and the patience to use it,
any form and every condition
can find temporal expression.

A pencil is so capable of
worlds that like Narcissus
in the silence of his pool
you can become lost in it.

This drawing, like this myth,
is about the power of obsession.
Drawn into a spiral of refinement
just one more stroke—obsession.

You meditate into the candle's flame
too long. A craftsman sanding until
his hands bleed. The poet searching
for just one more perfect word.

A penitente beating himself to divinity.
Brushing your teeth for the tenth time.
Michelangelo on his back in the Sistine.
Bach improvising fugal invention

until his wife drags him to bed at sunrise.
The clutter and mattering of anything
brought to the holy sepulcher
of full attention wholly without restraint.

Obsession—Only what we ridicule
or don't understand or medicate.
As an artist, where do I draw the line?

Look well into the eyes of Narcissus
It's your question too.

II. Sometimes an idea drops
straight from a deep unknown.
You can take no credit for it.
To metaphorize Narcissus

by making the eyes themselves
pebbles that drop into the pool,
form the ripples which spread
and interact, was a lucky grace.

Every human wrestles this myth.
To love yourself, but how much.
Your eyes dropping into the pool
as you read and as you look.

THE ANGEL OF BEGINNING

I. PERHAPS FRONTALITY is compelling
and disturbing because it doesn't
allow the viewer to be a voyeur.

You are compelled to engage the viewed
directly. Symmetry in nature is neutral,
symmetry in the human face is not.

II. The Angel Of Beginning, nucleotides spinning
ribbons of protein eddying in the primal ocean
and a mere billion or so years later, Shakespeare.

When you look into any face you are looking
at the whole history of life. Whenever you follow
a ribbon of causality, it will lock, intersect, divide

and dissolve into every strand. You follow
the ribbons of narrative that form us, like a destiny,
and know any other ribbon followed is a destiny as well.

III. The pastel candy-floss forms a few algorithms
that alter the plasm of becoming and allegorizes
"we" into a life mystery replete with stories.

The fabled recall of our worlds, soon more lost
than the anaerobic bacteria that electrostatically
charged into our grin at the first pulse of life.

How many bits of protoplasm working in concert
does it take to arrive at Iago, Hamlet or Falstaff?
What shadow play will we be in a million years?

IV. When at long last the lights went on
in the puppet show you are starring in,
do you find you are pulling the strings?

Of the you that is pulling the you on a stage
of things, are you pulling you, then, toward
the beginning of your own end or the final

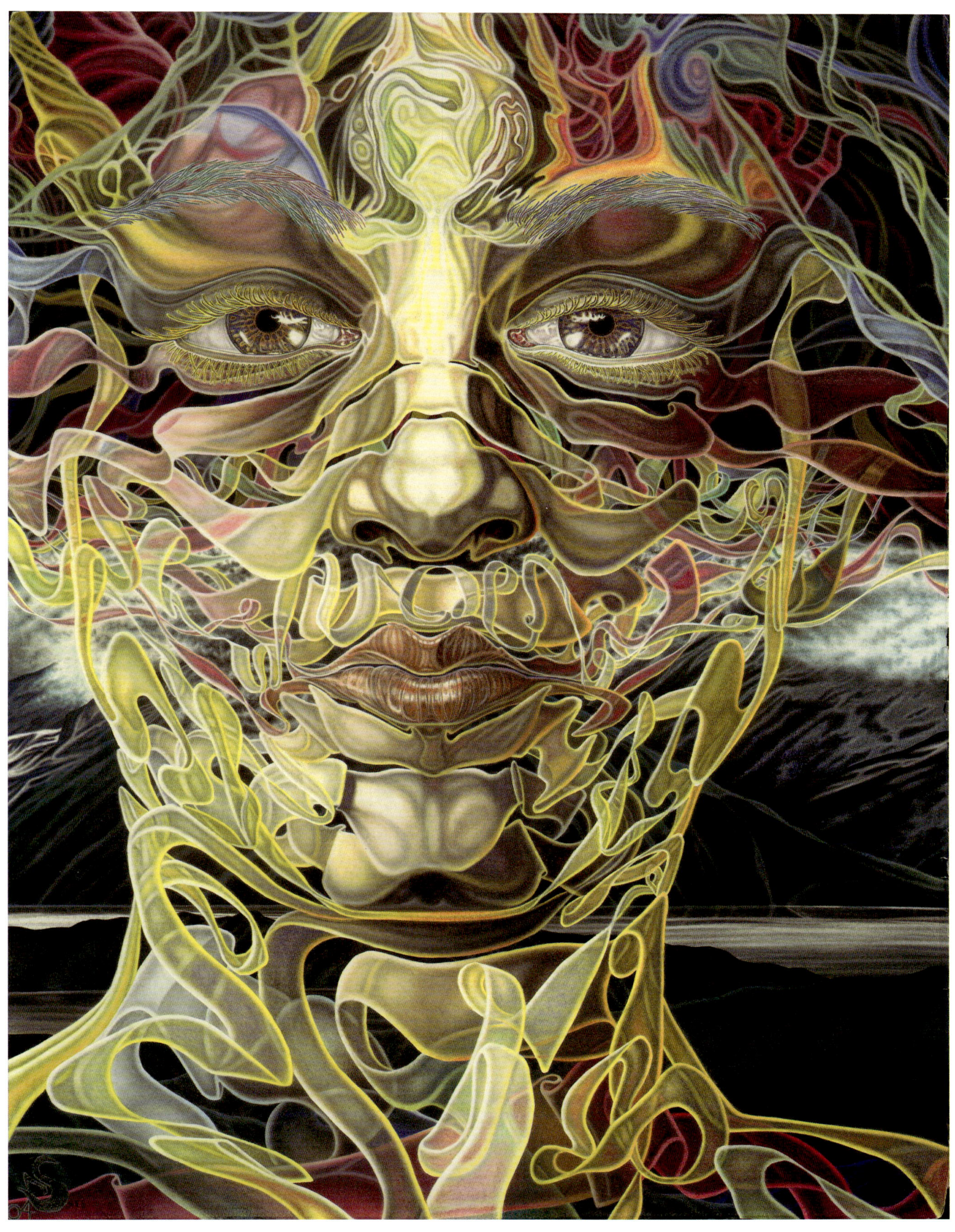

curtain on the end of your beginning?
How do you focus on the beginning
of the world, from its ending, through your eyes?

V. There will be an after you
after you are gone. And before
you go, going forward will be
the memory of the yous that

sheepishly played it safe
and passed on, and the lion in you
the stag and the raven of you
will also extend, and in the end

the beginning you, will start to
again see yourself in its forming.
The black landscape will push you
into the fright of existence.

VI. Beginning is always the A B C s
of blocks, building into complexity —
falling, growing, ebbing, flowing —

until beaten down by incarnation.
You see yourself seeing yourself —
see yourself, you smile, you smile,
you smile. §

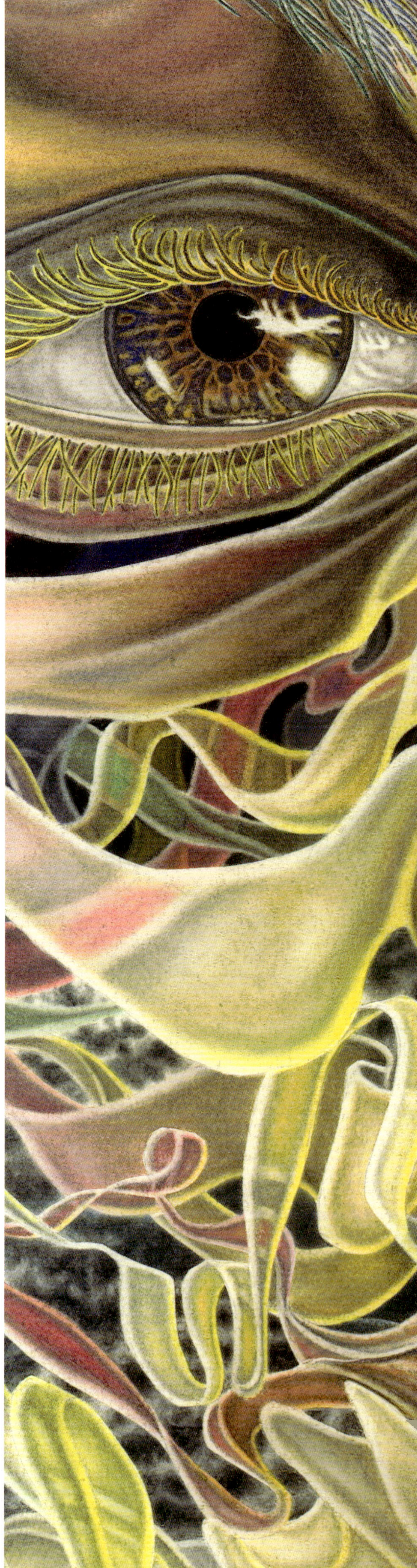

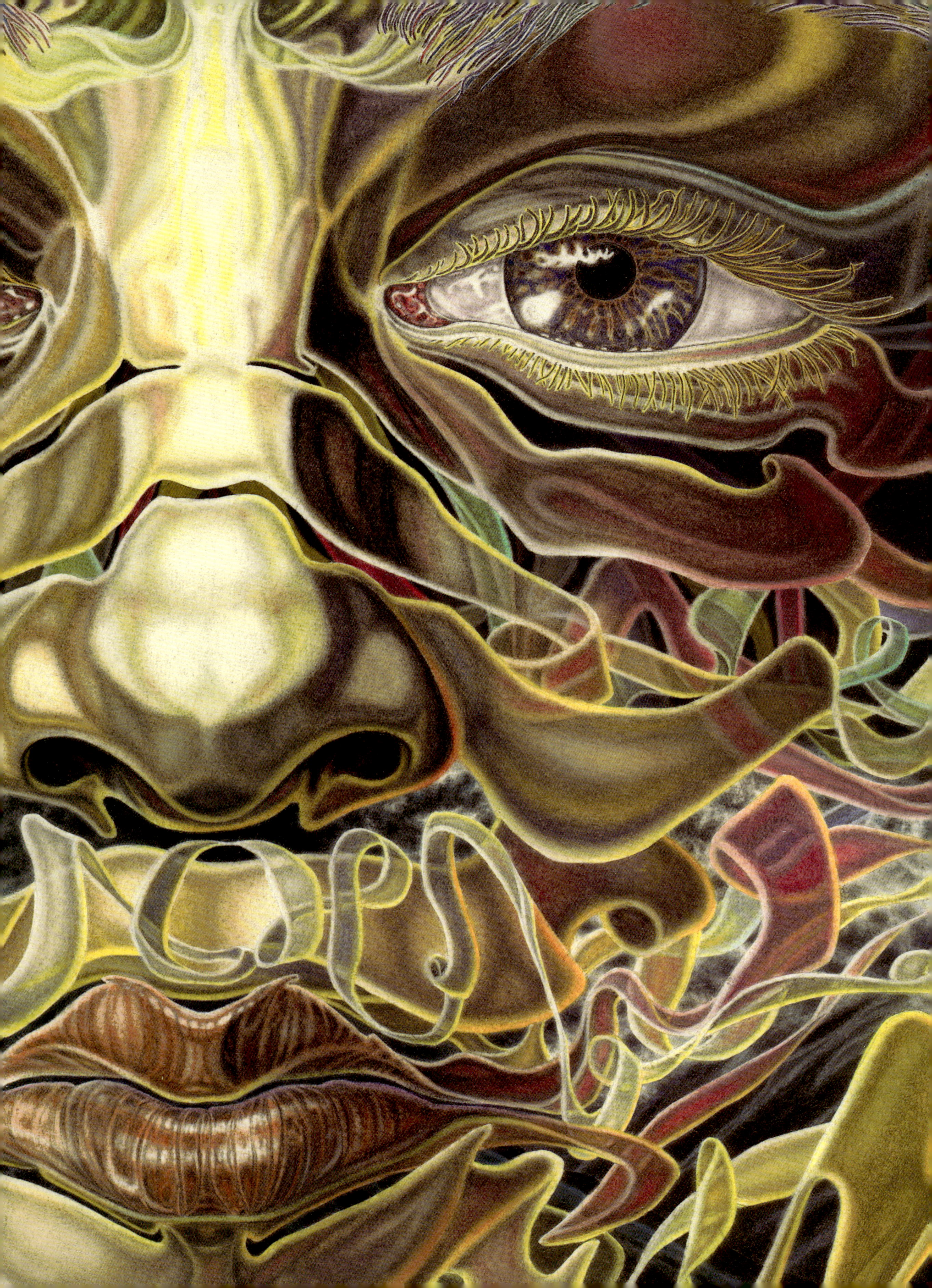

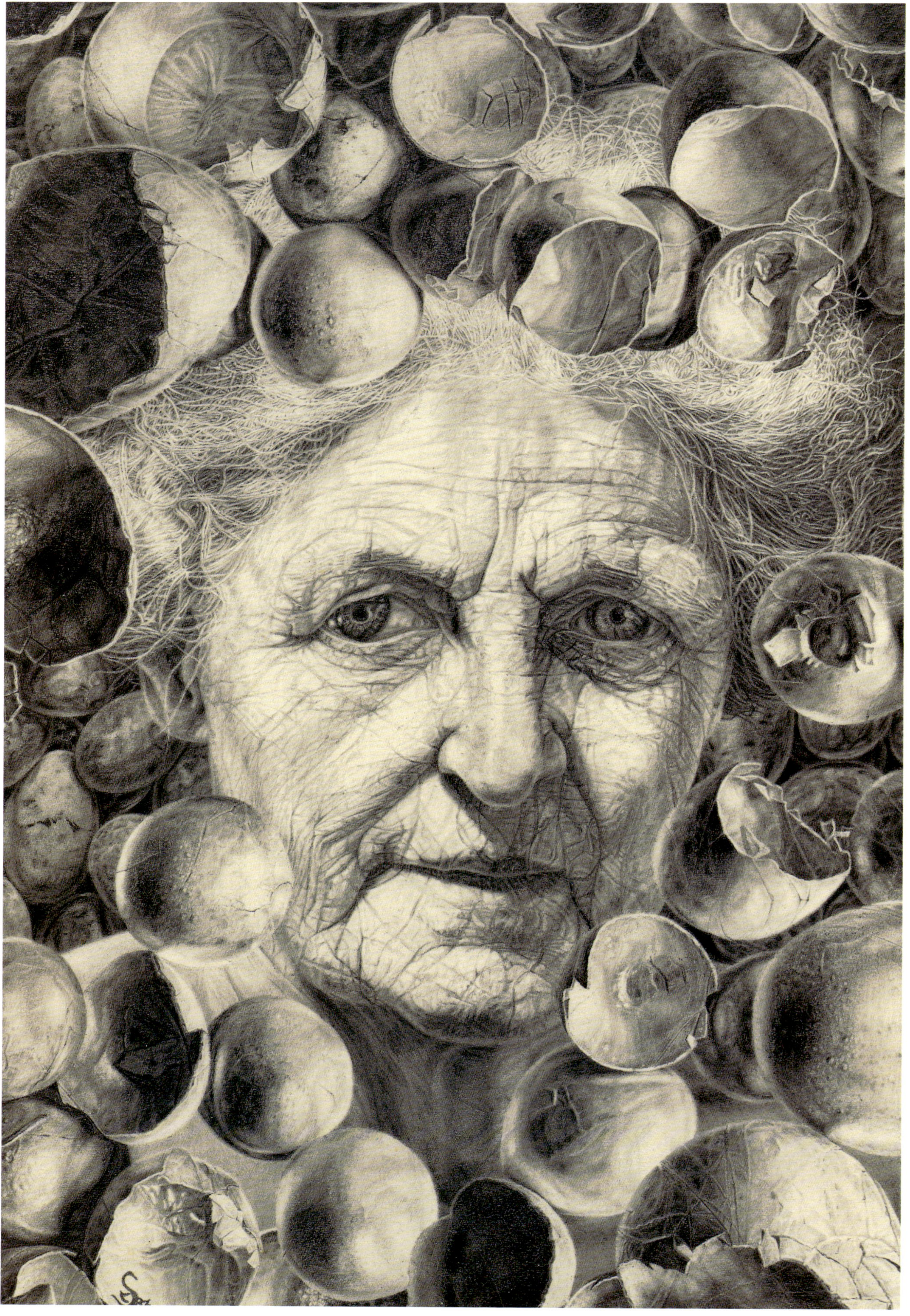

AGNES WROTE every line in her face
and at ninety-six, the Russian novel
of her century neared its final page.

With her at Freeborn County Hospital
I did the only thing I could, I drew her.
I drew her the way I would draw

a geological formation. I drew her
out of the shell of her finality,
and we both sat and patiently waited.

A stroke of the pencil very like a birth.
Great-Grandmother didn't die so much
as close her pages in the layers of black

Minnesota earth. Years would pass,
and the sketches of her phantomed
through my thought, and as all true

connectivity waits below the surface,
I feted a patience until a moment
would arrive, an analogy surface.

While eating a poached egg, I noticed
the shells with the slicked albumen drying
and the torture of small cracks and membranes,

like taffy-pulls of parchment, that held
the egg's life, *loco-parentis,* waiting
for removal. I removed myself

from breakfast and saw that these cracks
were identical to the cracks I had drawn
in Great-Grandmother's slowly eroding face.

A woman of fierce will and more than a dozen
children — what better metaphor than dry and
emptied eggs nimbused around her head —

like a last tomb, framing her face like
something hangable. She would emerge
from the formalities of life as we all

must return to its informal playpen.
Toys are played with, always in both
directions. We play with them

and they play with us. There is electric
energy in the symbols that static our hair,
and closet in the lair of our ticking days.

And to the end of them, toys will define us;
our uniforms, jewelry, artworks, machines,
land, our pets, pretty human dependents,

our self-delusions and hopes, even the liniments
of the body we sculpt or neglect, toys to cherish,
be owned by, and to choose and be chosen by.

I look at this portrait of Great-Grandmother
and see within it, two entirely lost worlds,
hers and mine, both mediated by toys.

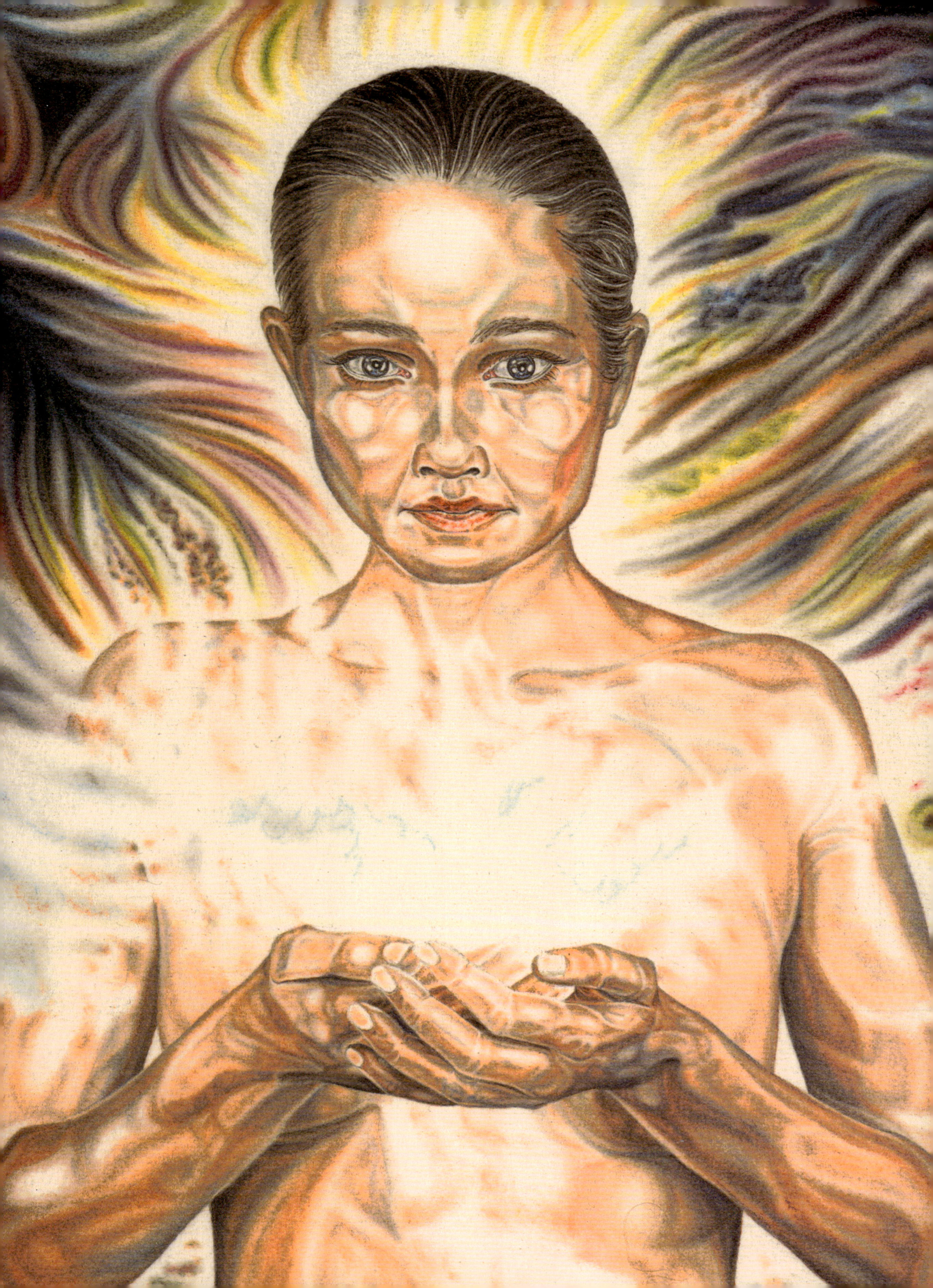

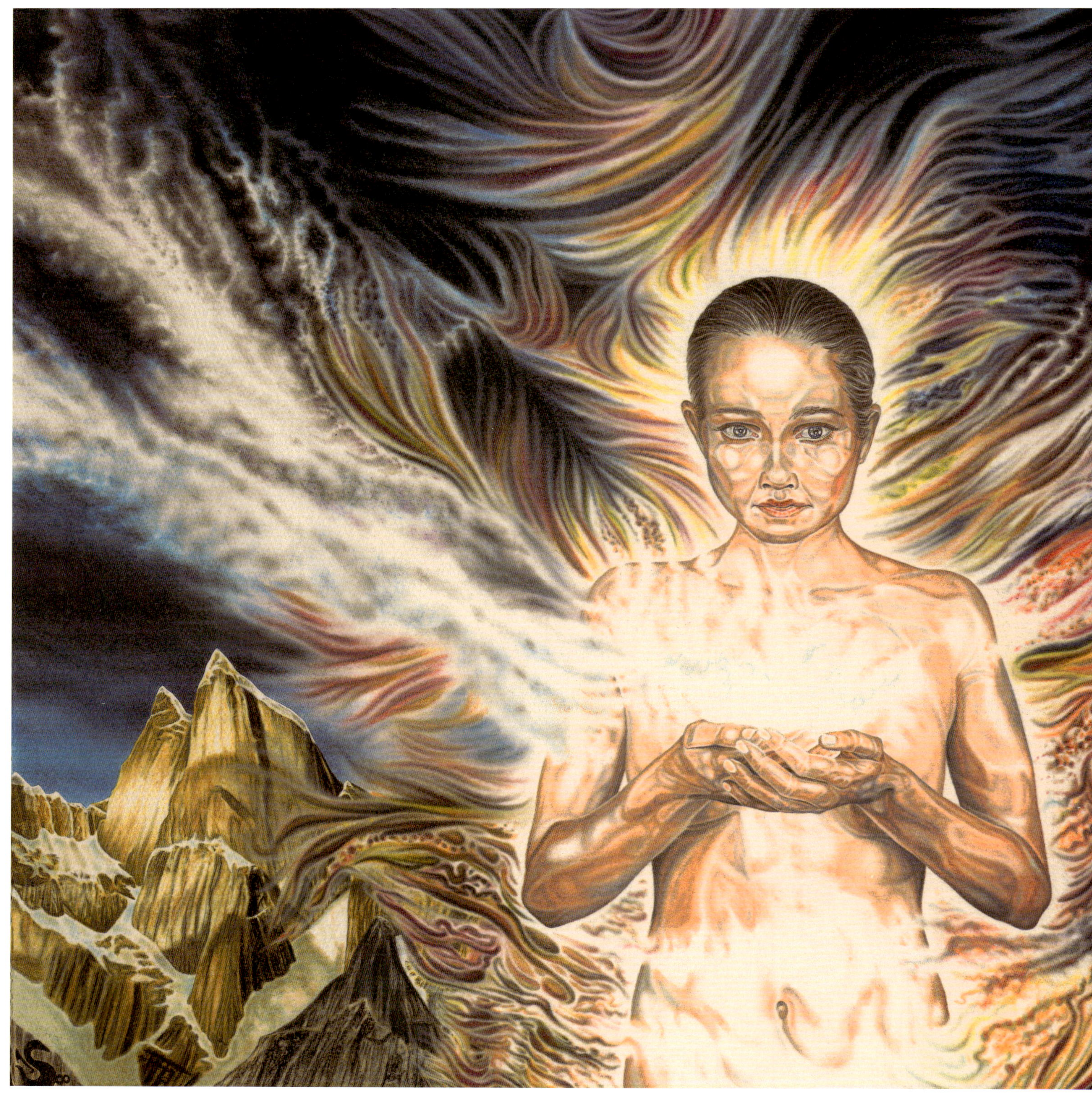

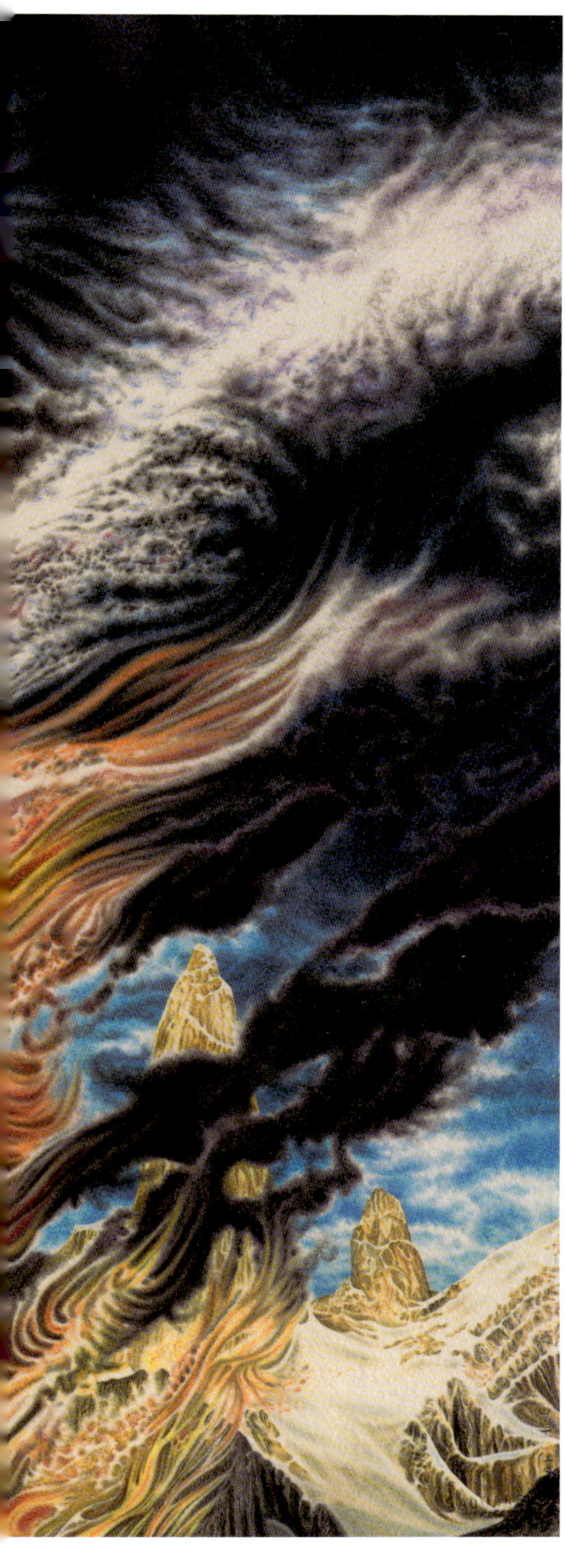

THE FIERY ANGEL

SHE WAS a woman of infinite grace
and she held her heart in her hands.
Her heart was light as all hearts are.

She would weigh that center in gossamer-
grams, and like us all, she died too young.
And so she passed the trivial indignities

of her actual death, at thirty-five, sixty-five,
and one-hundred-and-five. Birth and death
fell from her as the damper from a Victorian-

hearth falls from a reluctant measured life,
and she burst into flame. She couldn't be
engulfed, the gulf between her and temporality

spanned galaxies. Her fiery robes winged themselves,
she waited to fly. The rich life she would never know
burns in all who knew her. We must hope for the same.

Our deeds and actions, the fuel of our fire —
to make a work of art or a perfect act of life —
and in the end, oh how we will burn!

Not with the biblical punishment of a soul
that won't be a slave to a false choice, no.
We will combust like the Phoenix and return.

And never be forgotten or remembered.
When you are reluctantly part of forever
you're all that can ever be. . .

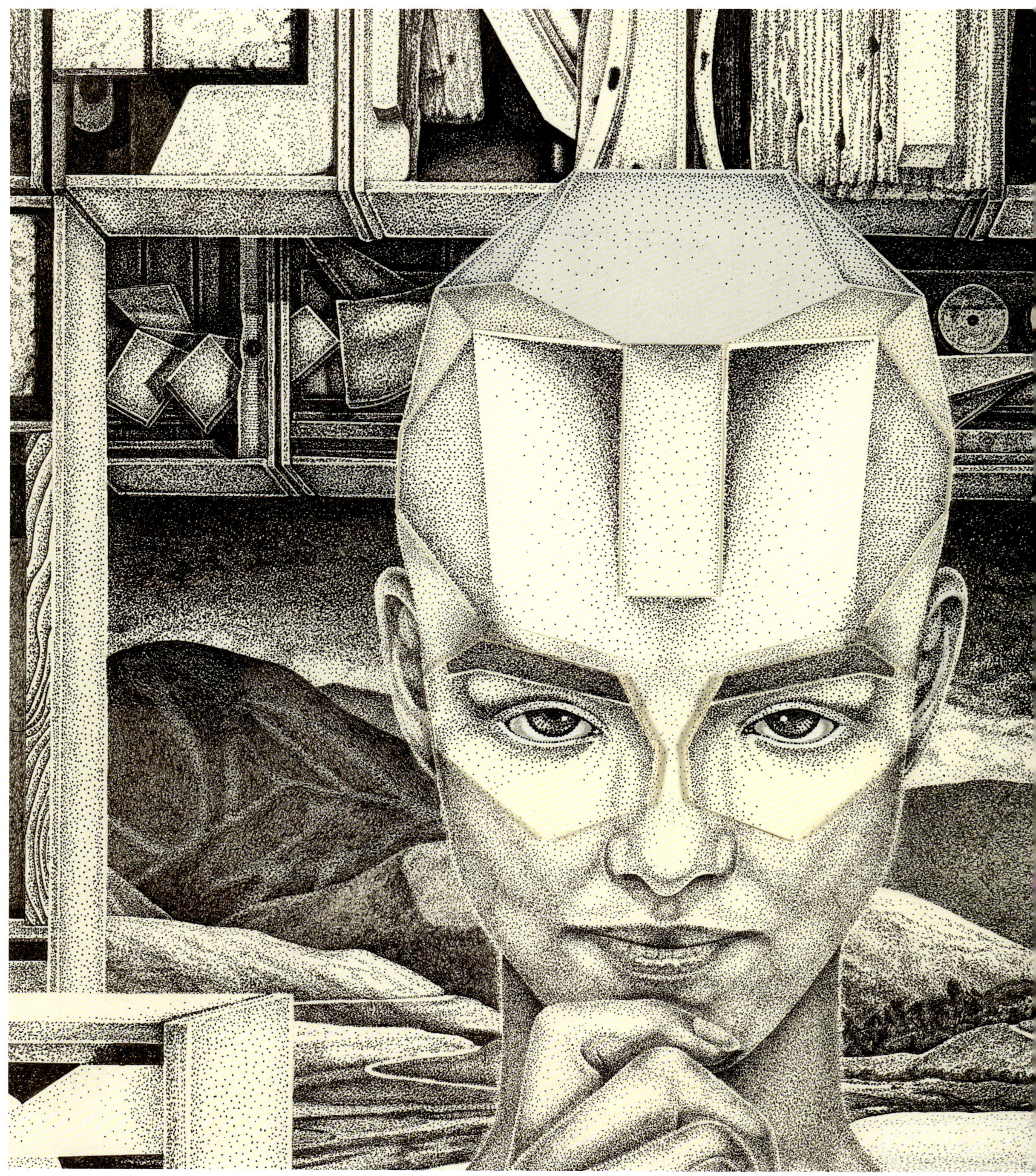

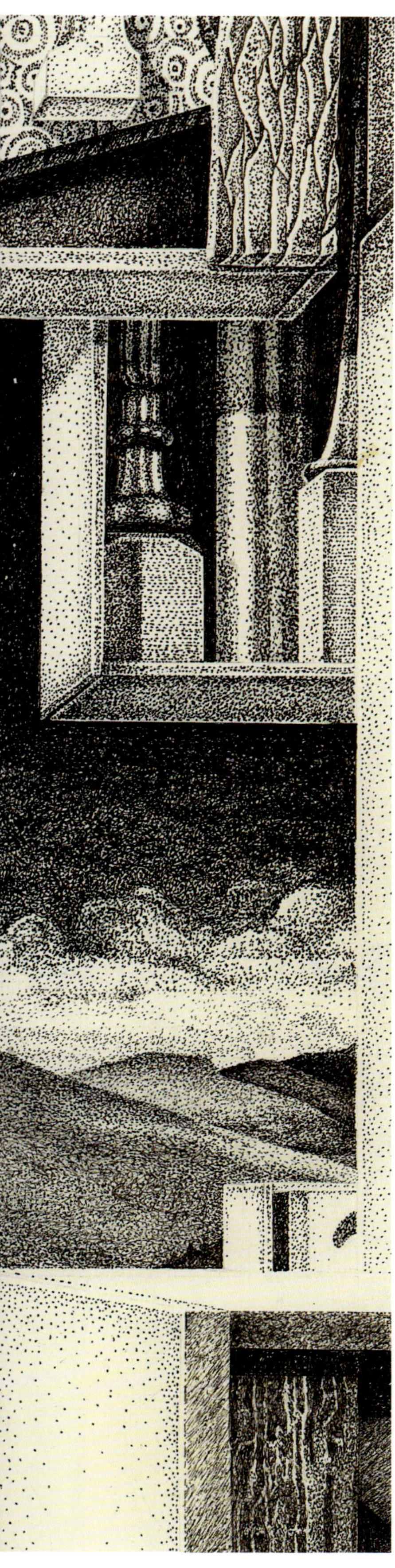

EQUIPOISE

IN A LESSER niche at Lascaux
a lost hunter or forgotten shaman
did not etch the great beasts of the hunt —
    but instead etched polygons of many shapes.

Nothing to control, track or hunt, no function at all —
and in their clumsiness, no romping aesthetics
like the roaring animal power painted all around him.
Yet there they are, something from a geometry primer.

 Drawn thousands of years before even public schools
learned to ruler a rap on the knuckles, and deliver boys
to the beast of those who know how things ought to be.
A first proof of the symbol-making power of consciousness.

We have been on the tightrope of this dance ever since.
Control and release, feel and think, belief and doubt,
the dualisms buzzing and swarming our heads
like horseflies, eager for the blood of our devotion.

But even the formal geometries have a lovely arbitrariness,
aren't quite square, lined up, battened down, or well-nailed.
The rational feeling and the bloody reason, all cobbled together;
Nature will not allow the ape that thinks to be one or the other.

We are instead a blueprint for the universe's knowing,
schematic and scattered, erasable and not the only one.
Equipoise, a lyrical balance, if we can only get it right.
In a lesser niche at Lascaux, who would have figured.

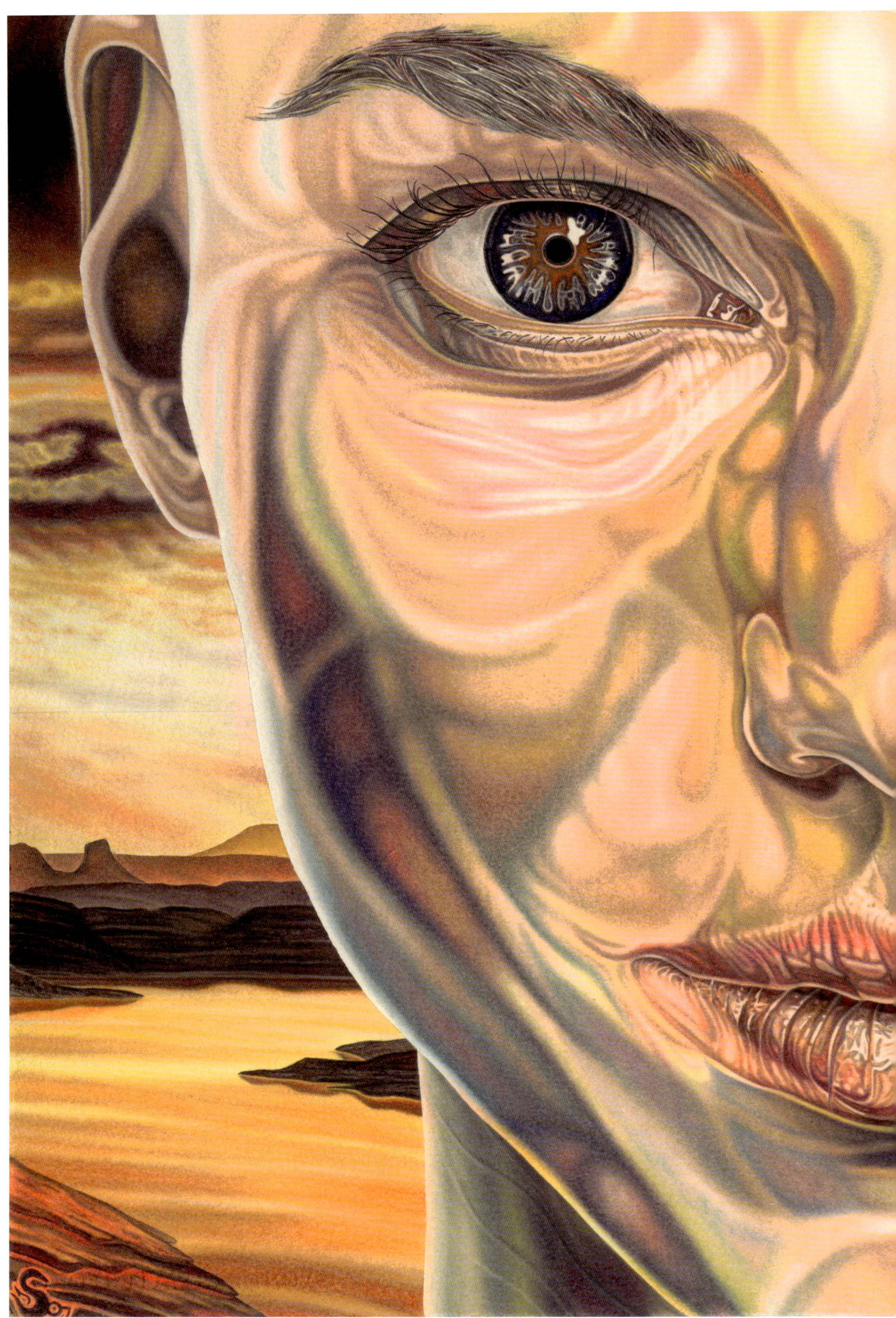

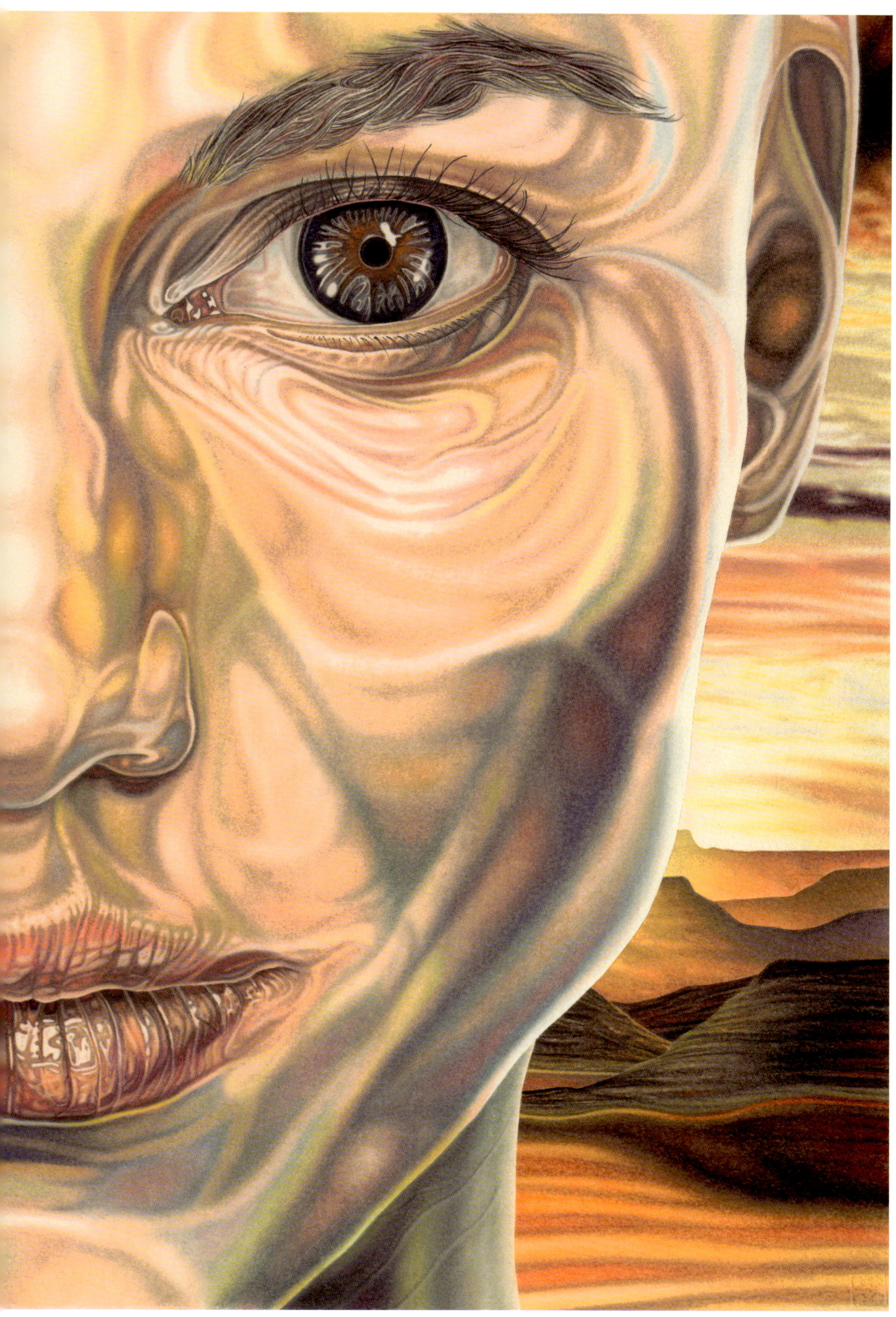

IT'S WHAT WE SUSPECT hides behind our smile.
The Greeks called it daemon, attendant spirit.

Pay no attention to the man behind the screen;
attend not the genius of place that will penetrate
the homespun of your origins like cobalt dye
in a wooden tub. For your daemon will be

with you, yea or nay. Find your dearest desires
and force them into your complacency. We were
not born to be neutral on the stage of action.
Pay no attention, for behind the screen you will go.

Dionysus, God of daemonic force, dangerous
only because venturing from any safe place
forces you to confront the power of your real
mask; the pallid natal flesh must be burned away.

The Romans make the panicked glitter of Dionysus
into Bacchus, a fat, harmless old drunk. While
the Pope turns daemon into demon, gives it horns
and exhorts us not to be seduced or damned by it.

Not to be corrupted by your essential nature.
It seems historically, the force of one's inner light
must always be controlled by outer force. After all,
the Romans literally turned prophecy into law.

Dionysus could not be erased, but he could be controlled.
Genius, one of our fuzziest and fondest words,
is always about good and evil. A Genie after all, is an evil
genius. The creative in you is owned by your daemon.

Call it familiar, muse, angel or trickster —
whatever euphemism tames your death, whatever
secure place you need to feel safe from the whirlwind
at your center, is fine and probably necessary.

But all the way back to the beginning of us
the real Guardian Angel didn't tell us to be good.
Our Daemon told us to be real, fully alive, creative
to the brink of danger and beyond, to risk

the coin of our short moment on something golden.
You may dress your daemon in a three-piece suit
or call him indigestion, or dismiss him as metaphor.

Science will help you erase the possibility of him,
and post-modernists revising the past will deny genius
entirely as counter-productive; even talent
is too much; just function, and process, and forget.

Yet whatever you think you are, the daemon behind
your smile is ready to upset the applecart of your
cherished assumptions. Take you on the possibility
of a somewhere, where genius is inside your skin. ❧

SHE WILL look into you
till the end of your time.

In the temporal now and ever though,
endeavor to draw a single contour line
that defines the arc of a breast to the belly
and down the architrave of the hip.

The myth of ease in drawing the young
is that they are perfect Tabula-Rasa,
but that is why they are closer to God.
To draw with a free hand a perfect circle

is almost a Samurai proof. And to draw
a young woman's flawless contours
is a proof very much the same, for
there is very little latitude for error.

But a lived skin is a seasoned landscape
that is wholly in time and of the earth.
The young have one foot still in heaven.
The old are planted here like enduring oaks.

The geology of wear makes of us an ornament.
Land-locked we are the forces that formed us.
We are the eternity of the moment and taken apart
and remixed even as we strive to still be here.

Look into the eyes of the long deposition
of a life of change and see how a soul can
still be firmly grounded *"I am still here"*,
yet be sea-changed on the shoals of space

An attic smile among the earned payment
of cracks and fissures and all along the way
the crenellate stratigraphy of use. The child
hums a lullaby without contradiction.

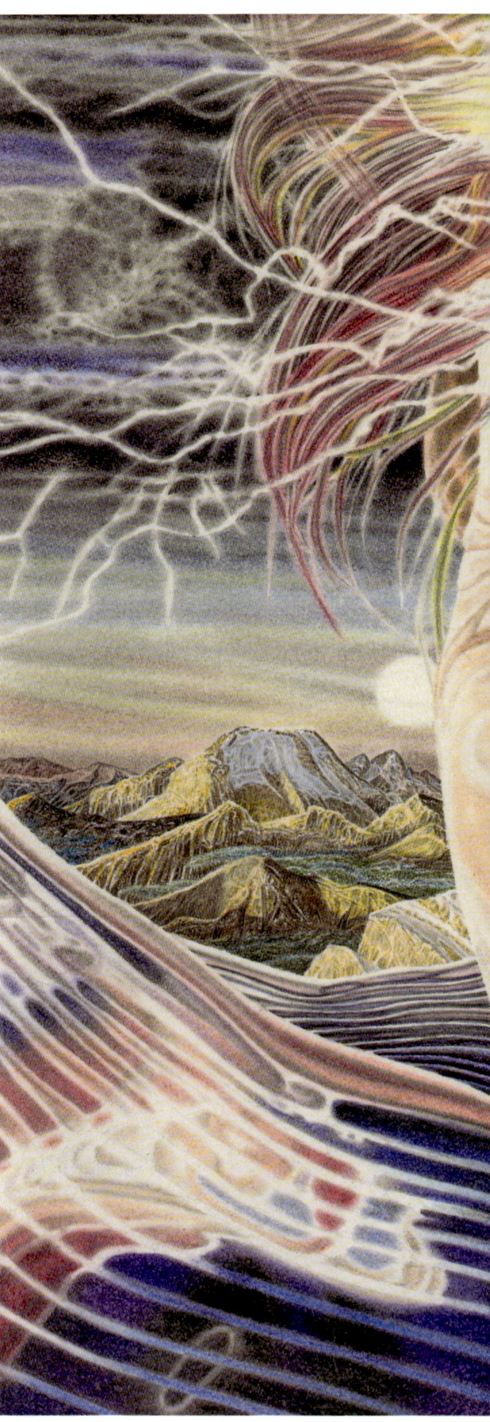

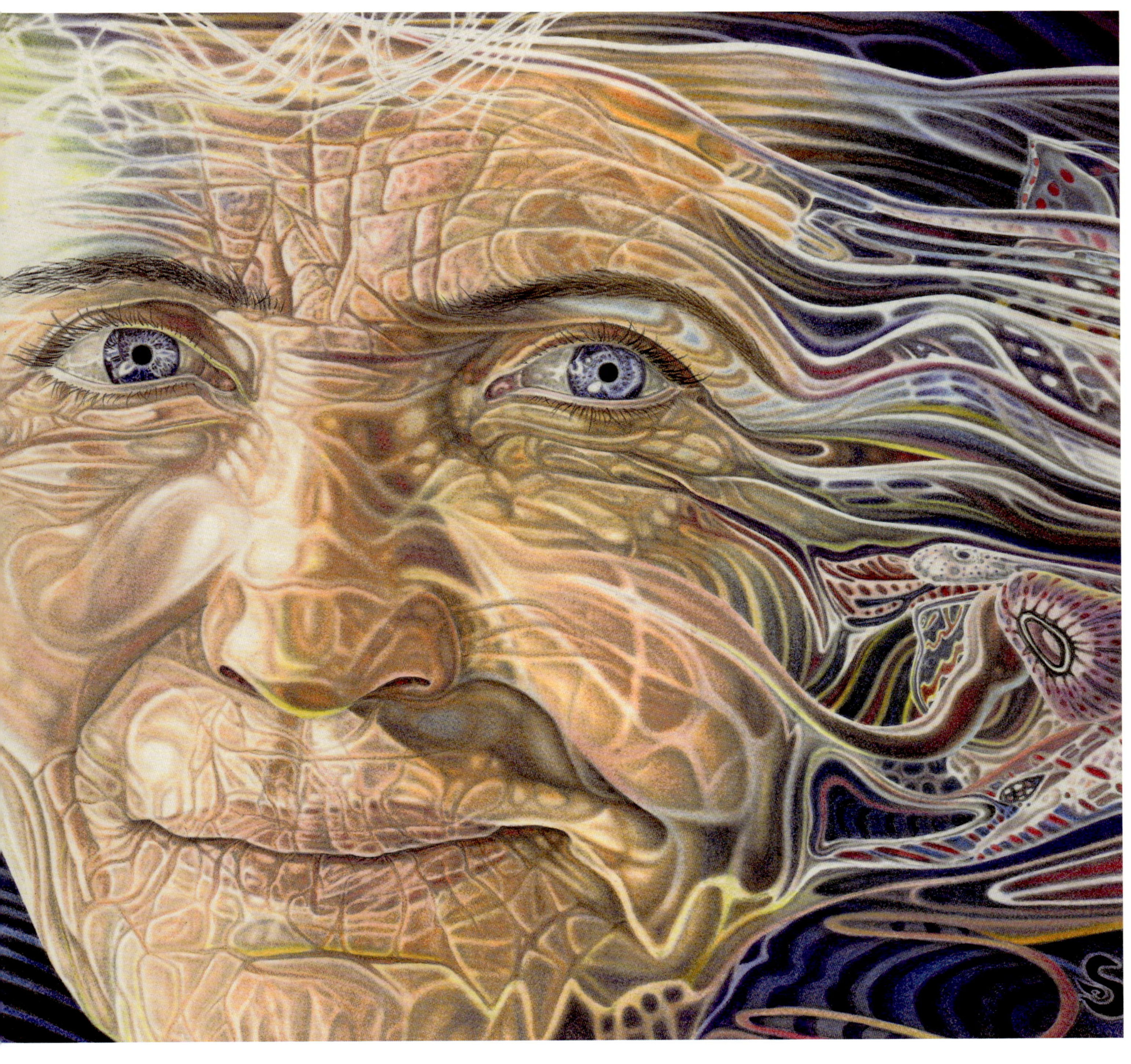

We will be mixed again in crystal, water,
and star-shine, re-imagined by forever, which
can afford to take its time with us. The woman's
curve of grace a sonnet without explanation.

The End Of The Beginning
where we will find one foot
in heaven again, and draw
with a free hand the perfect circle. 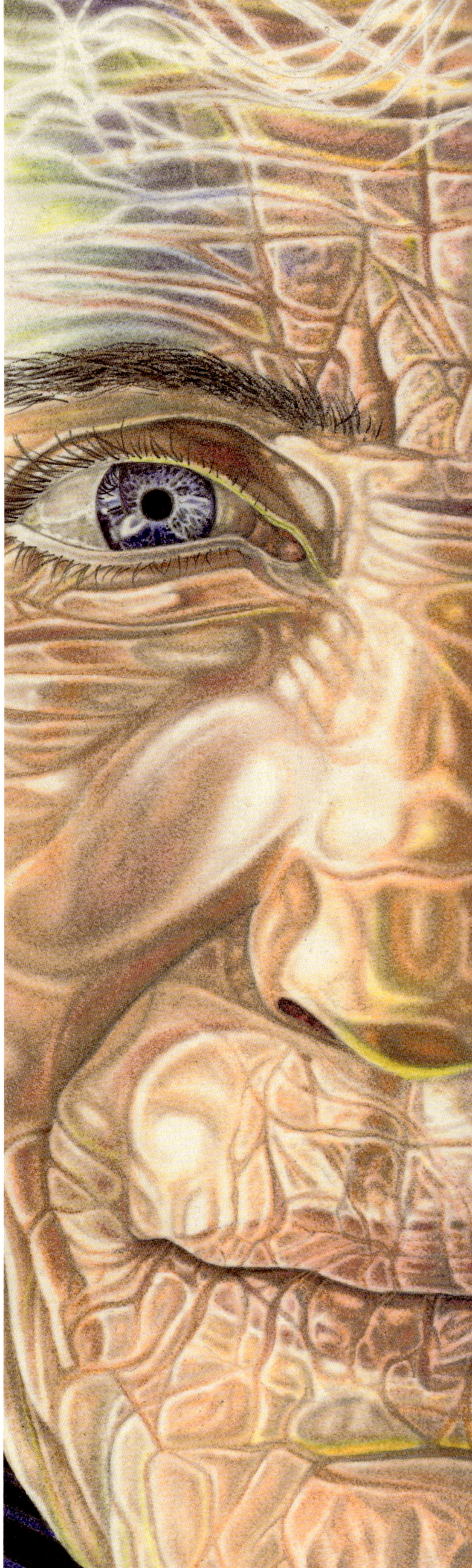

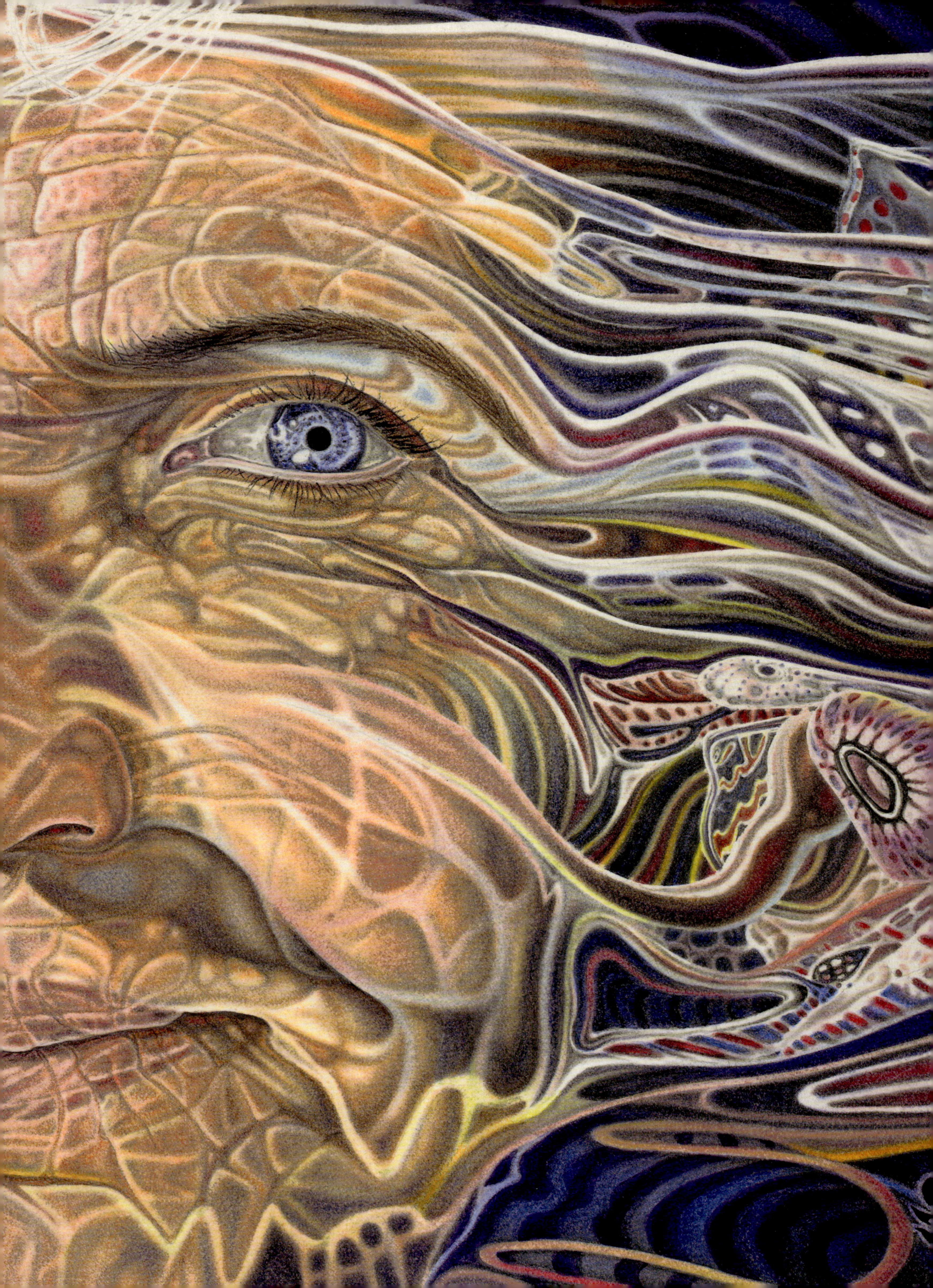

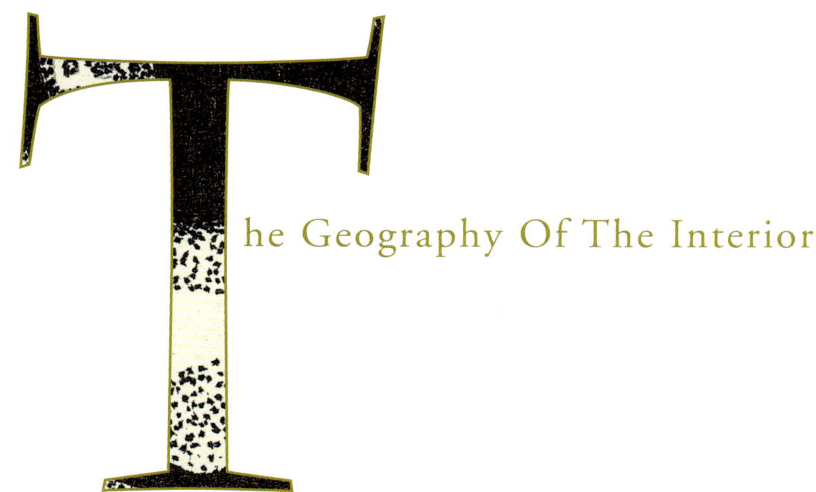

PART FOUR

The Geography Of The Interior

MONOLITH

A translucent gate in front
of a ripsaw of mountains.

Heightened awareness is always
about mystery, beauty and terror.

> To confront the extraordinary
> is to be drained from time.
>
> For a brief blessing,
> God becomes us.
>
> It doesn't last, of course,
> but the memory does
>
> and the memory is nearly
> the whole of our life.

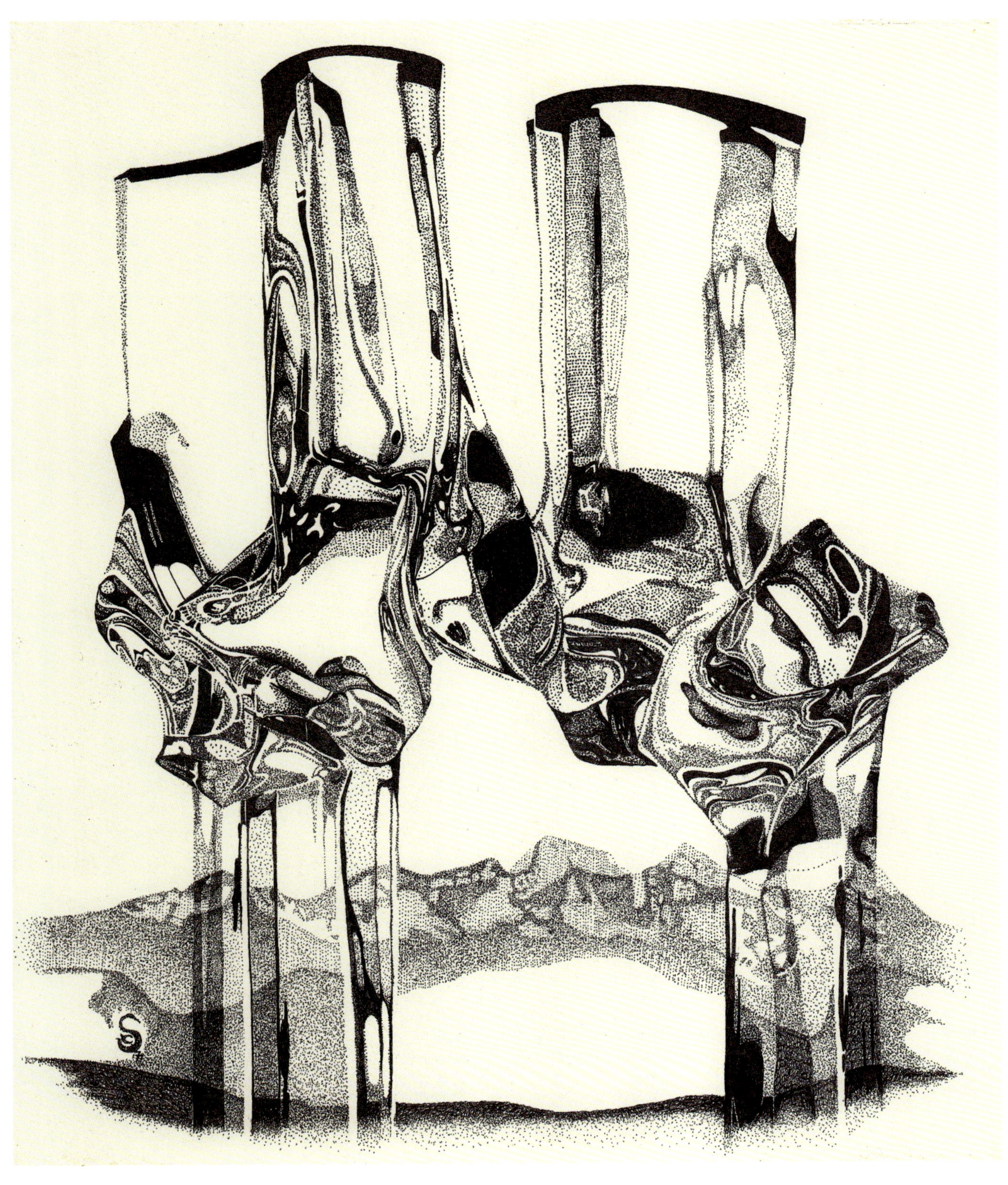

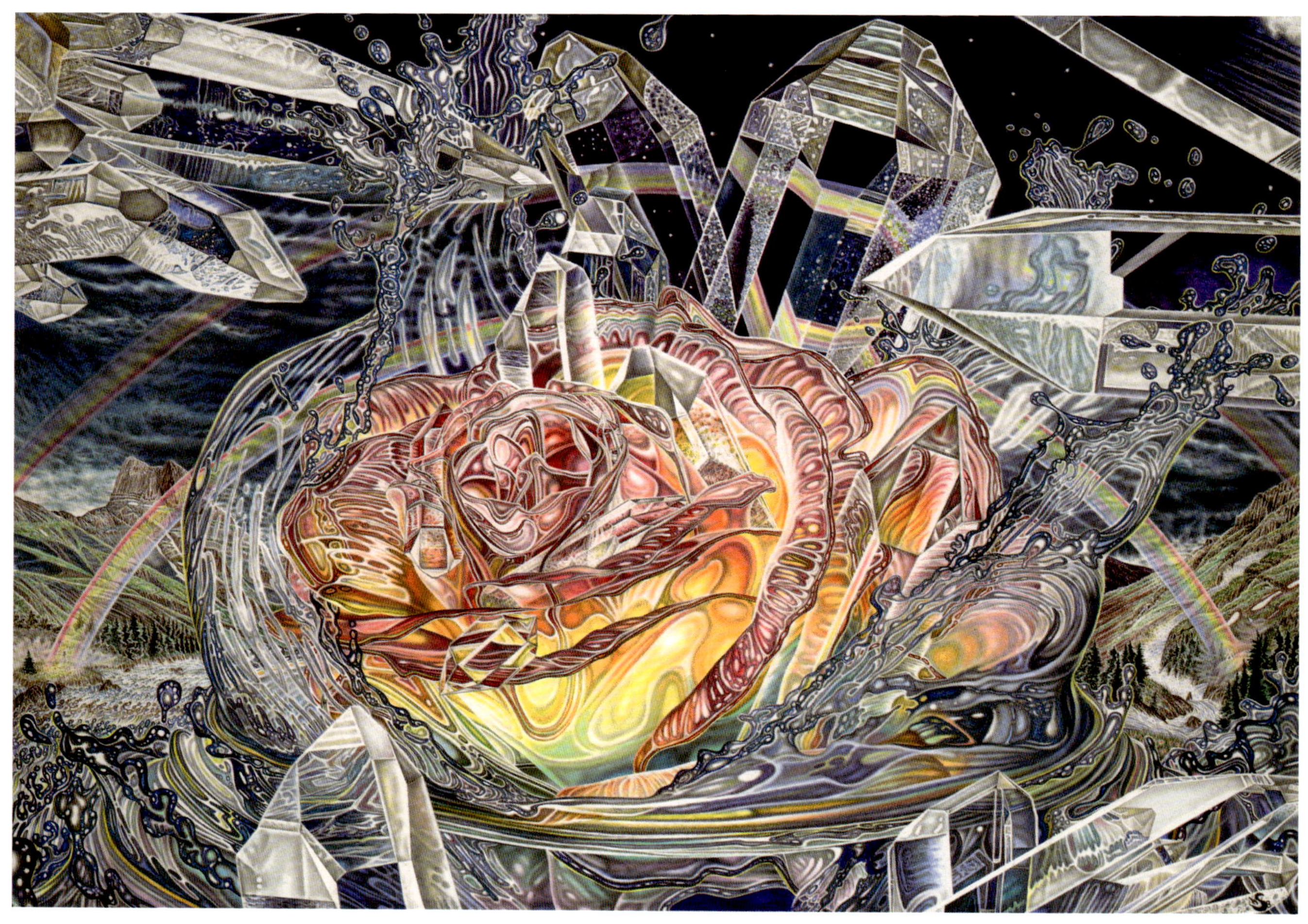

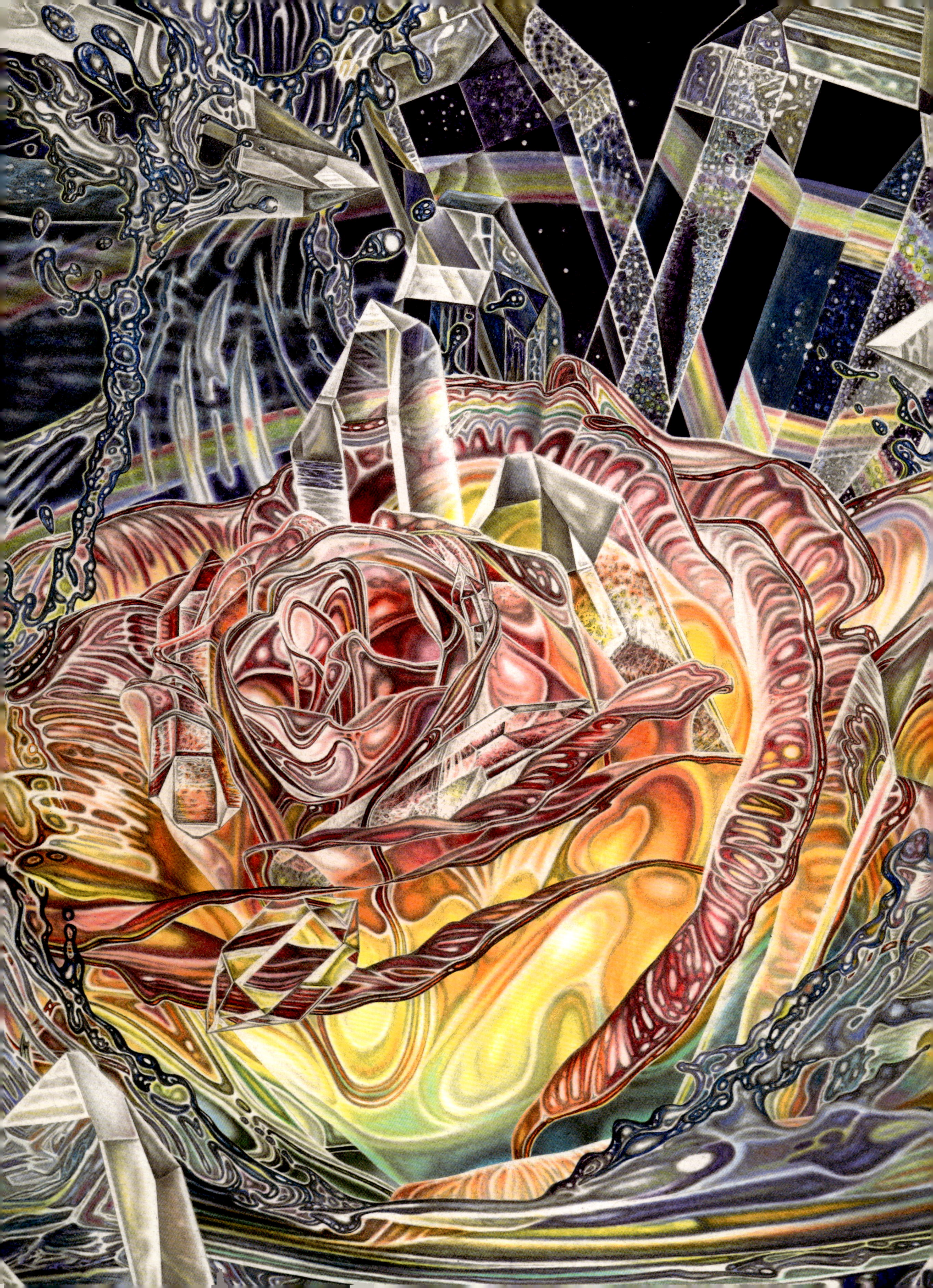

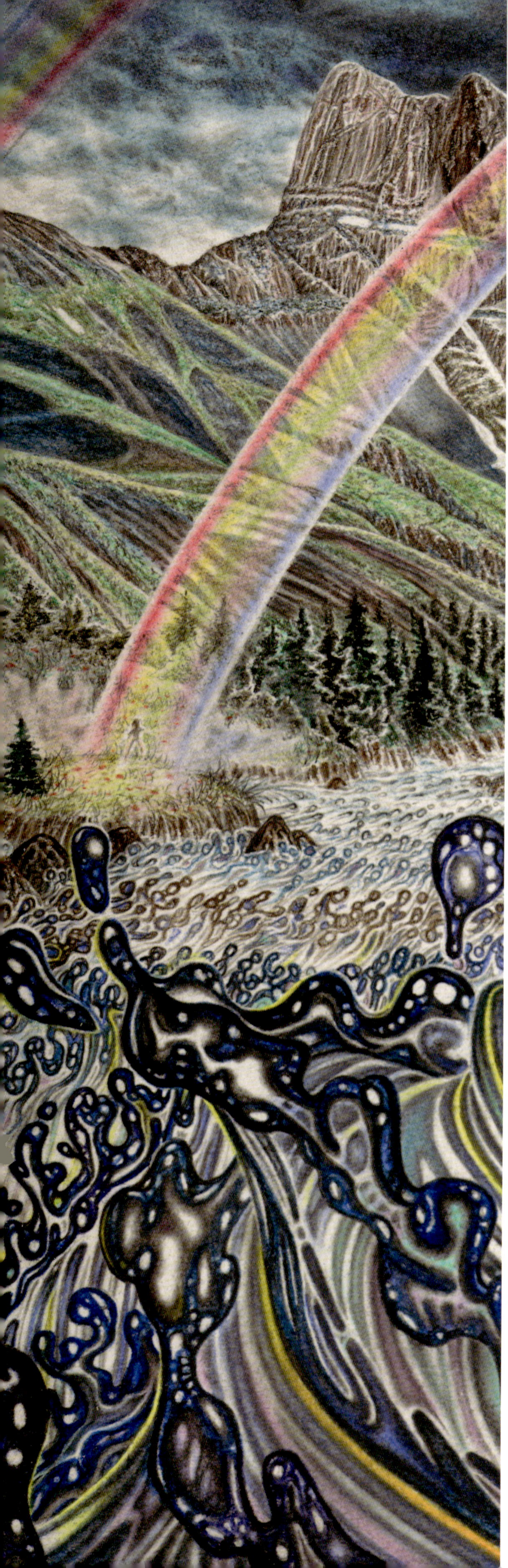

FOR DANTE HEAVEN was a constantly
expanding rose of light. His mind,
his poetic genius, could evolve no further
toward bliss, and really whose can?

When confronted with the drift of stars
on an icy midnight, or the points of life
in a lighted pond, the vivid meditation
you live is the complex clarity of joy.

Rhyme and the tinkerings of reason
won't help you bridge the distance
between one point of the rainbow
or the other. Between these points

all heaven breaks loose. Before you
is a cataclysm of color rearing in a tear-
dropping splash toward the everyday —
physic you can ignore, or find yourself

down the rabbit hole exploring. Trans-
lucence, what you see, through what you see,
the outer "I" possessing the inner vision
that is seen but not easily or fully believed.

It happens all the time. You hold, say,
a crystal of quartz in your hand and
for a moment undistracted by definitions,
or equations of shape, your fully

sentient "I" falls into the crystalline labyrinth.
Inclusions and bubbles, refractive angles,
prismatic cuts of brightness merry-go-round
you through a kingdom of distortions

each more fanciful than the last. Your mind
divides. You know the matter-of-factness
of everything and yet you're lost
in the endless elaborations of fear and delight.

Backlit water explodes in a necklace of drops
fountaining up prisms of borrowed color.
As a rose of pure glass strikes a transparency
transparently. These things are always happening

but are seldom frozen in time. Spend time here
and you will see a clear small symphony
polyphonically played on cut-glass petals,
land — escaping and all things moving.

There is praise-singing offered to the right
kind of chaos, organized by a willingness
to put the neoclassical blinders away
and swallow slowly the hard candy

of random possibility, wedded to a precise
moment. Think of this as three-dimensional
stained glass, broken free from the coffin
of its cathedral. It moves and spins

like a galaxy of ice. When the world was new
and freshly washed, all the glitter of creation
greeted us in this way, the shock of seeing
forced into an immediacy with all things.

When we civilized our wildness, when we
perceived in a fundamentally different way,
we glamoured away the garden, we gained
the Faustian Power, to Will in the world.

But from time to time let's take a moment
to offer ourselves the supreme luxury
of remembering what we misplaced.
A lost world is merely a rose away. §

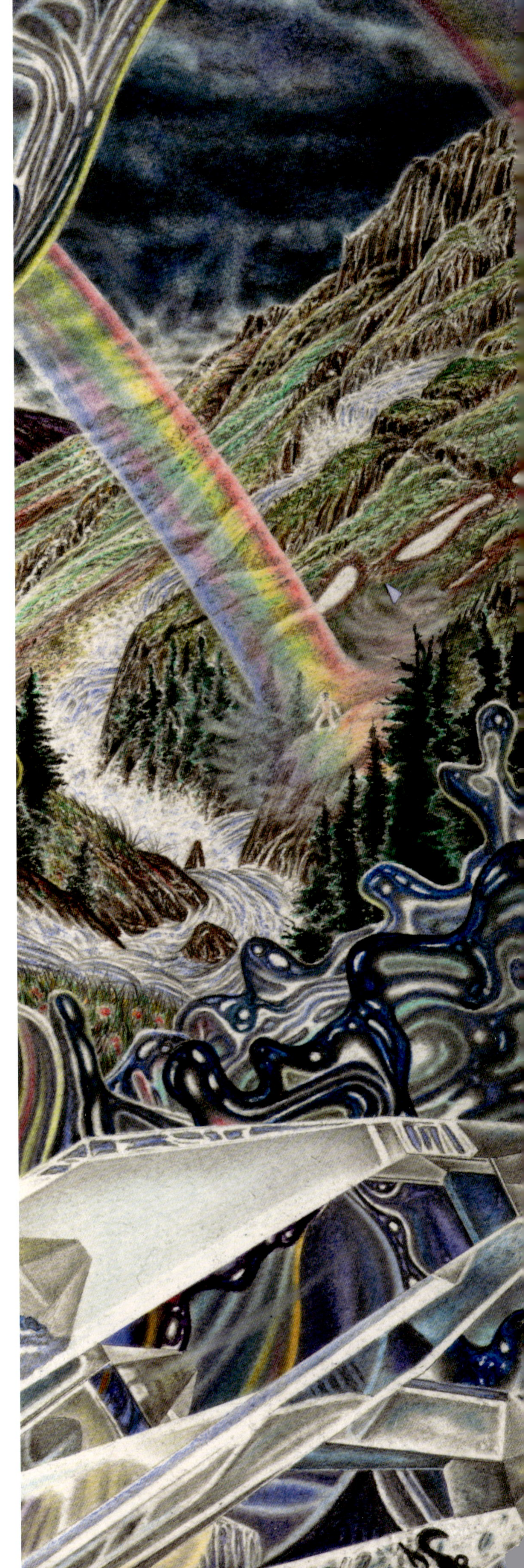

SILICA SEASCAPE

GREEK BUILDINGS catch shadow,
are white, and might be seen
jellied in pellucid brightness
by simply blurring vision.

A crystal goblet turned upside-
down, becomes a parasol or tree.
A silken shawl shimmies free
of itself, escapes ordinary wear.

A moiled full curve of water
like the oiled gossamer of ebony.
A bruise of ripe darkness
heathen as the disc of a vanished sun.

A world without stolid opacity,
all surfaces diaphanous or vitreous.
Why does natural hocus-pocus
lodge imagination in dazzlement?

If you enter the unknown
you will become known to it.
To travel you must leave yourself,
otherwise it's just movement.

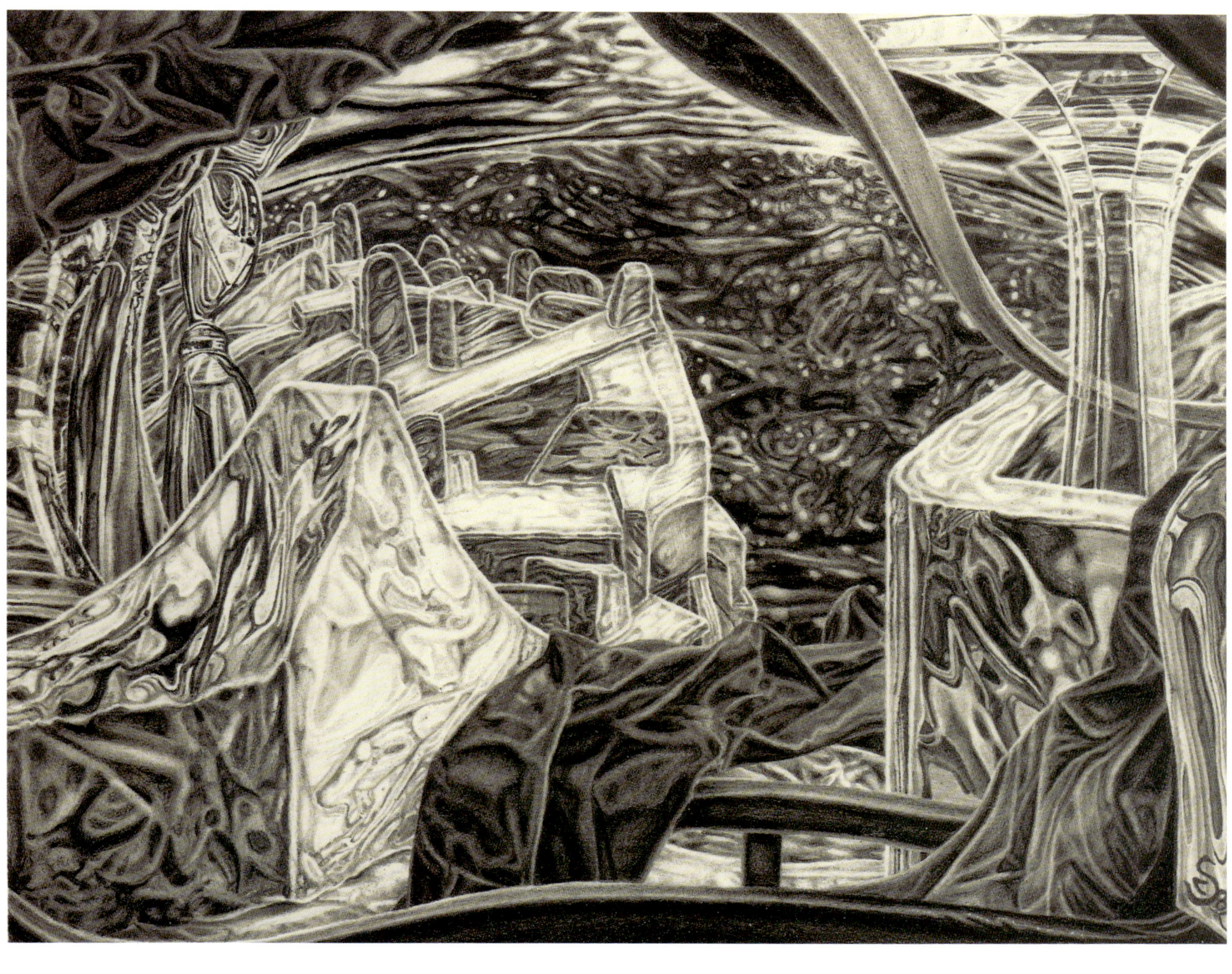

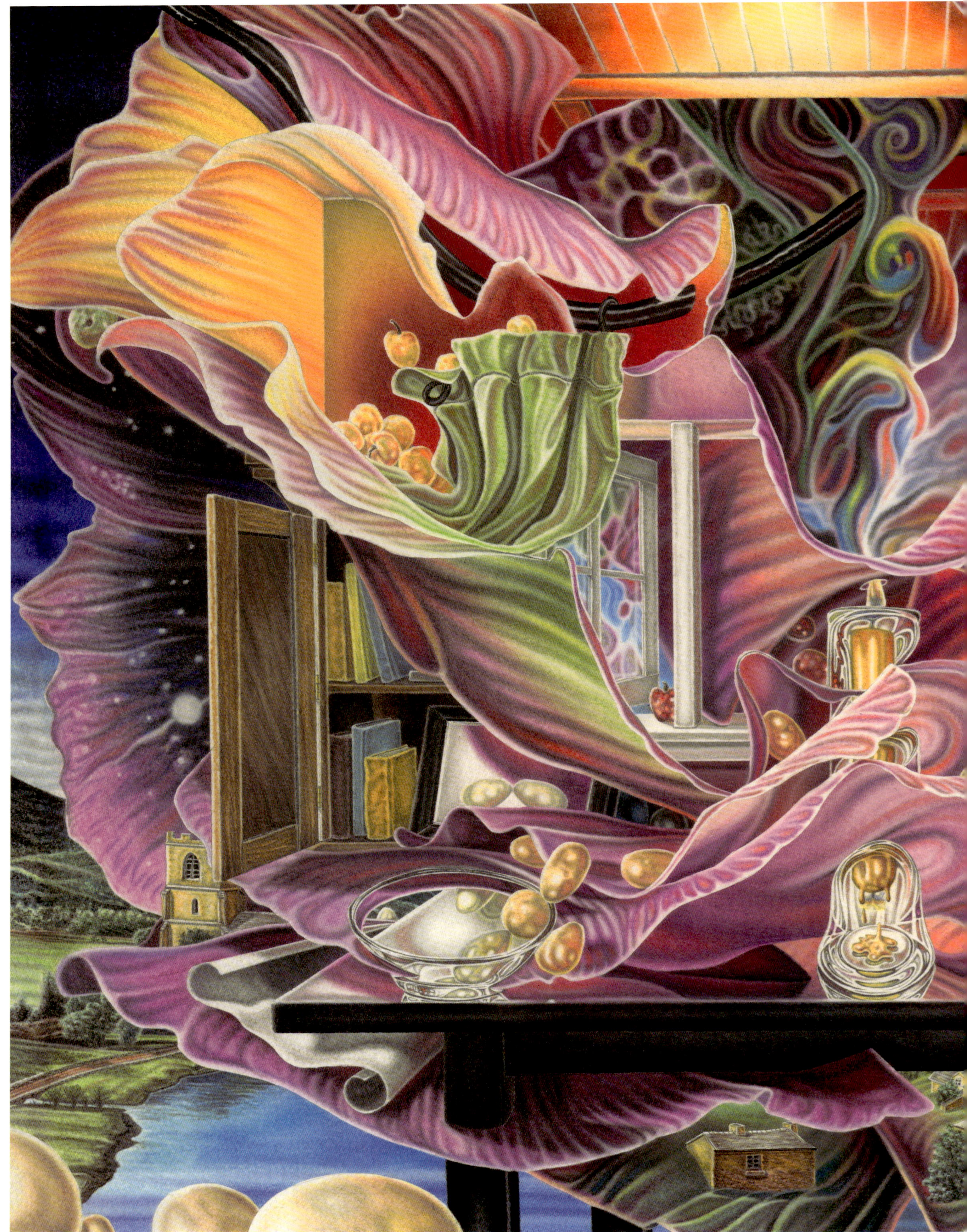

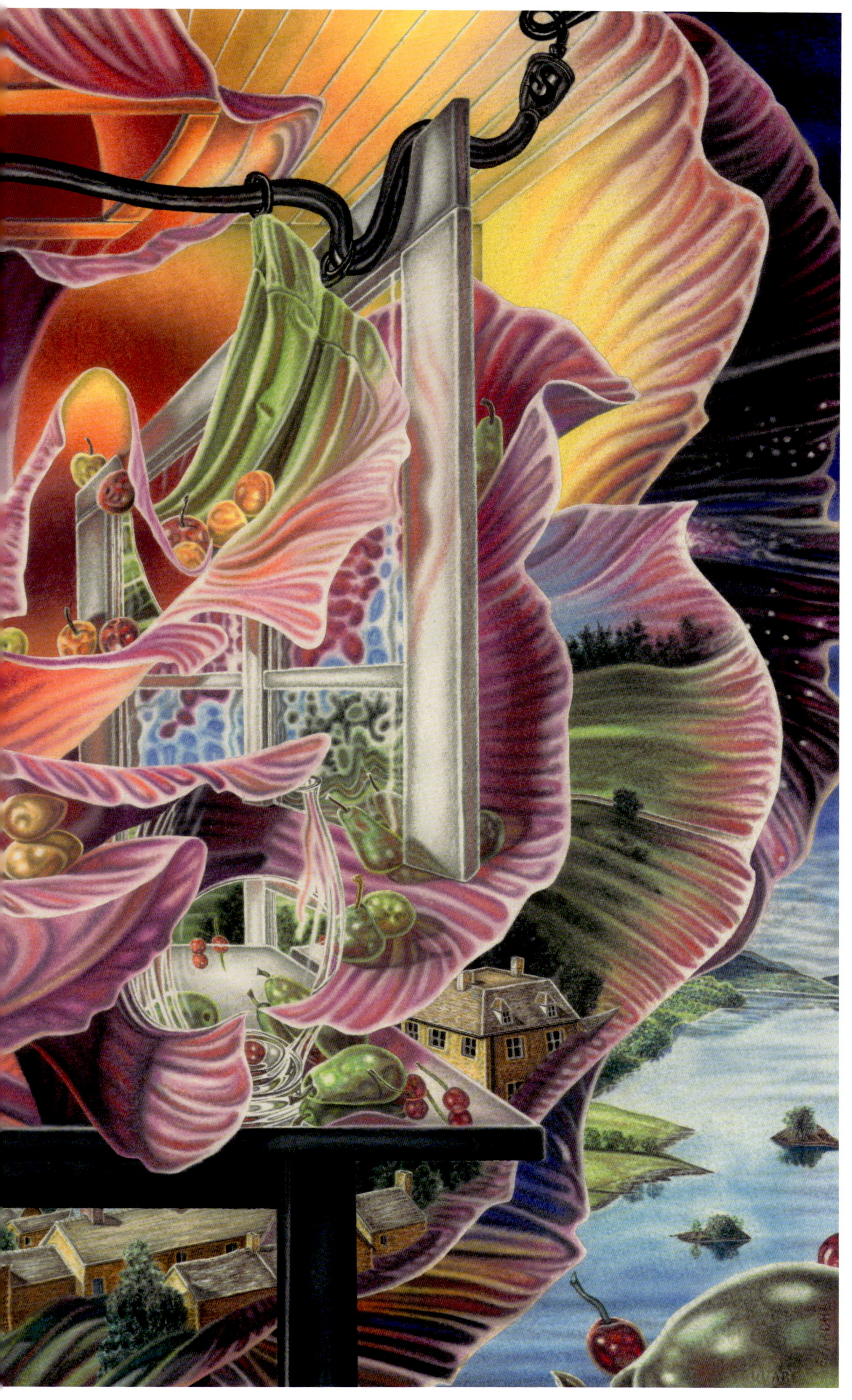

THE ROSE OF MEMORY

THERE ARE villages to explore,
paths past steeples, eggs to be
cracked, fruit to eat, windows
to open and books to be read.

Candles that burn at both ends,
boats to be taken to islands
to be boated to, green grass,
and the promise of hills.

There are ripe daydreams
in a furl of curtains and a red
rose to see them through.
What remains of you is what

you blossom with. What you love
and affirm lives beyond the term
of days. Malice will linger a bit
but, like rain, will soon disappear.

Memory hordes like a miser
and what it wants is what
sweetly pleasured it through
the brief wound of incarnation.

THE ROSE OF MEMORY
stores all cherished recall,
even the future of you is here,
remembered before it occurs.

Some buds will be blighted,
some flowers fail to open,
frost and drought may take you
but most roses fulfill themselves.

It is so easy to want more than beauty.
Deep meaning, serious discourse in dim
existential halls. To be gluttonous in things
and the tabulation of things seen —

the conquered flesh of many lovers,
the broken failure of others, you've
successfully broken. It is easy to fall
to ashes in the complexity of desire.

A flower opens, is brief and full of
sense. Whispering *"Attend to all I offer
and receive all you've lost."* The rose forms
a lace spiral to its unopened center.

You will return to memory;
the slow crush of ordinary magic
is a trick that never ever fails.
But the conjuration that endures

more deeply is to grow into
the rose's heart where all recall spirals —
where it's not just what we were
but where everyone else was.

Back as well to unfathomed waters
and to drink deep in sleep, and when
you waken, the rose is there until
the world removes you to its grindstone.

Some day you might find yourself
hopelessly lost at the center of beauty
and not remember how to
grow into your own death.

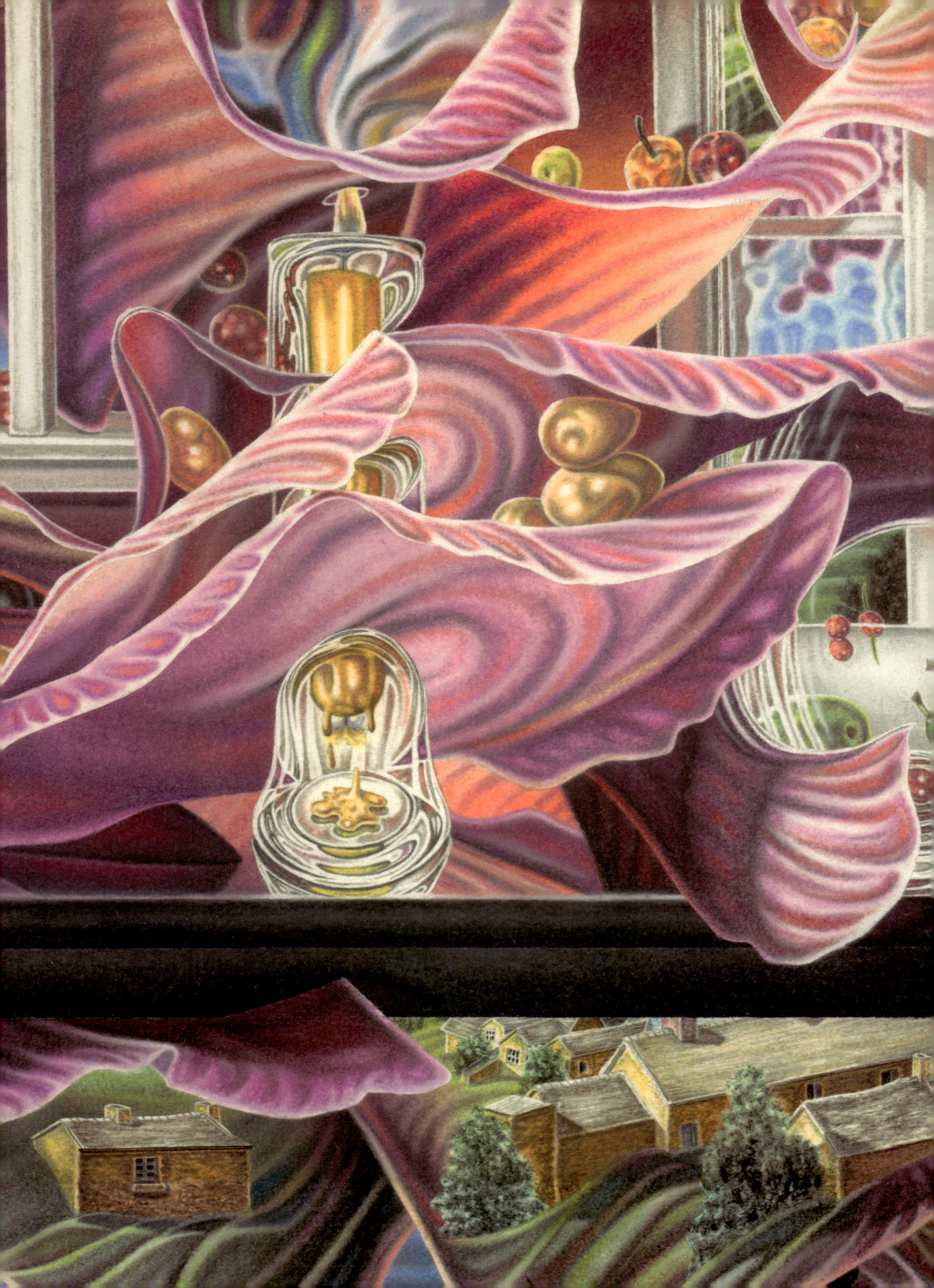

A VILLAGE IN Penzance with a seawall
like an eardrum that silences the sea.
A room in a tavern with old glass bubbled
by rain and a salt cellar of wind.
A field or two of pitch black dirt stunted
by a cliff that tricks a farmer's ambition.
A pastoral like an onion peeled down
to a sanctuary for plain and simple gods.

In such a place lives have been lost
and found. A place with a beach of cobbles,
a shingle for shellfish and tide-pools
a school for properly mannered fish.

A lovely picture framed by the Machine.
Even if you love it, you know it. Modernity
inserting its modifiers into every love song.
A tessellation of ebony squares filled

with the black magic of information, if not insight.
A keyboard of cylinders waiting to impress,
elegant ambiguity on your very concrete needs.
You can drape it in art, but not escape it, in fact.

A meteorite of crystals might disrupt the frame
or be absorbed by it, lend randomness or order.
And frames contain and are defined by what
they hold. In all tipping points choice is possible.

A lovely village in Penzance, the heart's desire.
A Machine to build an idea on, the mind's requirement.
Can you choose both? Do you want to?

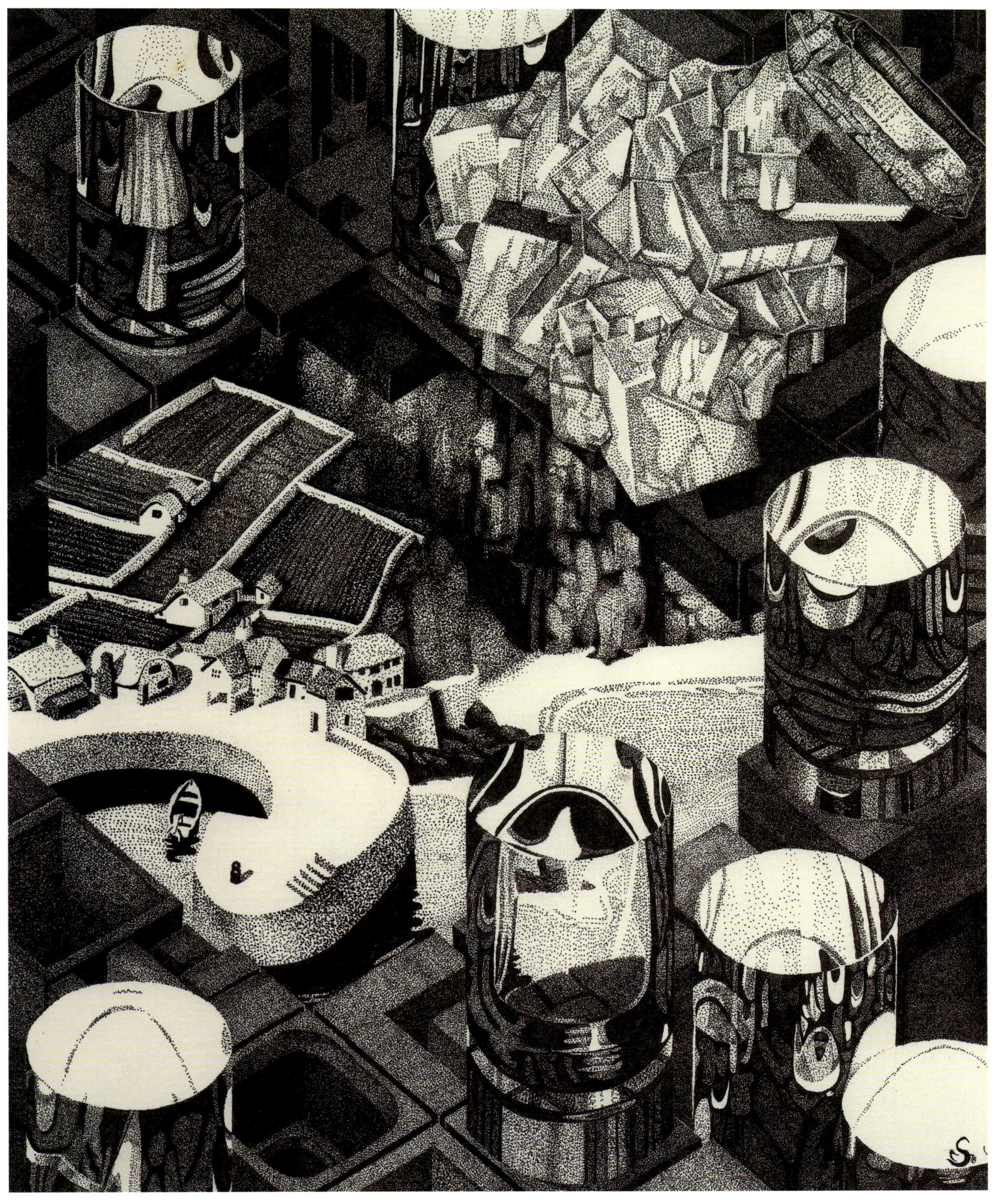

ON A MISCELLANY of beaches on any sea
the size of a pea or large enough to bail
a boat. Interred or dug up they embody
the same dizzying surprise, the spiral.

Their mansion rolls around a central
logarithmic principle of growth. All
mathematically precise. The very
golden-section painters have sought

since Apelles put brush to paper.
As any of Nature's buried treasure
shells drape their secret in an outward
embellishment of color and form.

Captured by the mind of Da Vinci
the Thatcheria Mirabalis became
the spiral staircase and the wind-screw.
In Japan the Precious Wentaltrap is so

prized, rice paper copies are made of it.
The Conus Gloriamaris elicits waiting lists
of eager lovers hungering for a prize
that may never be found for them to bid on.

And still the real history is the coiled
secret, opulent or plain, that they contain.
If you increase their scale, they are the despair
of sculptors. If you give them to poets

they will moon about the ever ascending
eternal reoccurrence. Scientists turn them
into equations. Engineers noodle out drills.
Theists make a metaphor for the City of God.

Or undiscovered, they nest in a tide-pool
awaiting a slow dissolution back to sand.
The secret of their form coiling back-
sliding into the very mind of Nature.

To live with the room they provide requires
a wholly different symmetry than the balance
of the mirror's hallucination. You must arch,
 curve more, become more sinuously rhythmic

and circumlocutional. You must top yourself, spin
into the luxury of the long arc. On earth they are
modest in scale, change that and they measure us,
make us scale the limits of our own straight lines.

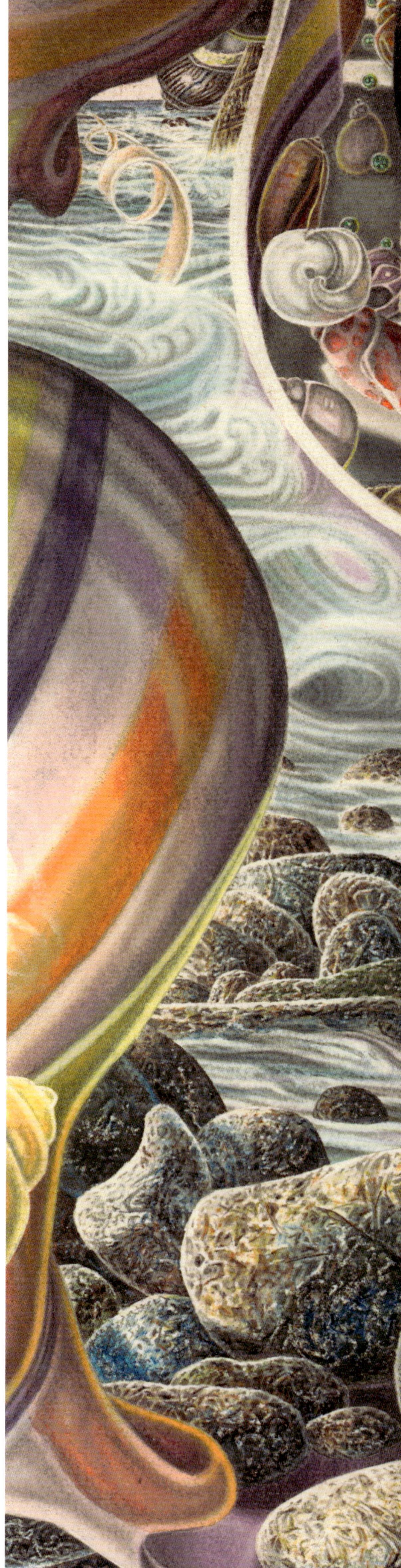

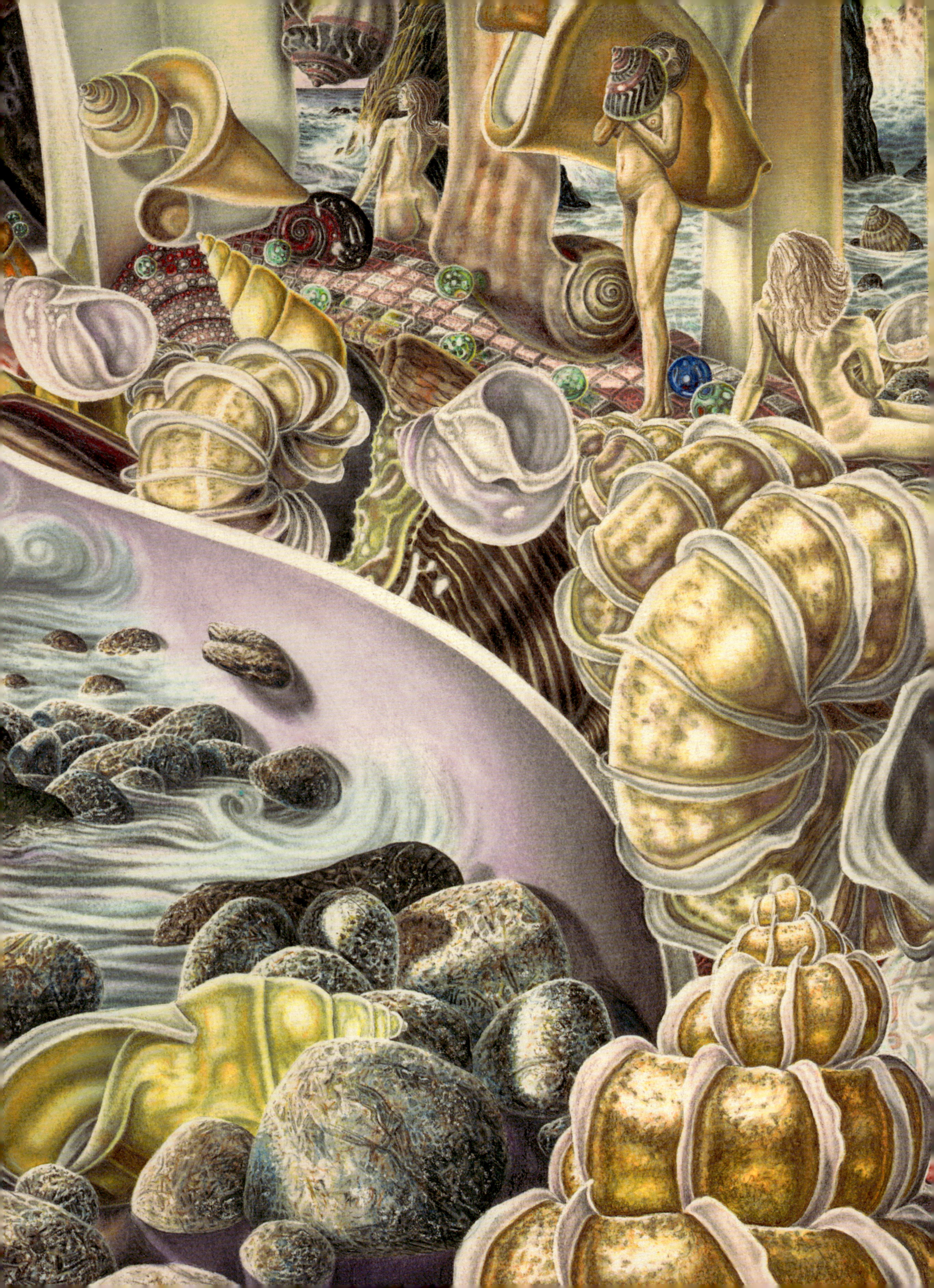

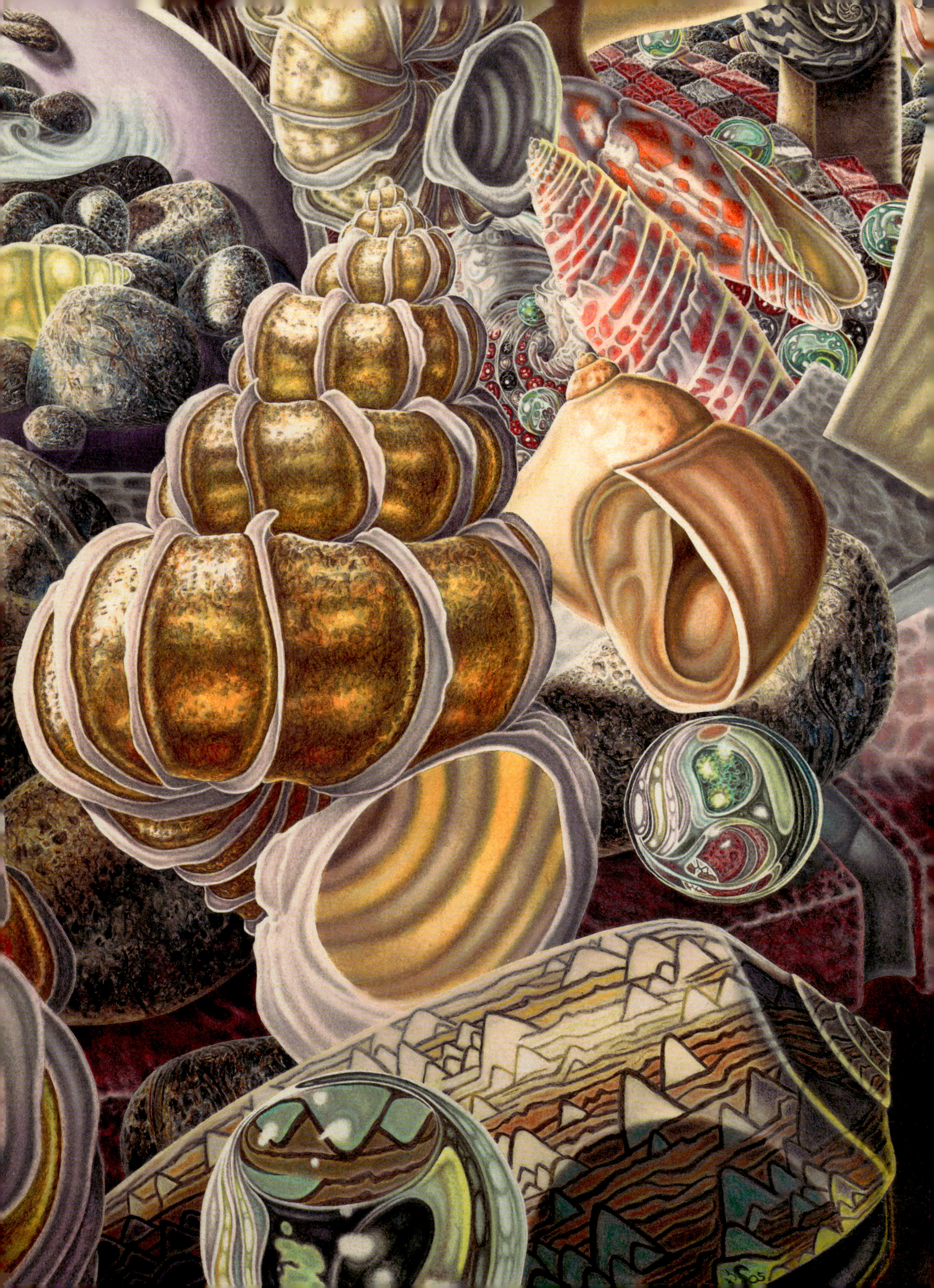

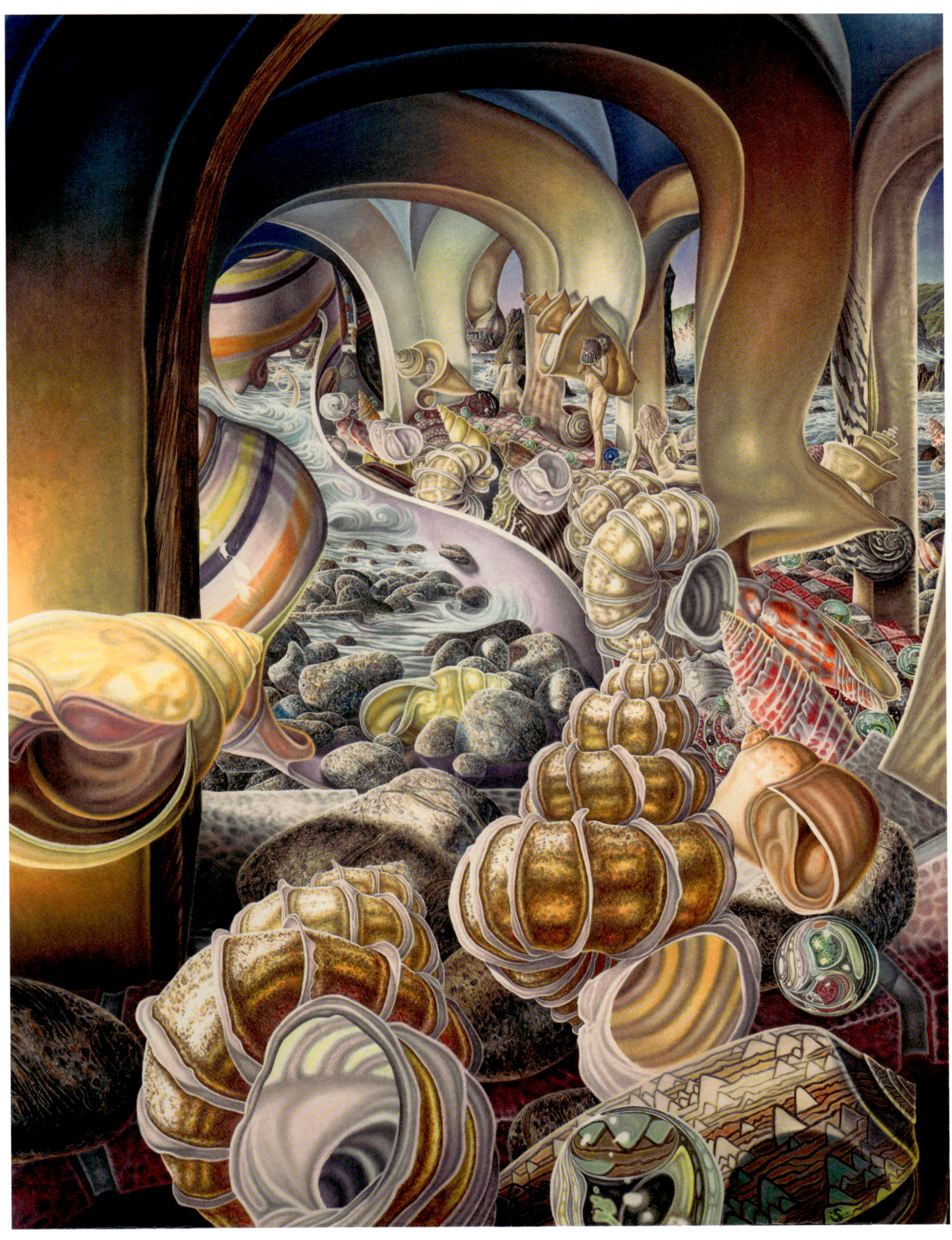

CASEMENTS

OLDING AROUND the fresh possibility
of rain, pocking up the moss reflected in
glass as it lakes the sky vertical. Casements,

house windows and doors, that also house
outside and in. Whichever you are in
is the polar opposite of what you're without.

Casements and rooms and floors and more
are the ways in which we make
recalcitrant space play by the rules.

Botryoidally speaking, concave and convex
are also nurseryed by window frames
and in and out depend on how you look.

Some Casements enclose the infinite
and others merely dead ends. These
permeable membranes are the only way

our sanity makes sense out of one side
or the other. Are we not moving between
the passages of our own lives? Backward

and forward at random, more random
than dream, unless we arbitrarily choose,
this is this, and that is that.

With a good Casement you can go either way.
Be outside looking in, or inside looking out, or
inside viewing the outside looking in, simultaneously. 

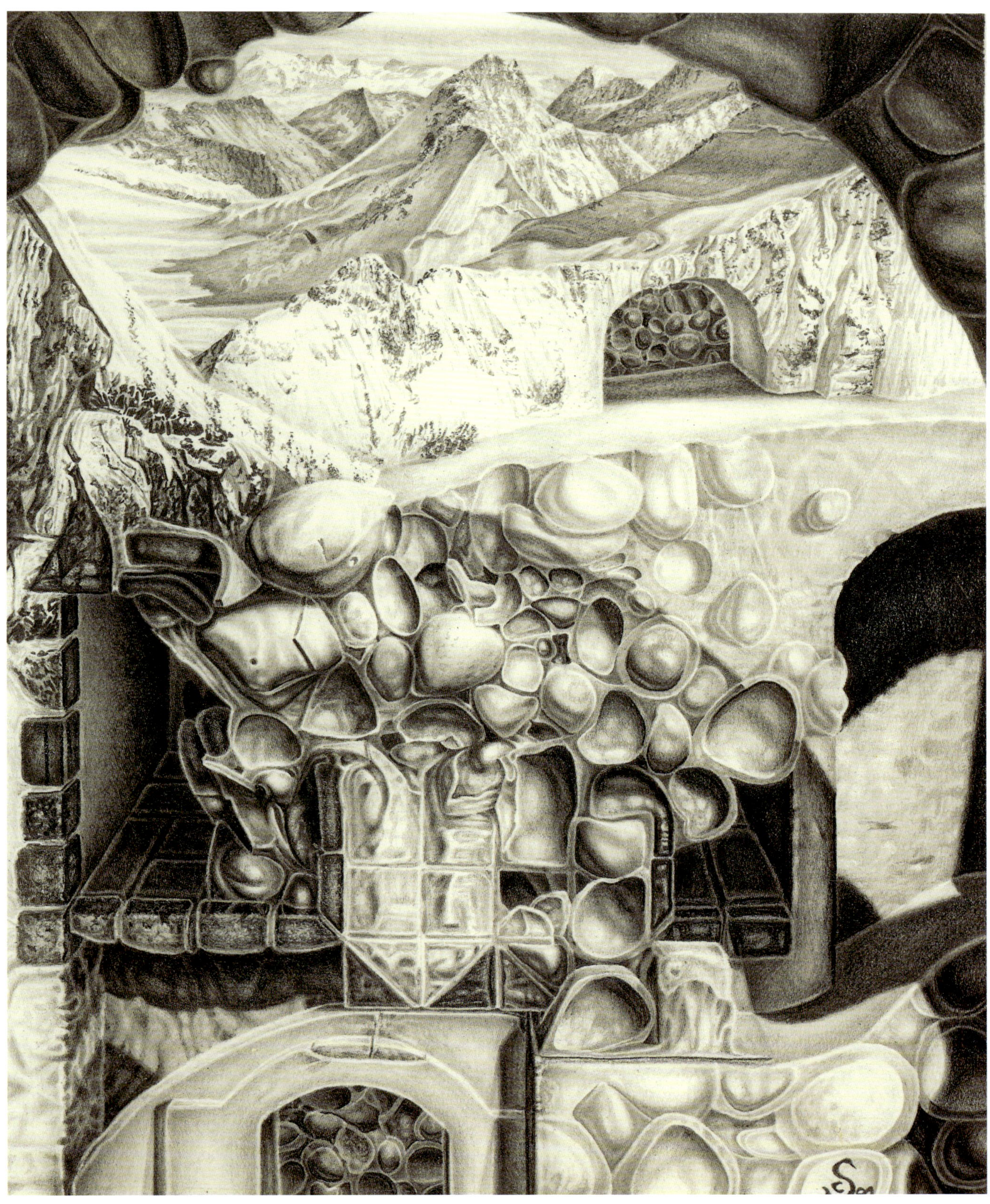

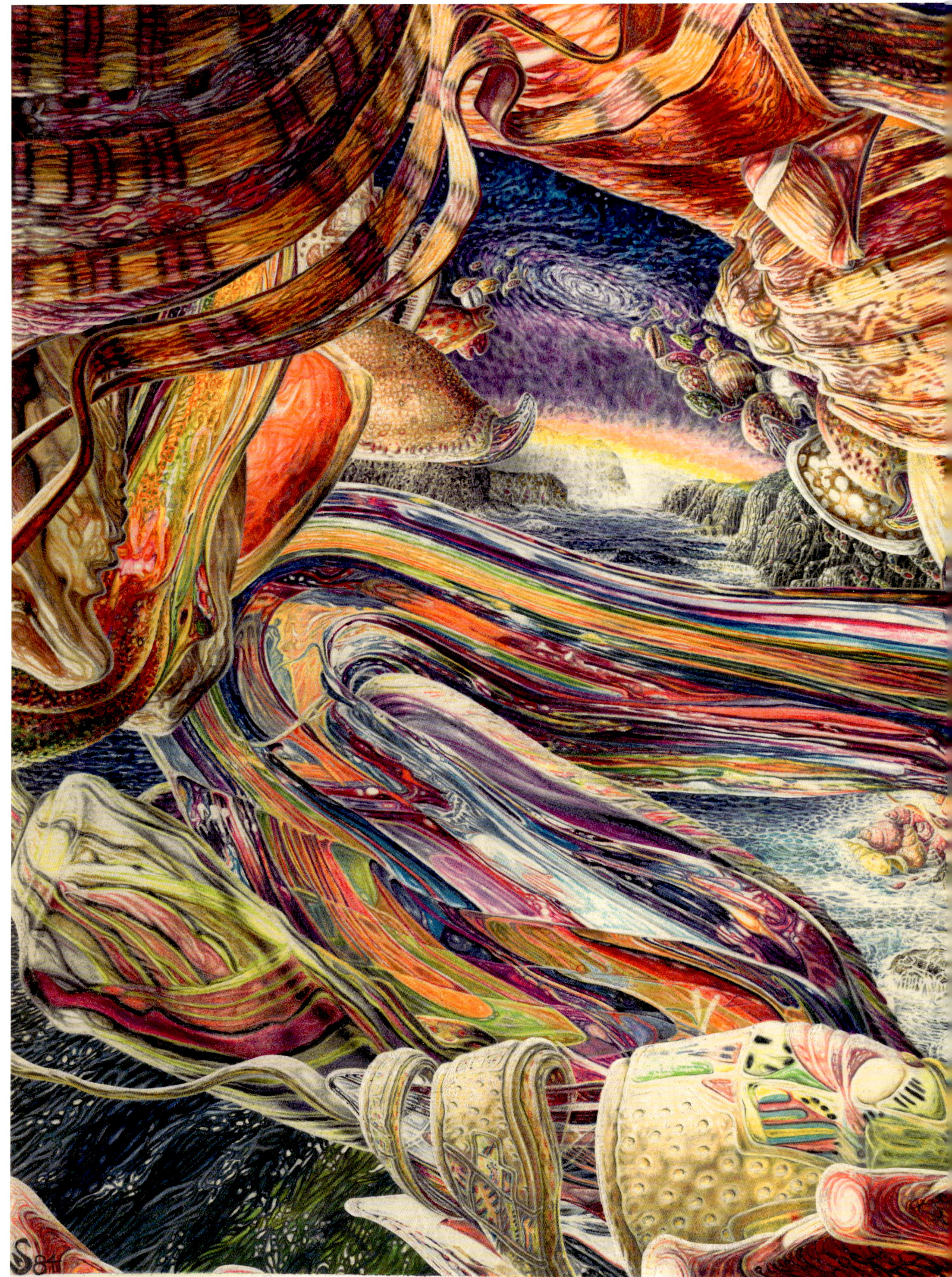

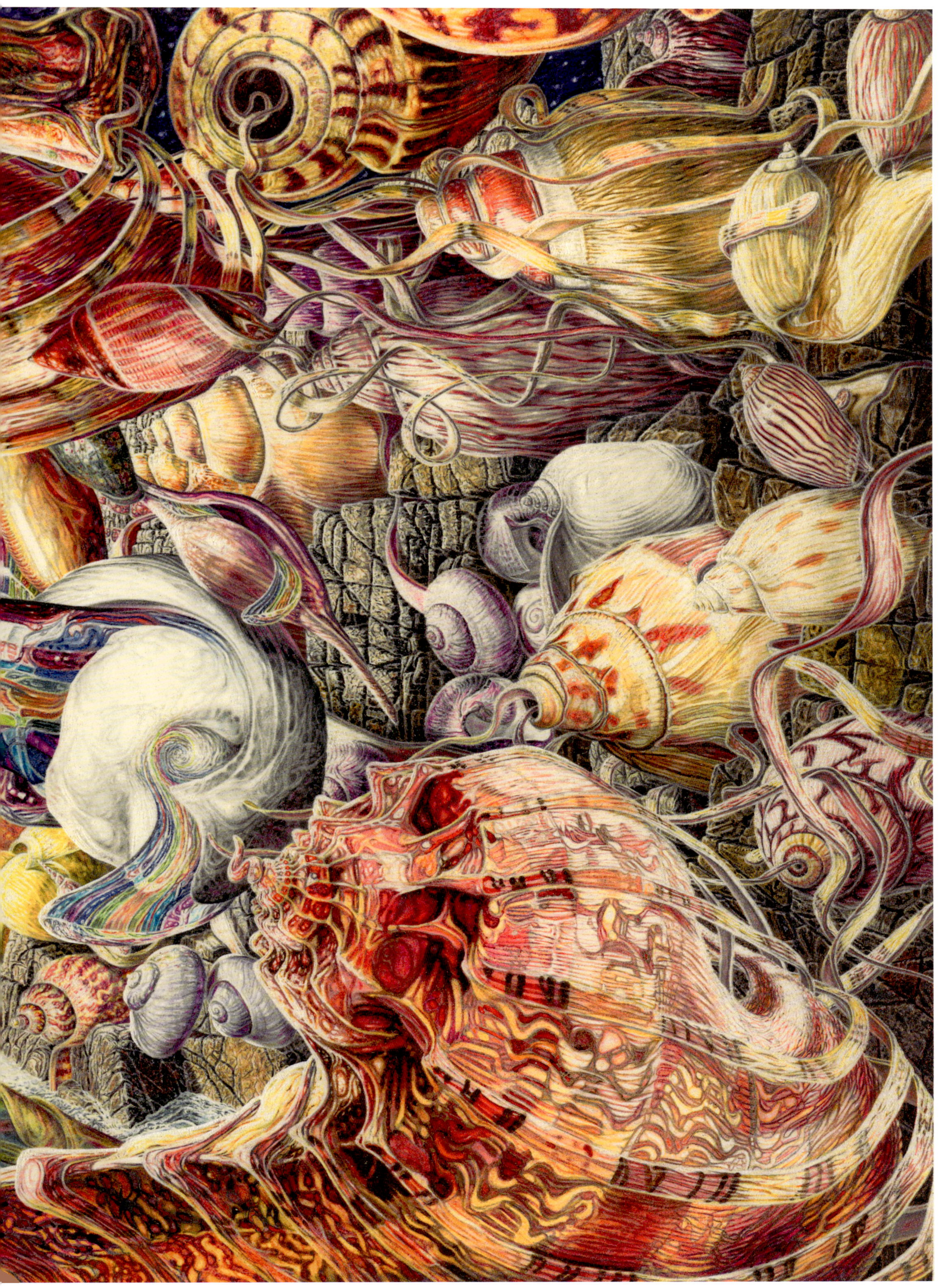

SHELL FUGUE

PATTERN IS A LANGUAGE. Without a Rosetta Stone
its vocabulary is infinite, its grammar fluctuates.

A shell will write a sonnet to itself
just by the shapes and lines on its enameled face.

Shells of the same species will chatter among
themselves like spinster aunts in full gossip.

Families of shells have dialects, different oceans
different inflections, but a common iconography.

It is said you can hear the sea in a shell
but really, you see the shell's voice in its glyphs.

It makes a sound because that's what you expect
to hear. It obliges your lack of language skill.

In the Torah of Malachology, the prophetic
Conch, spins the numeration of Paradise.

What does heaven look like for these
voluble mussels, what do their valves

and opercula whisper at the bottom of the sea,
or the crest of a wave that gives them flight?

There once was a Volute that circled
with a Cowry and spun the air between them
capturing the sugar of the rainbow.

The deliquescing snails moving faster and faster
become a glaze of glass, and their ripples of
transfiguration glaze the mollusk menagerie.

Rippling toward the Milky Way, the hosannas
of their fugal invention could be clearly heard —
it sounded just like the sea, a final Amen.

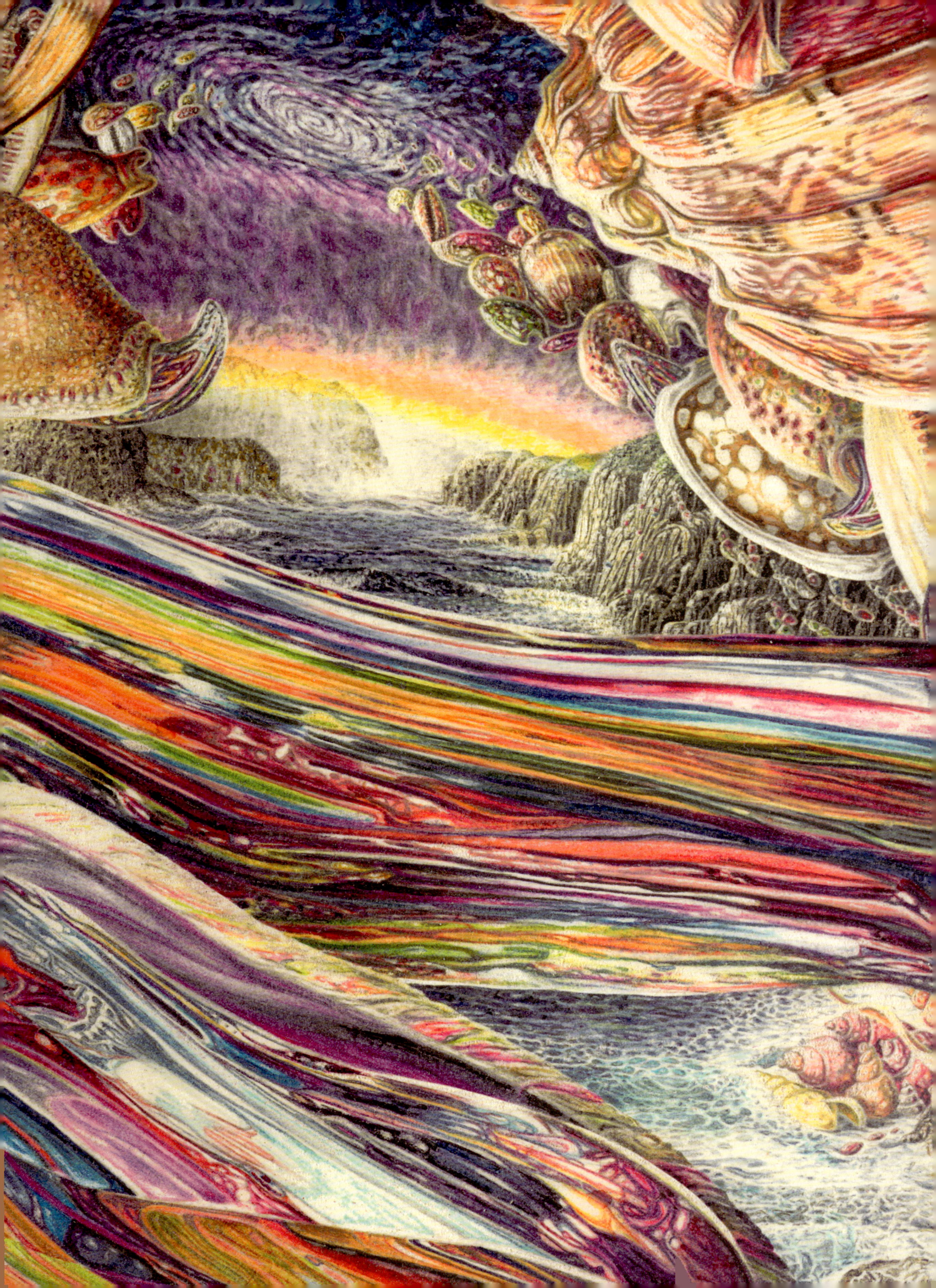

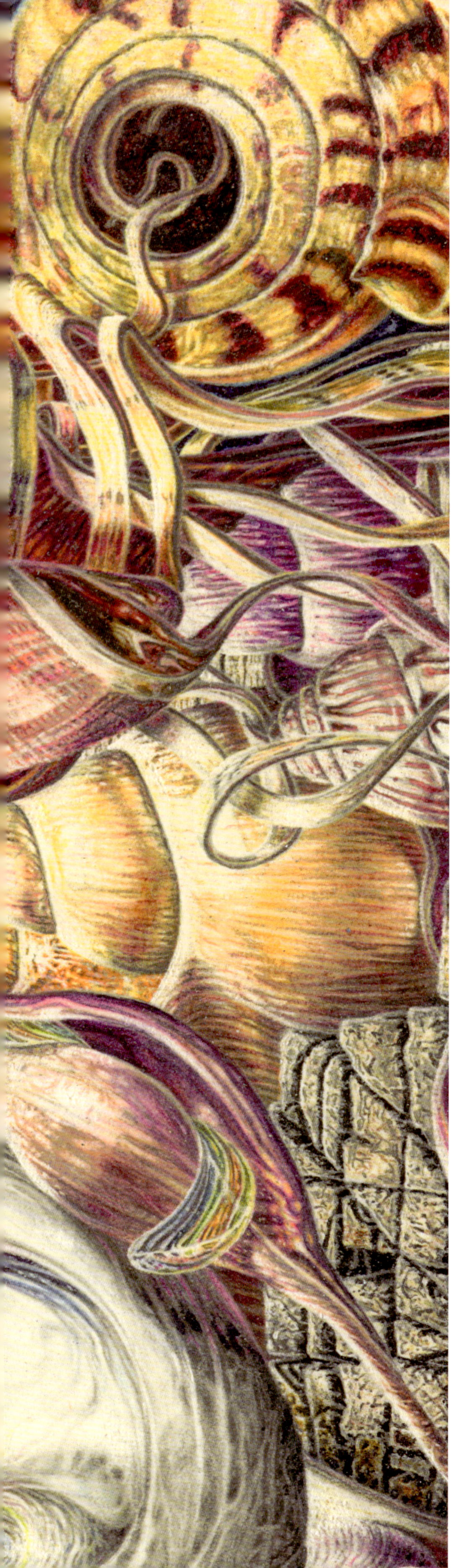

Color is the map of a fully-realized geography
that can be inferred but cannot be discovered.

A shell will paint a landscape to itself
just by the chroma and hue of its tinctured skin.

Shells of the same species will stratify among
themselves like colorful priests in full dispute.

Families of shells live on different peninsulas
with different tints, and dye to a similar palette.

In the Pentateuch of Mollusks, the gentry
of land snails stain the crystal Rock of Ages.

What does the big rock candy mountain
taste like for these colorful abalones and clams?

Once there was a will of fire coloring through shells
at the speed of delight; the spirals spun primaries,
split complementaries and triads, and the Light stayed.

So when the tide rolls in, a last judgment of night,
it will roll out just as readily, and the bright sea tops
will send out color and pattern to extend again. ⚘

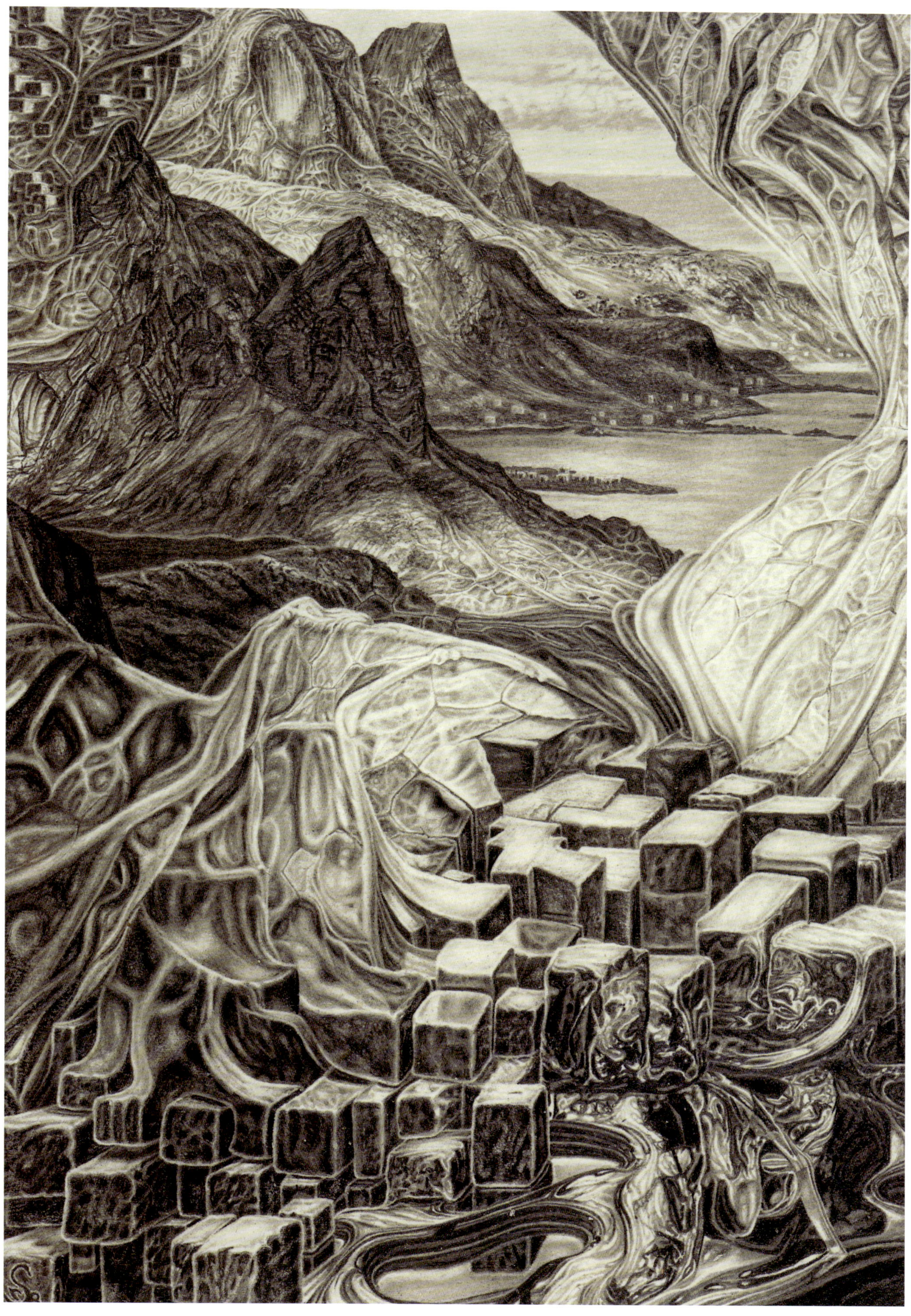

A T THE SKRAGG END of the gray North Sea
Norway's rotted stone teeth rise up
from eroded jaws. Chew into the foam and chop
of a cold comfort of fog, bitten by the wind.
A few houses enameled like children's blocks
tumble over the steep pitch-black basalt
un-erodable even in this terrible fist of surf.
At the end of men's grasp the rock resembles

the corded dendrites of cabbage leaves.
Draped they are, the wilt and weavings
of these vegetative leavings. Cold-slawing
and chewed up by the Wurm of the Norse.

The leaves cube like lead crystals into an ocean
of brass. Surreal is not about what's impossible,
but about what's ignored and not connected.
A moment will come when reality finally

gives up on you. Without the logical imperatives
that make each day follow the next and the next,
gone will be the gutless goosestep to the grave.
Re-forging link by link, vision re-remembers you. 

THE BONES OF CREATION

SOME TIMES it's good to recall
how little of forever
you have spent time in.

A picture can distract you
in its closed system of eternity,
seduce you to waste before it.

You have no large choices. Will you
look at this painted tangle
of rock, cobbles, glacial ice, or not?

I'll be the first to admit it is
just a few square inches of paper,
dust, carbon and a bit of gum Arabic.

Still it's just as real as you are
and more real after you.
You could find a worse dalliance.

A day offers so many choices, why
list them, they're endless, why after all
not dwell for a spell in an artist's dream.

Yes, I grant you, I'm essentially no one
and hence this painting is by a nobody
and therefore is basically nothing.

My work is not famous.
But then are you? Go on,
a little peek won't kill you.

There's a lot to see really
and at least you haven't seen it
a certified, pontified thousand times.

Aren't you a little bored by what chooses you?
Well go on then, bootstrap a choice
that your credentials haven't approved of.

Don't bother trying to look me up,
you won't find me, I haven't won anything,
I'm not owned by anyone you've heard of.

Bells and whistles are playing so many tunes
but some of us are a bit tone deaf; we sit
in our rooms and hear birds we can't identify.

Are you a little like that too?
So I can't be threatening; like you,
I'm invisible and likely to stay so.

Look how much I've written
and not talked about this piece.
Well, it's just a picture after all.

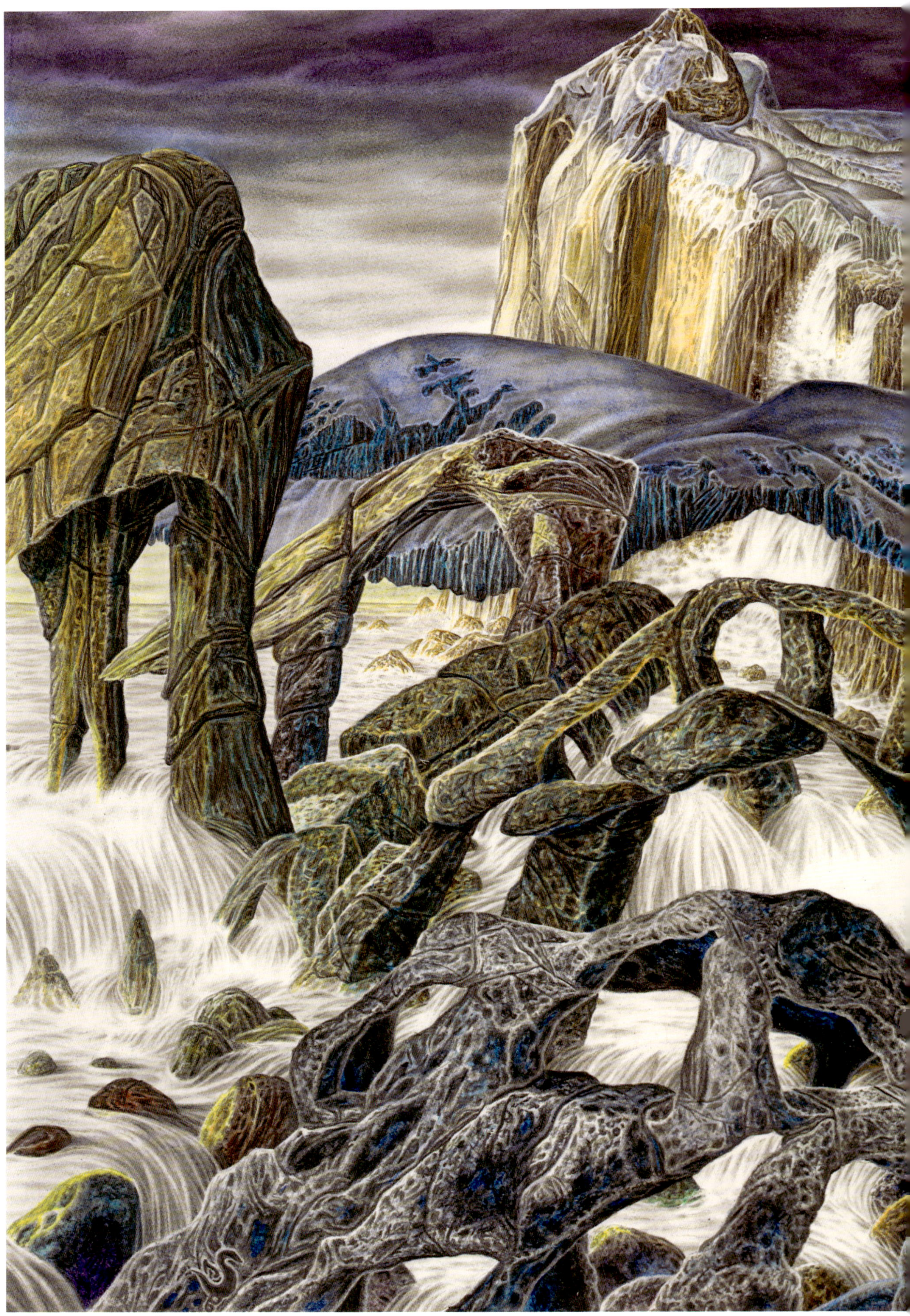

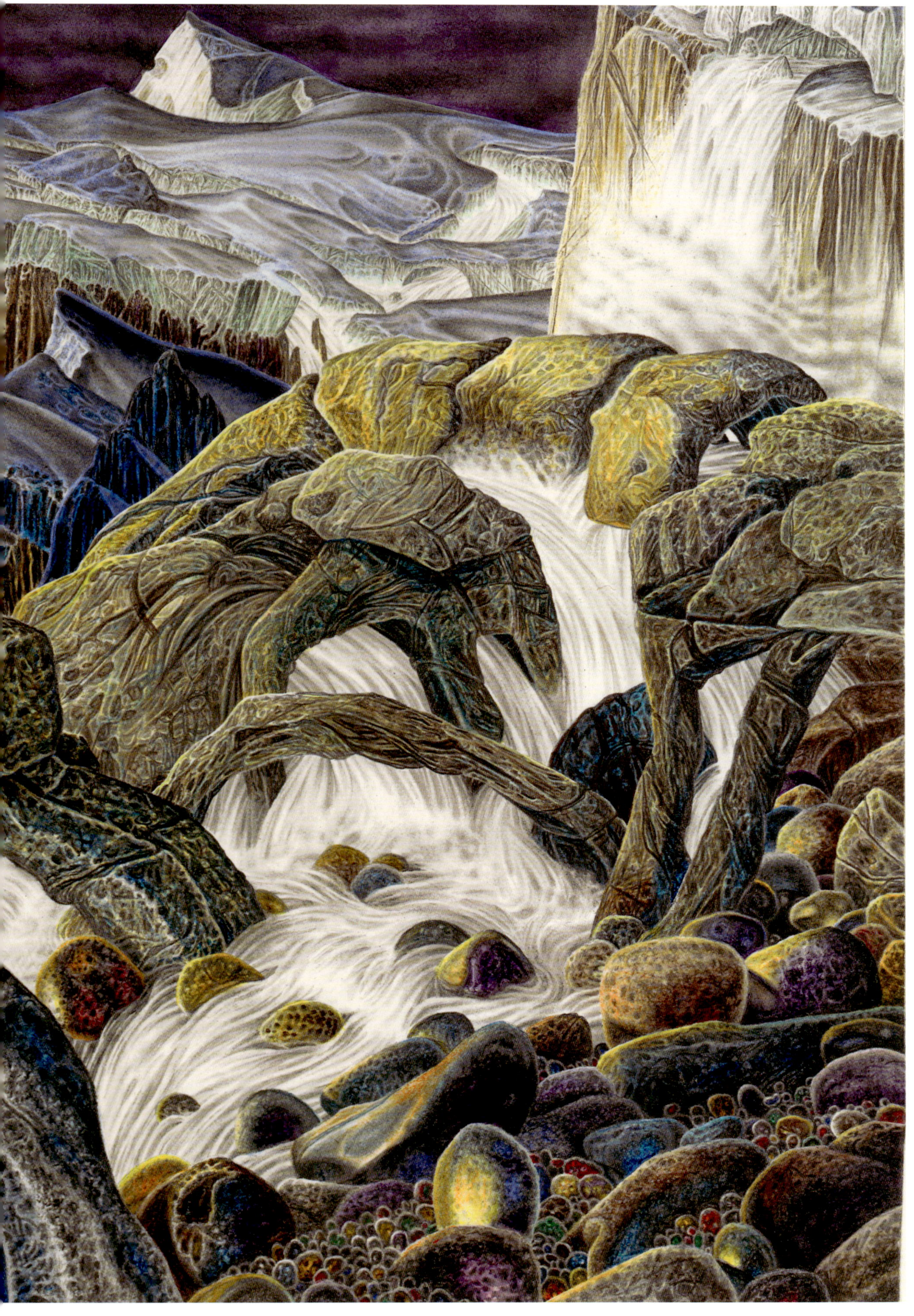

THE PREMISE is simple enough, what if the
community itself were alive. All I need do

is work the proposition to its logical conclusion.
But as Michelangelo said, *"The devil is in the detail"*.

The dragon of the cathedral was first,
with its vault of teeth unzipping from

the clearstory, arcing off to the Empyreum.
The lower jaw of windows rolling up like a scroll.

The nostril of the rose window inhaling
the incense of town like a cheap perfume.

And the steeples jacking the sky
like the opening bud of a stone Forget-Me-Not.

As you leave the cathedral's portal and stroll
the high street, the center of the hurricane is calm.

The Renaissance entry gate is as substantially
engineered as an Aristotelian syllogism,

although you do notice black bubbles of glass
petitely floating through the loggia.

To the left and right, buildings are bulbing
and shrinking, roofs are scaling off like gutted fish.

Walking out of town has become dicey,
the retaining wall under your feet has blown out.

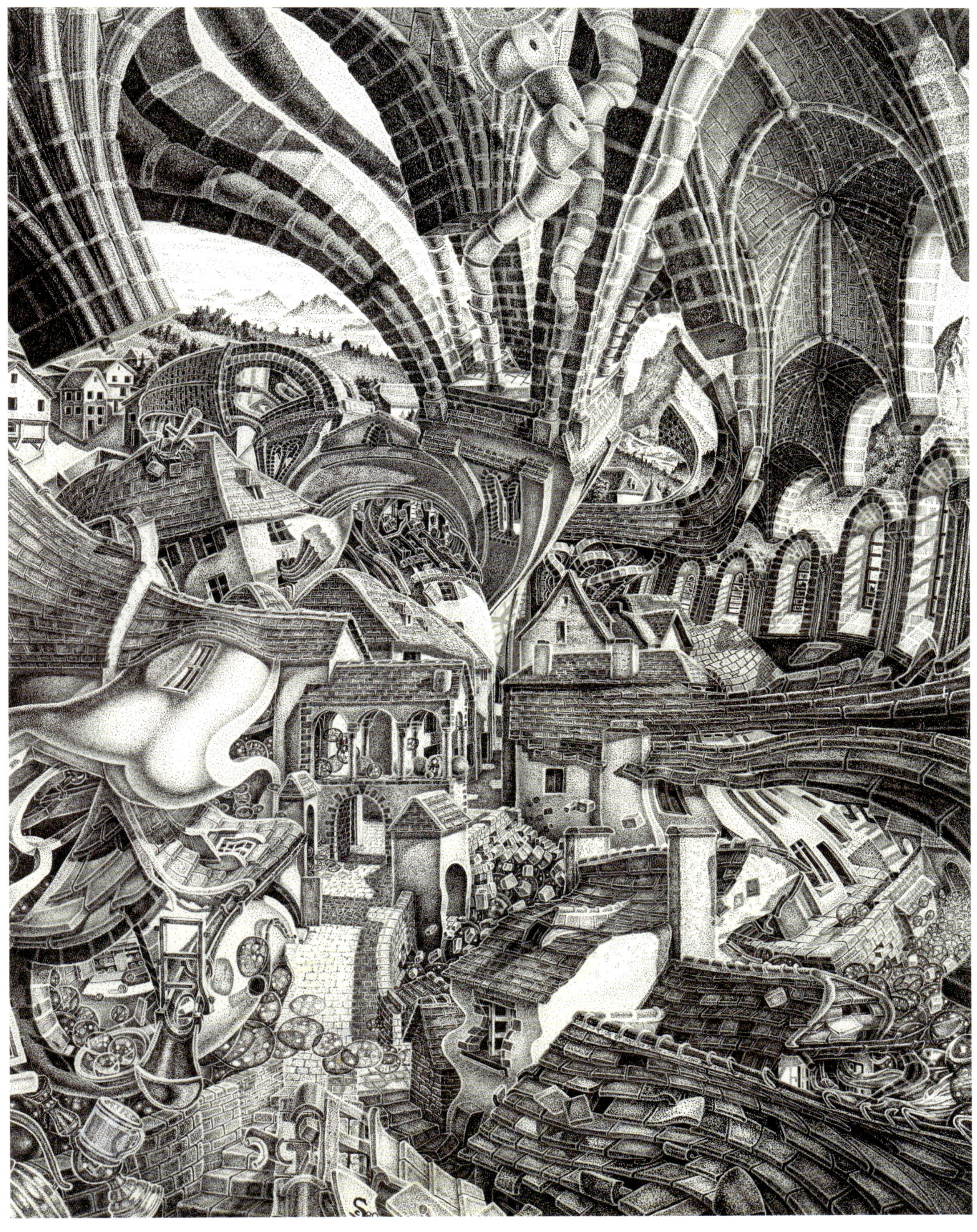

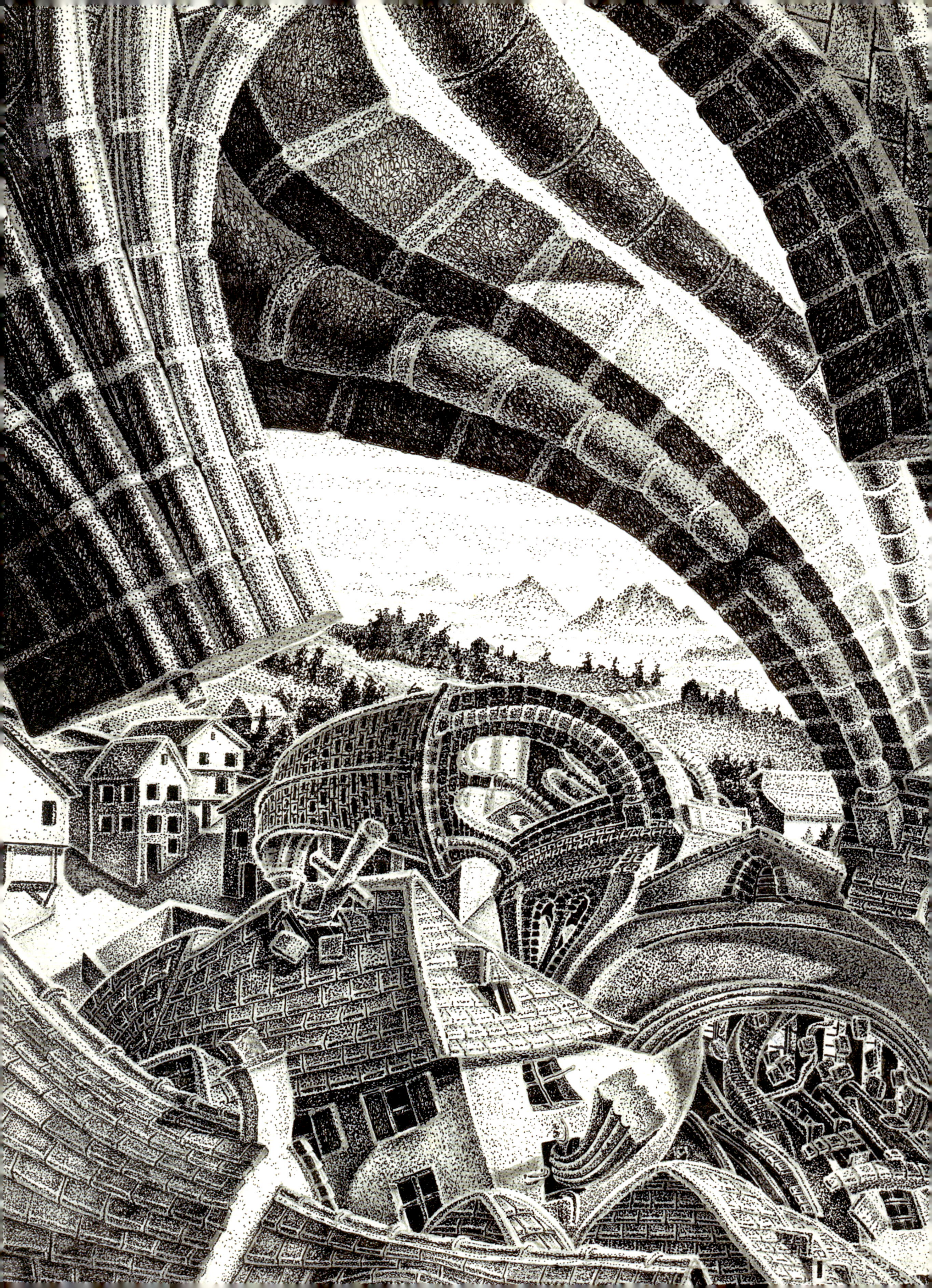

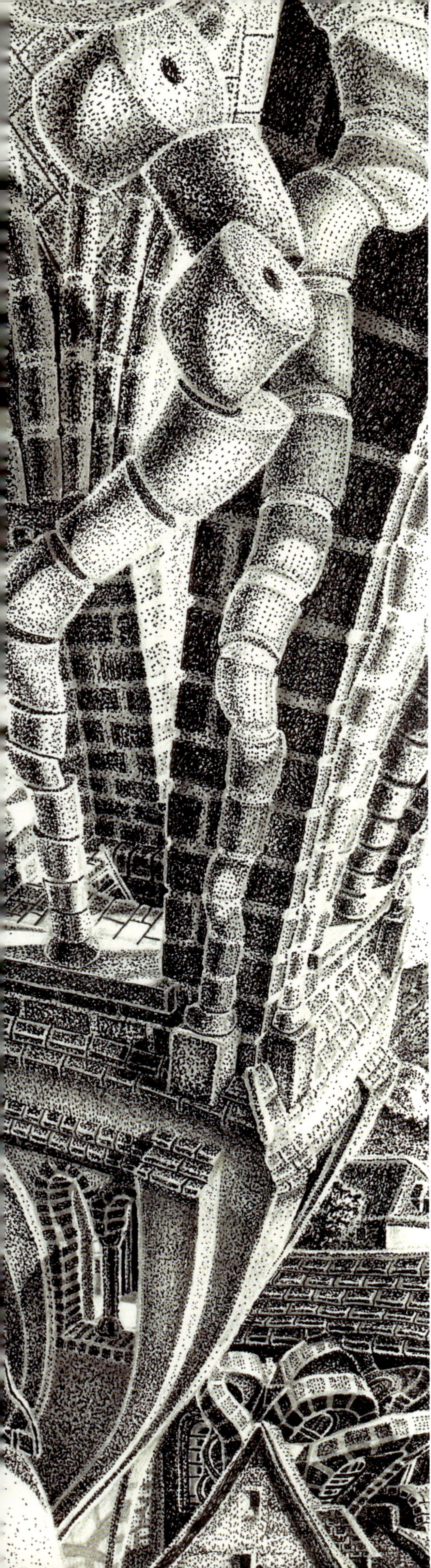

Spheres of sooty crystal are flowing
into the estuary of the street like a mob at a hanging.

To your right, structures are unzipping
the uncorseted bulk of their housing authority.

One house vomits out its interior, lobbing trays
and cups, dishes and plates into the countryside.

A final gooseneck of wavy adieuxing to an exit
into a, perhaps predictable, usual ending.

Does flux ever bend or end itself
or send itself to an early retirement?

Heraclitus said "All things flow."
You cannot only not step in the same

river twice, you can't step through
a door if it doesn't stop bobbing about.

We think we own things, but the things
we think we own think they own themselves.

Towns let us live in them, but sometimes
they just have to live by themselves. §

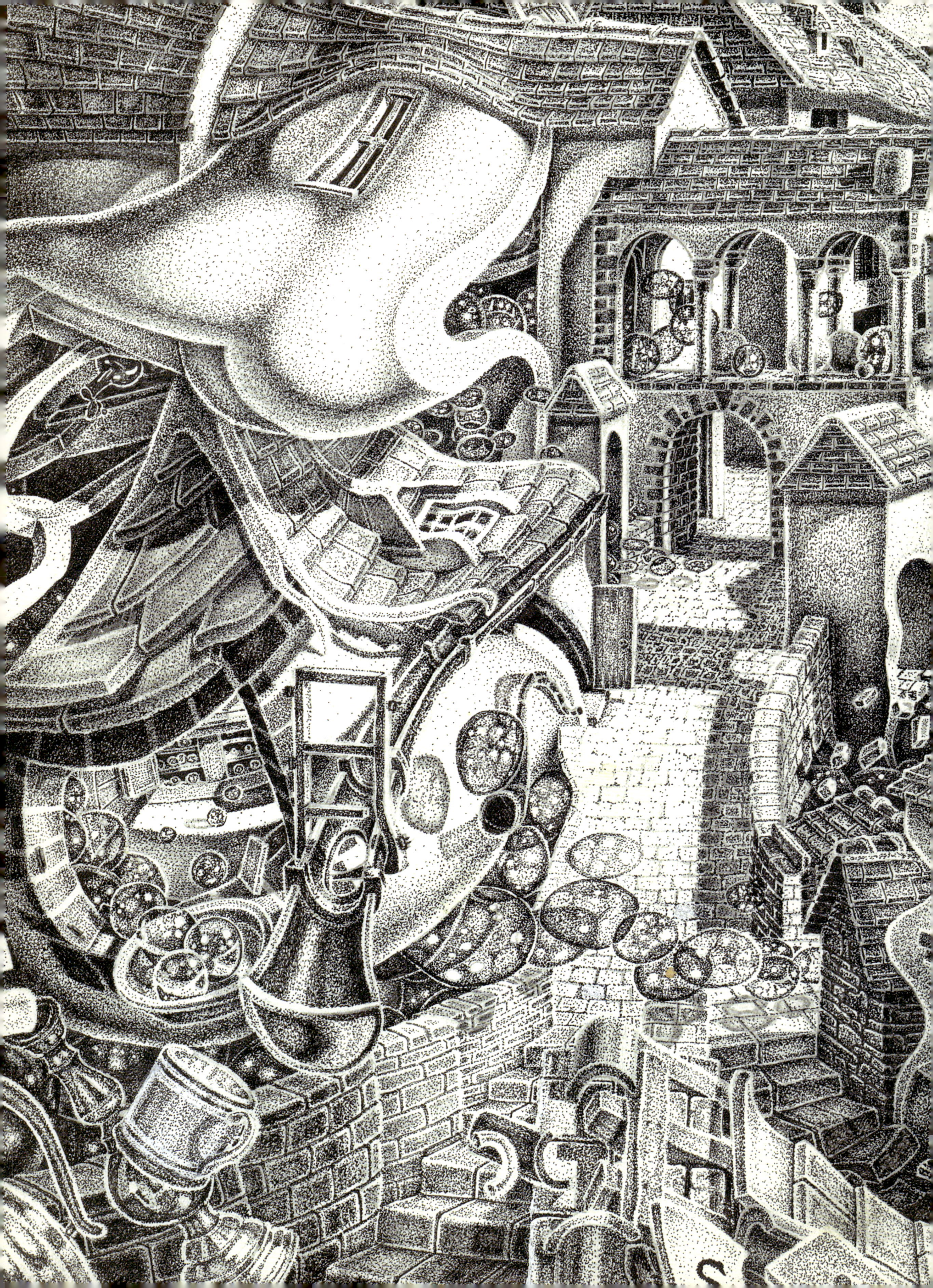

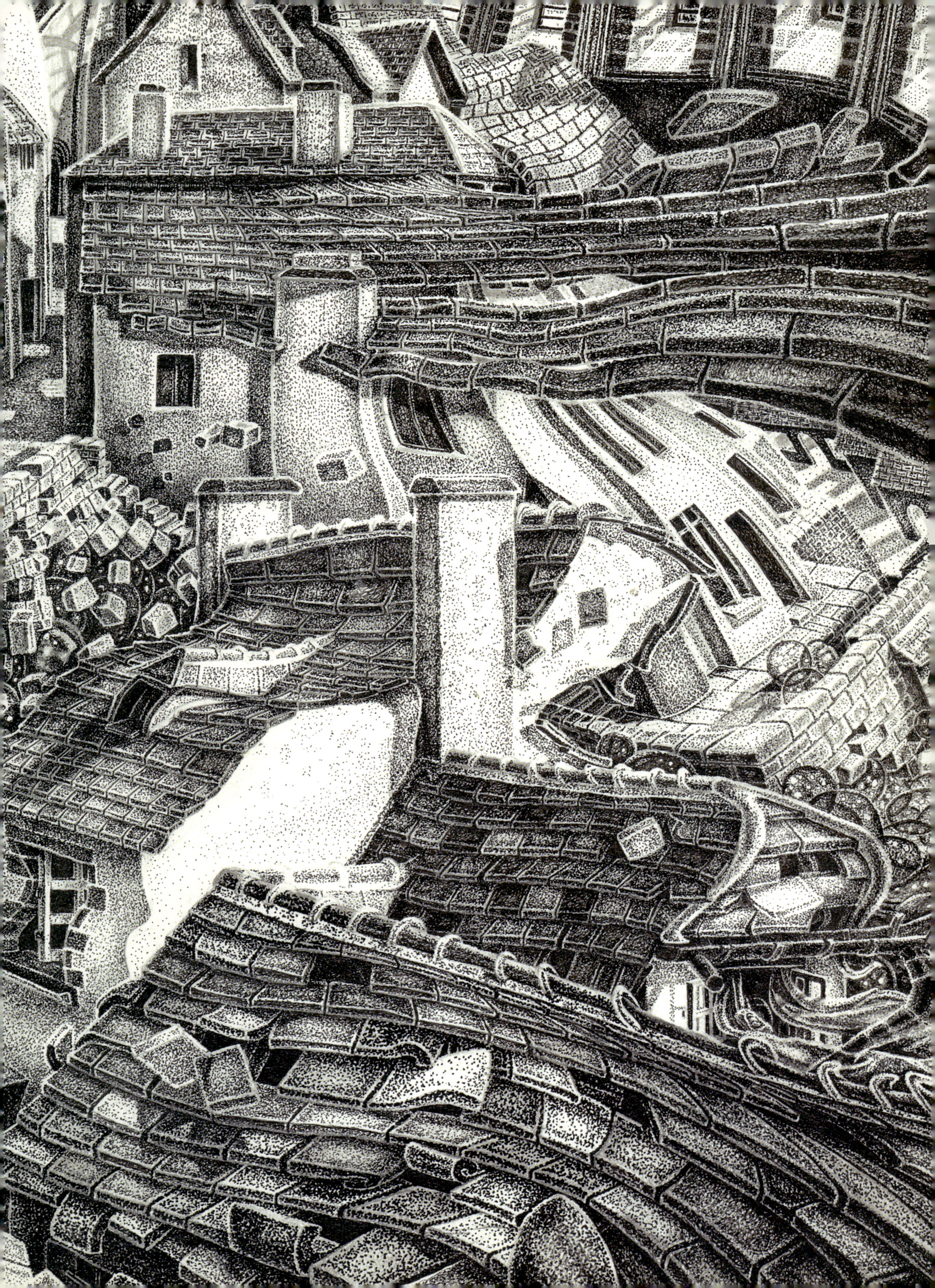

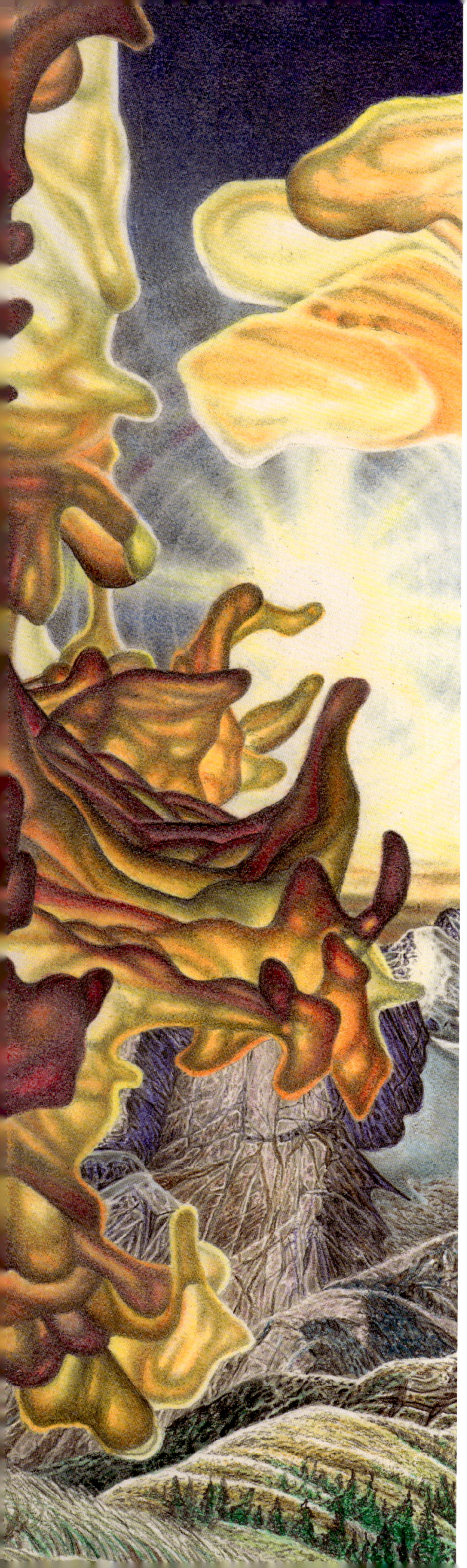

THE SKIN OF MORNING when dreams
are at the end of themselves and
all the richest imagery has been
written into the soul and forgotten.
All that remains is the membrane
of ghosts and furies, Dutch uncles
and centaurs, clowns, horses
and homilies by teachers asleep.

The residue of bird flight is here
by herons asleep in the blue blazes
of morning light. The epiderm
of departing myth bubbles
and squeaks soap bubbles fragile
as the last phantasm before eyes open
and the threshold of a possible
landscape enters your believing eyes.

Just like dream, a sun can perihelia itself
to sublime imminence. Forests chartreuse
themselves like a chanteuse in the bright
club that night has been erased from.
Rock, glacier, grass and the grace
of so much beauty. The fabric of eternity
will return to natal our sleep back
to beginnings and the tatter of memory.

Cloud will bring us down to another day
and another, and when we die in our sleep,
as we all must, and the sheet draws itself
over our bed, we find we are still wed
to carnivals of dream, seeming to go on forever.

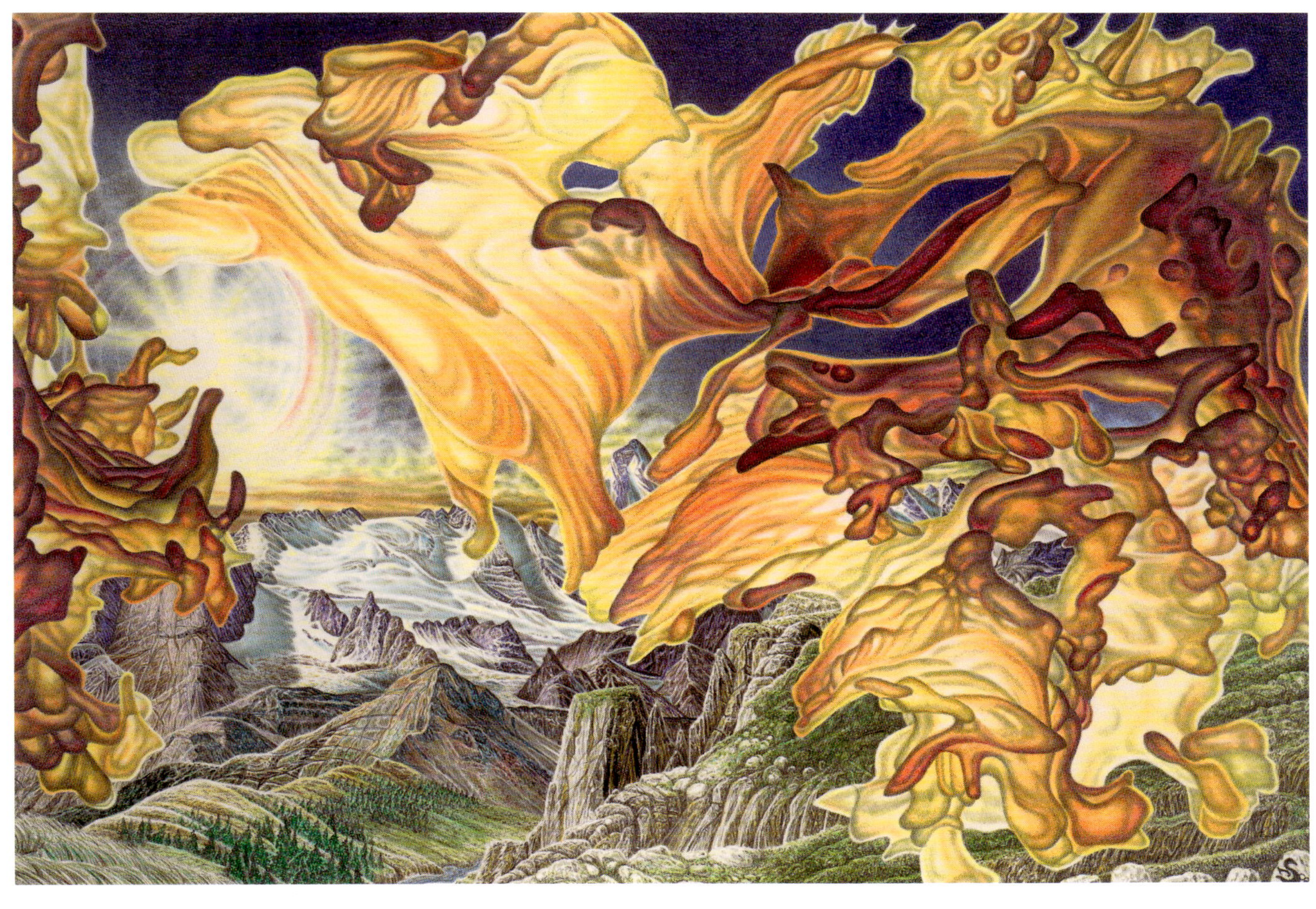

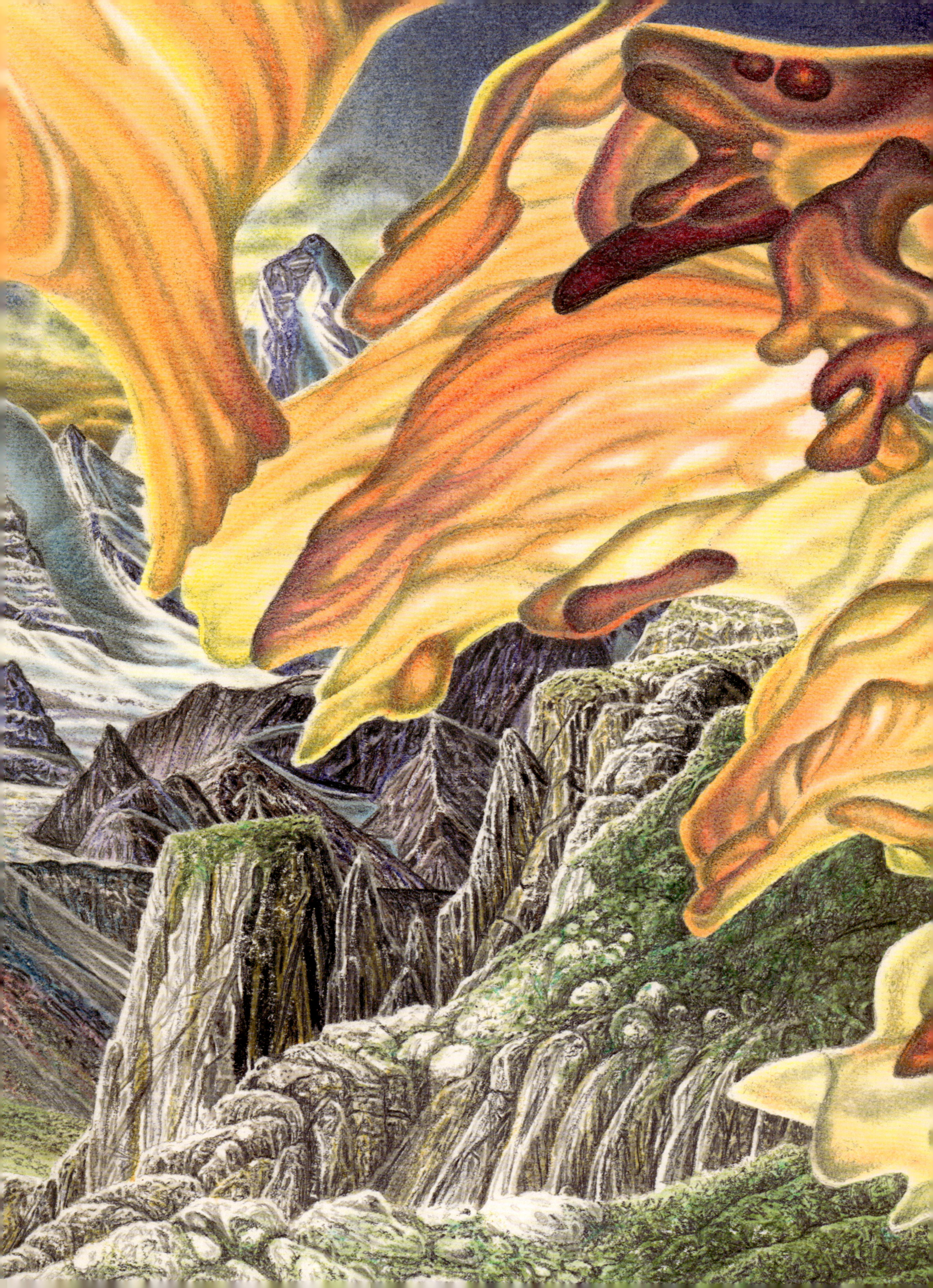

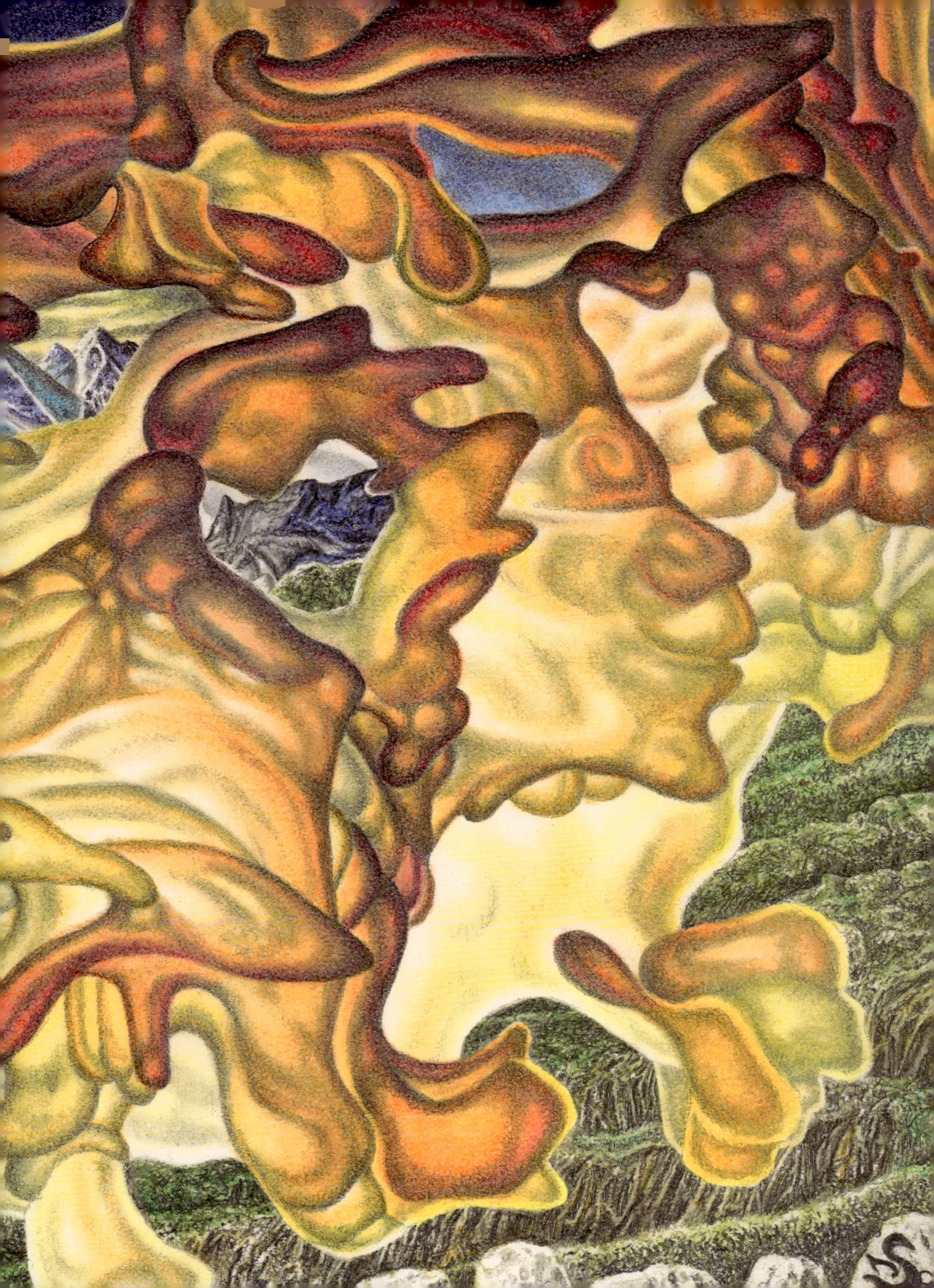

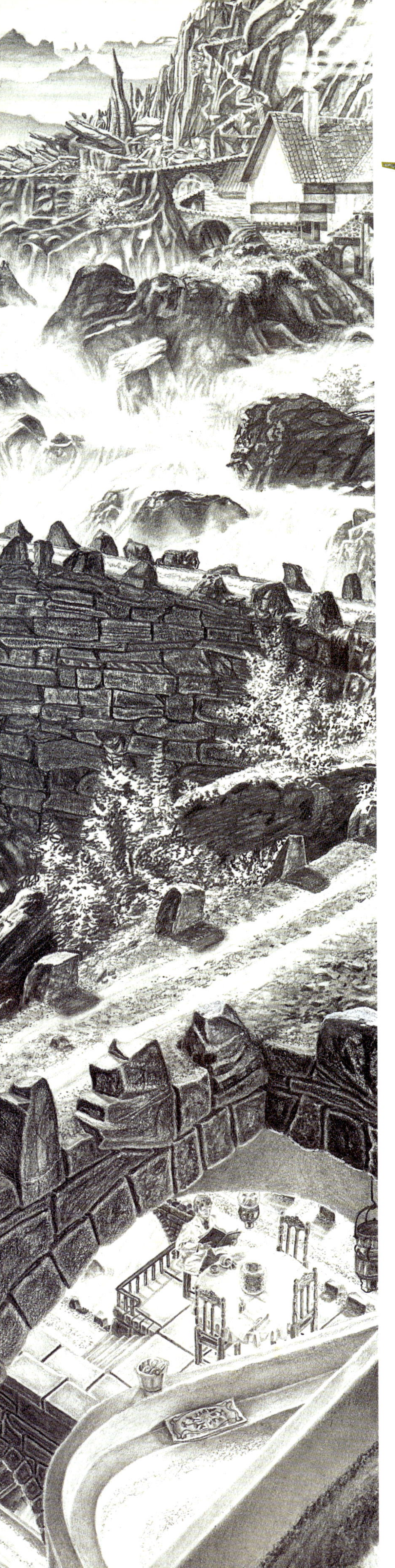

BRIDGES

WHILE WALKING on a footbridge in Norway
I fell to my death. I was awakened
on a footbridge and promptly fell to my death.

Upon awakening, I bridged the contradiction
by falling to my senses which I had been
falling away from for quite some time.

Nexus, finding connections. You've probably
noticed that making a leap of faith is easier
with a bridge. Bridgework even improves speech.

I walked under a viaduct every day as a child
not realizing I was being Rock-Island-Emmons-
St.-L trained over head. The Golden Gate

was a willing suspension of disbelief.
Ideally, Bridges should be made of stone
like Roman aqueducts. Bridging worlds

should be done by granite and slate.
To cross a void avoiding pain one needs a…
To cope with a ridge to nowhere, a span

leads you there. For either side is the other side
of the side crossed. Of course that's profound.
It was found to be true that the jump

above or below, back and forth, foreword
and back, is a conduit to otherness.
Even the unbridgeable is crossed in the mind.

The Hindus know all dualities must be bridged.
The space between memory and prophecy
can be crossed easily on a Bridge.

There are many ways to be double-crossed,
you can criss-cross the globe, star-cross lovers,
cross the line. All are more classic on a Bridge.

Frequently we are uncommitted between worlds.
On Bridges you can go either way. They are not
a means to an end, they're an end to a means.

If you stay in the middle of their arc as, say,
on the Rialto in Venice, the canal winking
below your feet becomes a ribbon of sky,

with each scintillation a star. Venetians
sleep-walk across, not knowing they are
crossing from one Venice into another.

Oh, and of course, lest I forget the Bridge
from birth to death, if we wait in the middle
of the span, it is called life. ❧

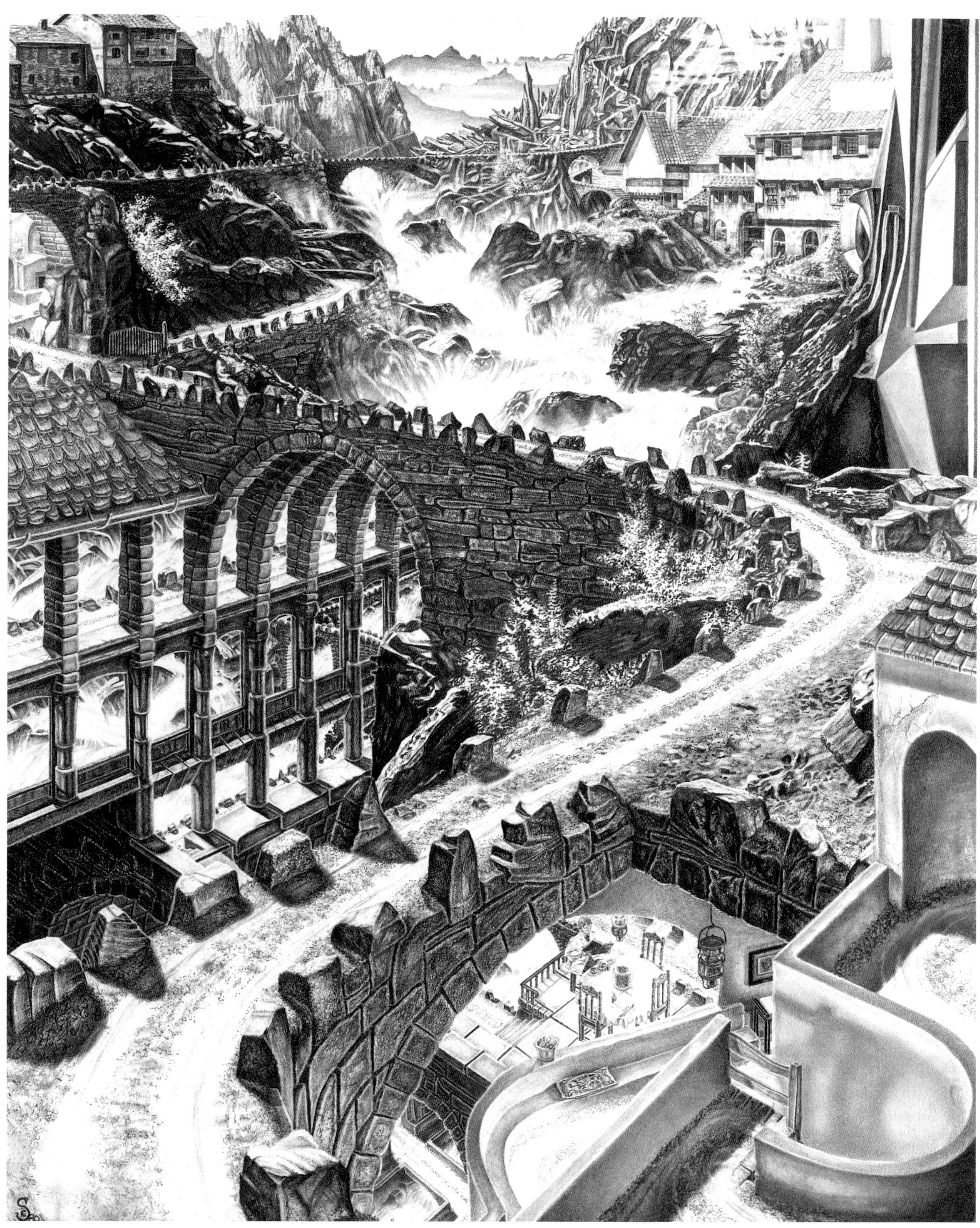

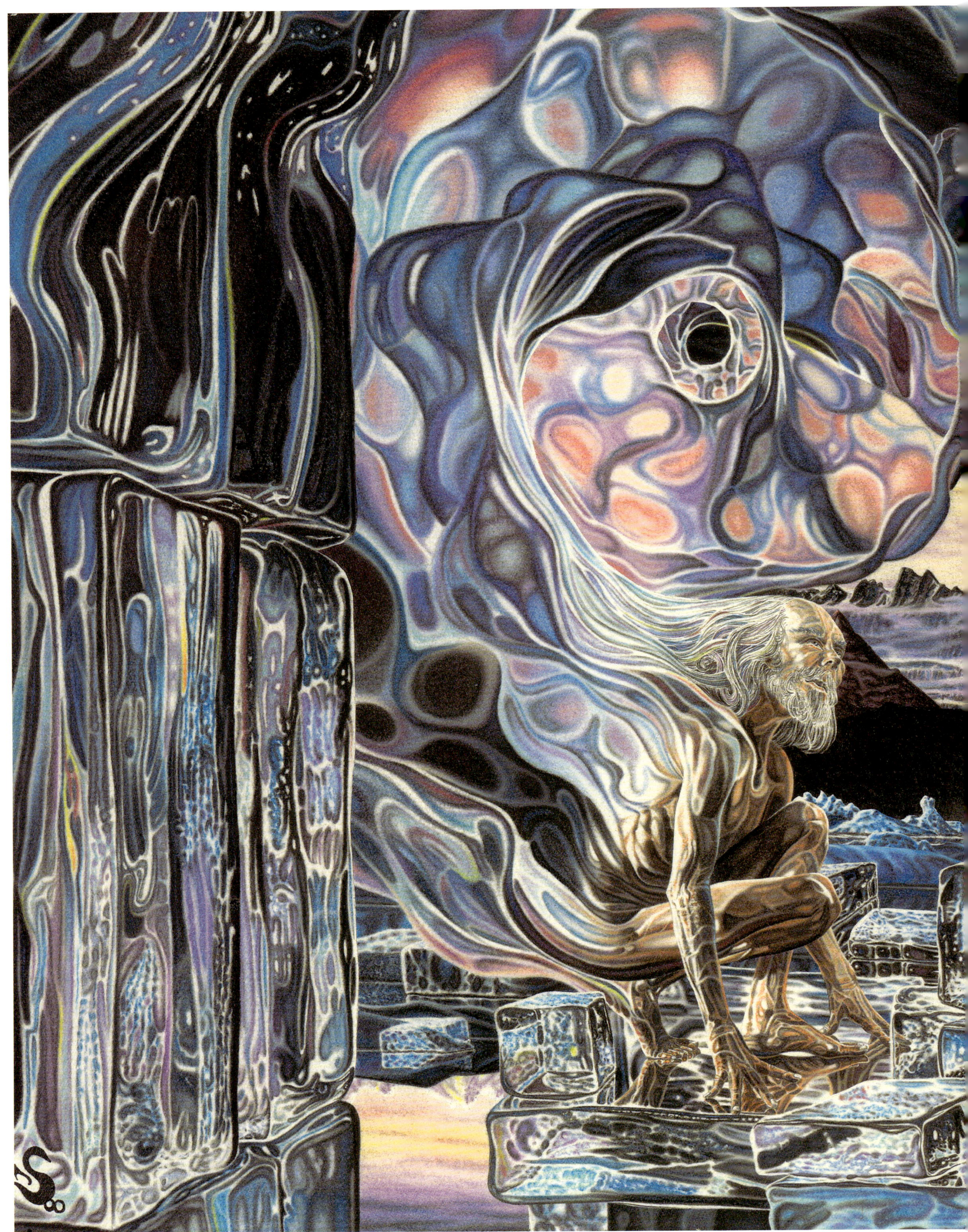

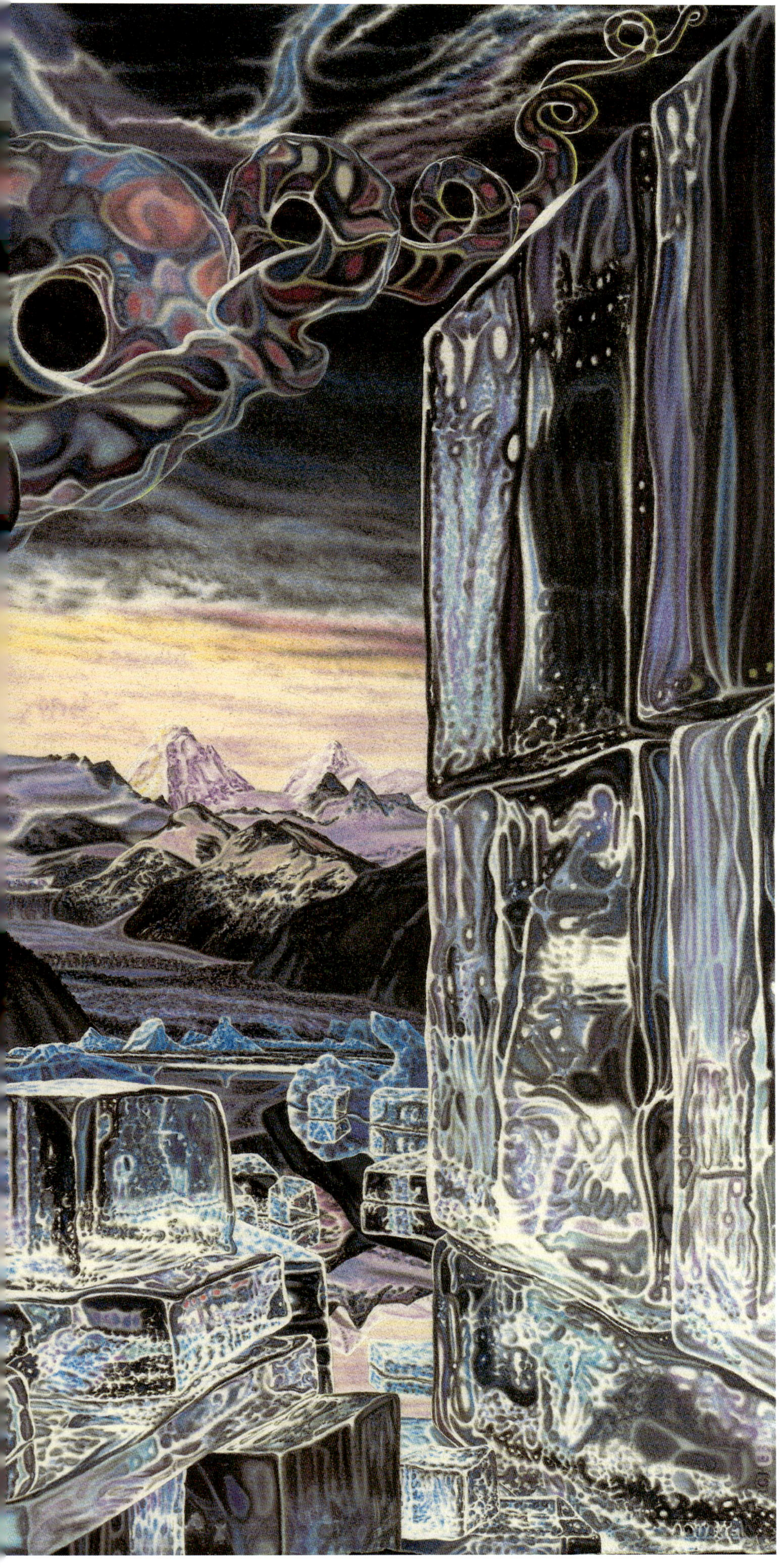

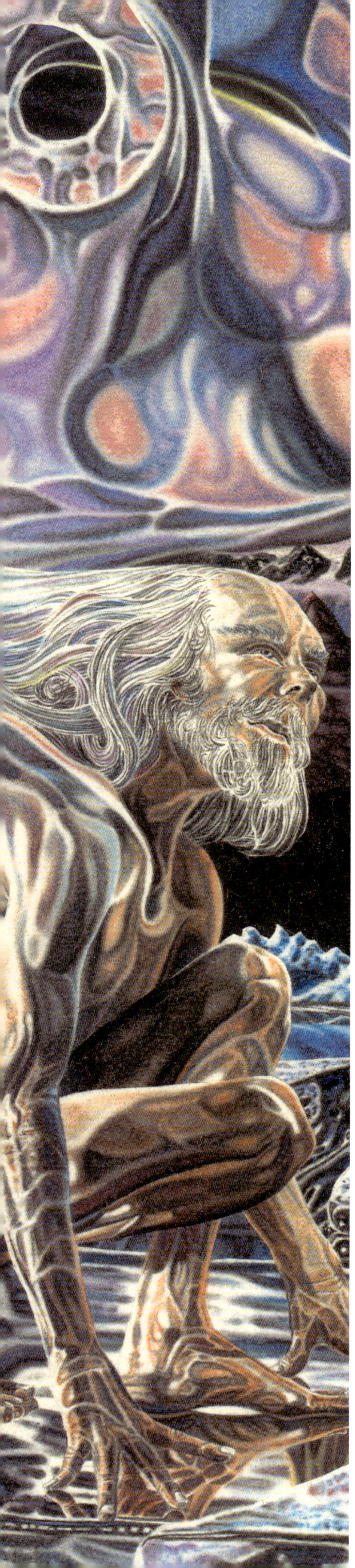

WHEN THEN the narcotic of everyday routine
wears off. When the bread and circuses run out.

When the consolations of religion seem vague.
When the boundaries of age break down—

we may find ourselves for a quantum of time,
the briefest moment, for that's all the soul can allow,

confronting the Mysterium Tremendum. No matter
how transfigured, holy, or disembodied, there is at least

a micron's worth of belief in the possibility
of our own extinction. And for the less enlightened

like myself, it spans galaxies. I can easily imagine
your extinction, but not very readily, my own.

There is a famous, brief, Chinese poem that runs:

> I always
> knew
> that I
> would die
> but
> not today.

We can see the terminus of everything. The cycle
of regeneration writ large goes on and on and on

and yet excludes the individual. What are we then,
a body of work, a mote of racial memory,

a few anecdotes friends recall, even a few crumbs of ash
in an all too real urn? And so at some necessary level

we don't believe it. So we are back to that
brief moment, the Mysterium Tremendum.

It's different for each. For me, it's a vast field of ice,
naked, and taken up in a vortex. An Old Testament

Prophet, puzzled, not masterful and without tablets
waiting, as we all must wait, to see what happens next. 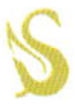

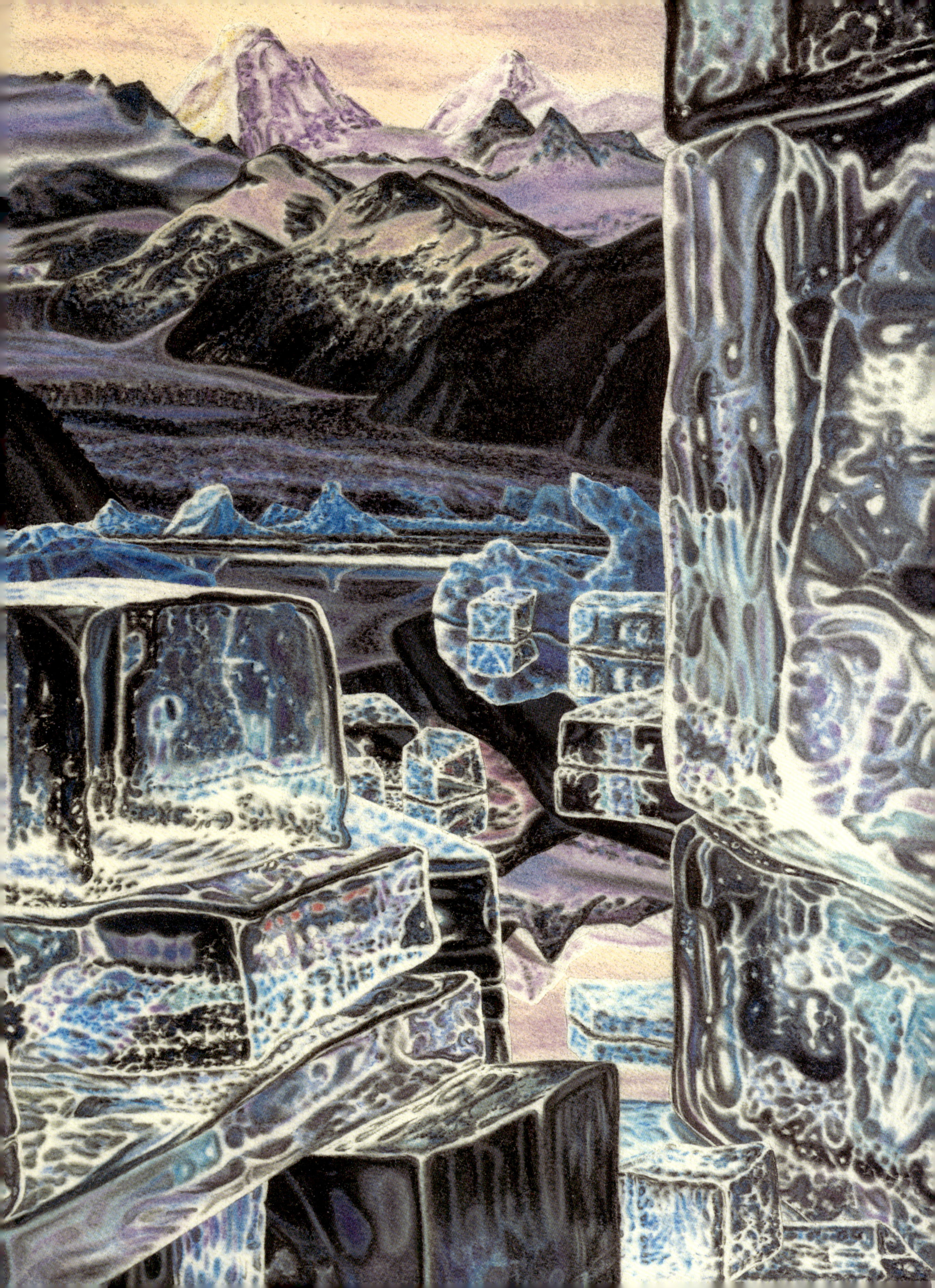

BIRCH TEXTS

IN THE PICTURE gallery at the end of Time,
when earth is a burned-out question mark,
something survived from the Age of Counsell.

The frames compress themselves and huddle
together in a single drawing for warmth.
Trees and crystal and ice and architecture

were dragged along as well, and compressed
in one work of art. The trees split their bark
revealing more frames, more trees, dimensions

multiplied until there was no more room at all
in the whole of this pictorial space. Everything
just had to stop. Preserved in amber, well out of

Time's proof, against the dread of dust, this drawing
made its way into the gallery at the end of Time
because it survived. Culture is about what remains.

All the other bits have been recycled
through a myriad of guts. This is all that remains
from the Golden Age of Counsell.

A few million years after this pictures Maker
is a particle of stellar debris, Steve finally got into
a museum. All his life, he made stuff like this

and no one much gave a patoot and here at the end
of everything *"Birch Texts"* hang just before
the lights go out. In life there was no Age

of Counsell, not even a bronze plaque,
just a bugger-off here, and call later there.
But now that the earth is carbonized ash

he finally gets his due. The thing is, it's
a very good drawing, but it wouldn't
much matter; every archeologist knows

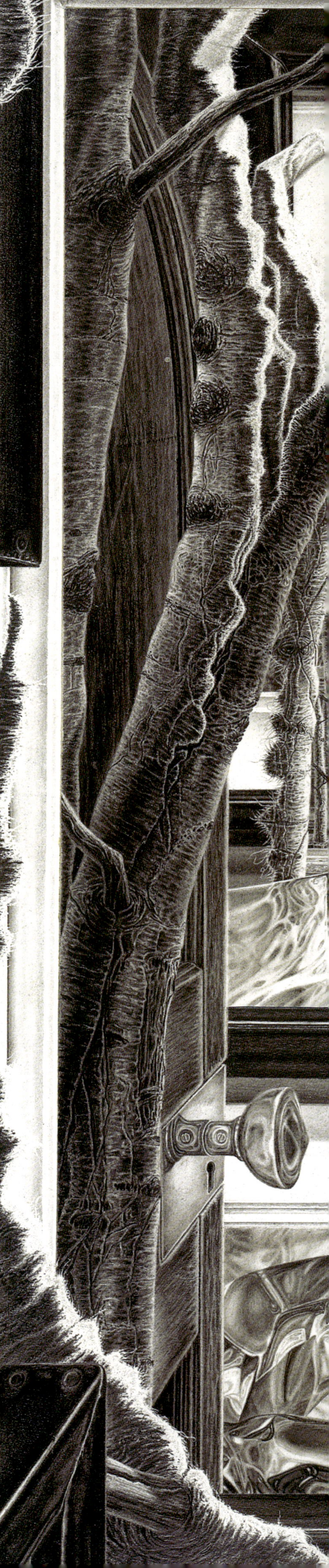

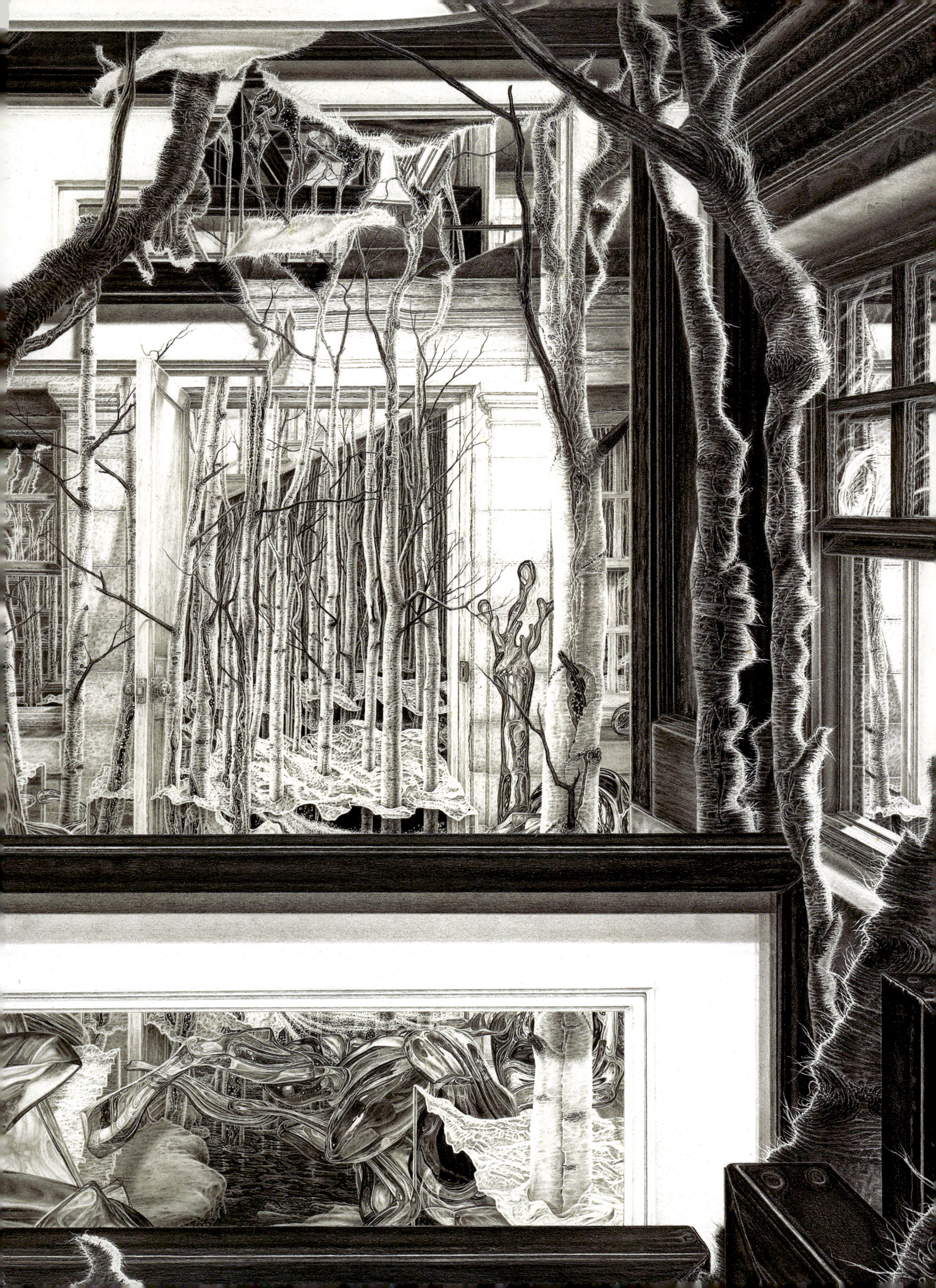

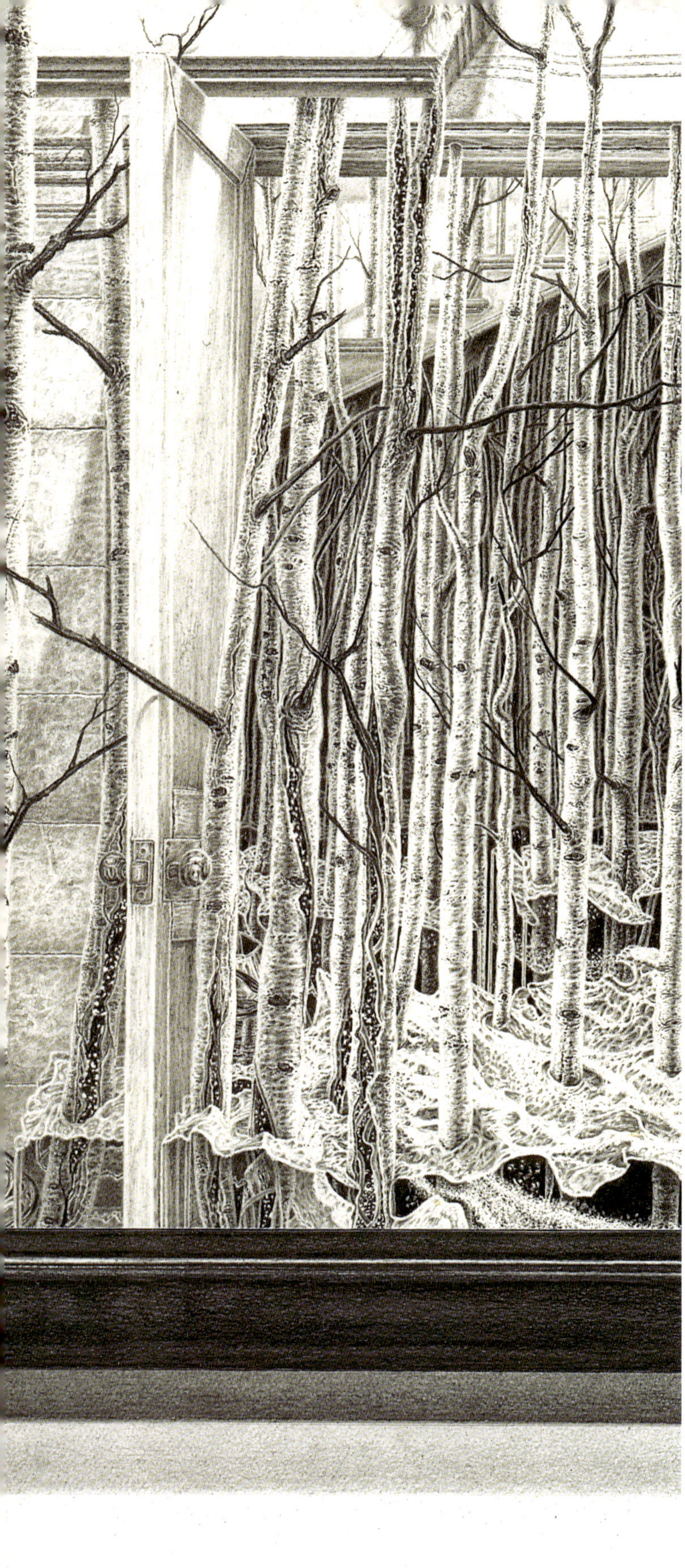

that what persists, survives, is significant.
The thing about being at the end of Time
is it tends to fully focus your attention.

This drawing could generate a novel or two,
no really, and now that it's the only one left,
if there were viewers, they would have the time

to see its birch trees emerging from crystal,
myriad gelatinous objects, several dozen
frames, windows and doors, of course,

occupying all three or four dimensions
simultaneously, and merely seeking a bit
of respect. Time. To see. The artist's lament.

If you're reading this and looking at this drawing
in this moment, nothing else in the universe exists.
You are in the picture gallery at the end of Time. 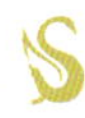

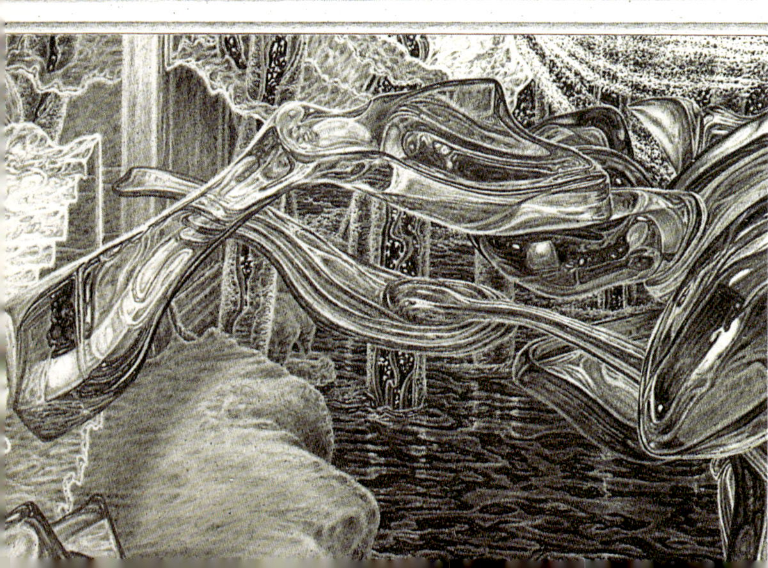

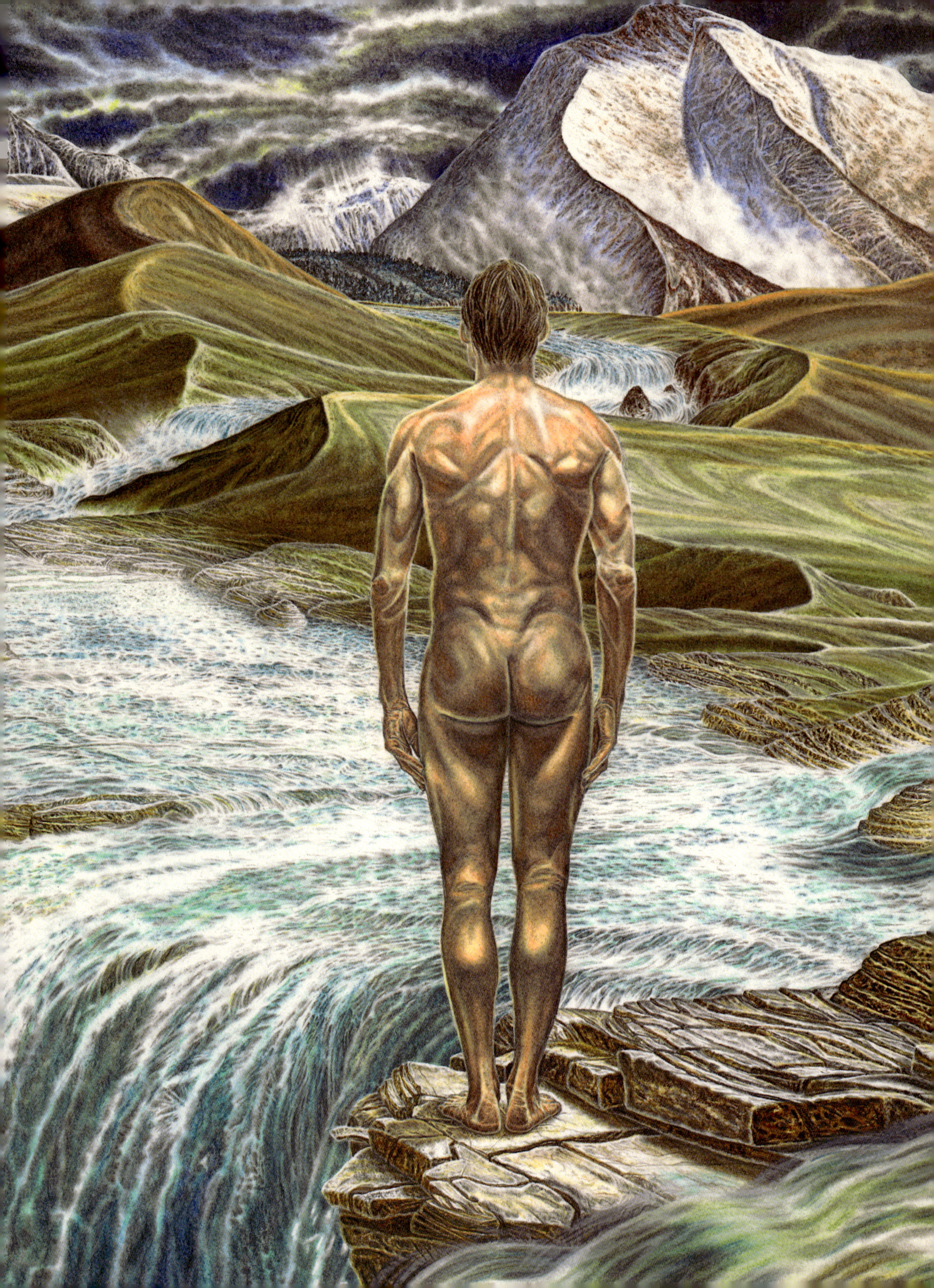

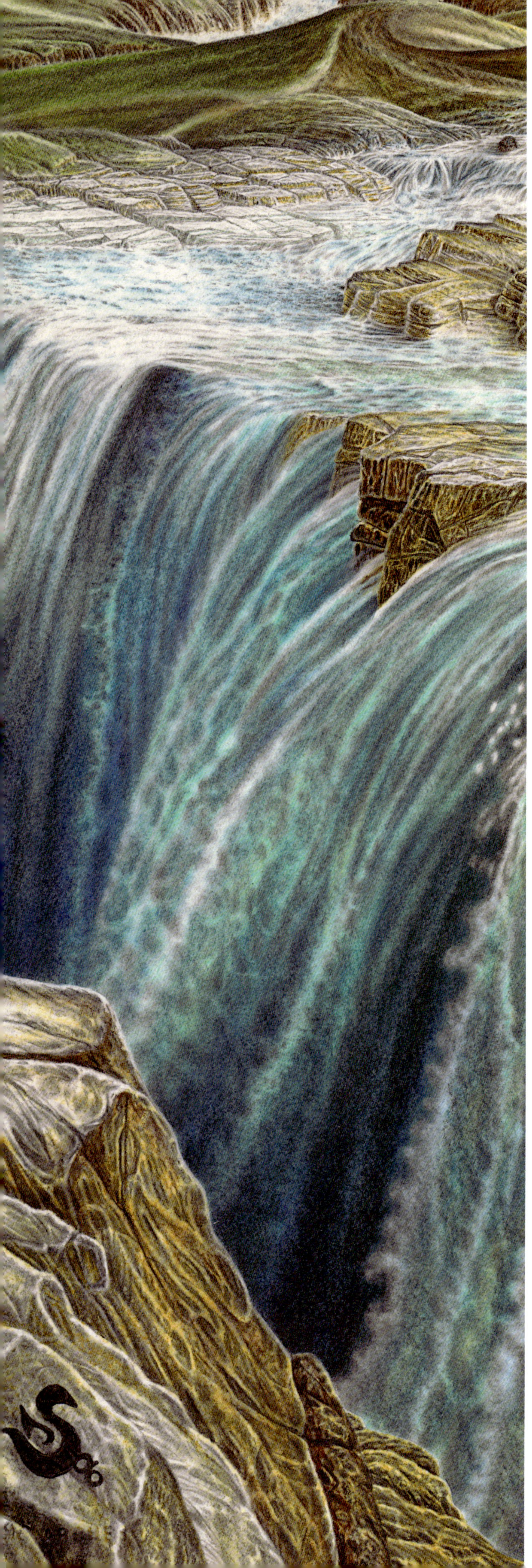

THE ETERNAL
LONGING TWO

I. PITCHED INTO the light and blind
longing for home and fearing it.

A moment as a literal precipice,
    the burn of all time in every breath.

    Stumbling into myself on the road,
a look of amazement in my eyes.

Memory bittered by wrinkles, wizened
out of Apollo into caricature.

Mirrors must deny childhood.
Eden blooms toward sunset.

II. Terrible and wonderful forms rise.
I seek myself like a drug.

Ask questions of a God only offering
answers. I bleed in boundaries.

Keys rust and my clues have burned;
everything hoped for waits unlocked.

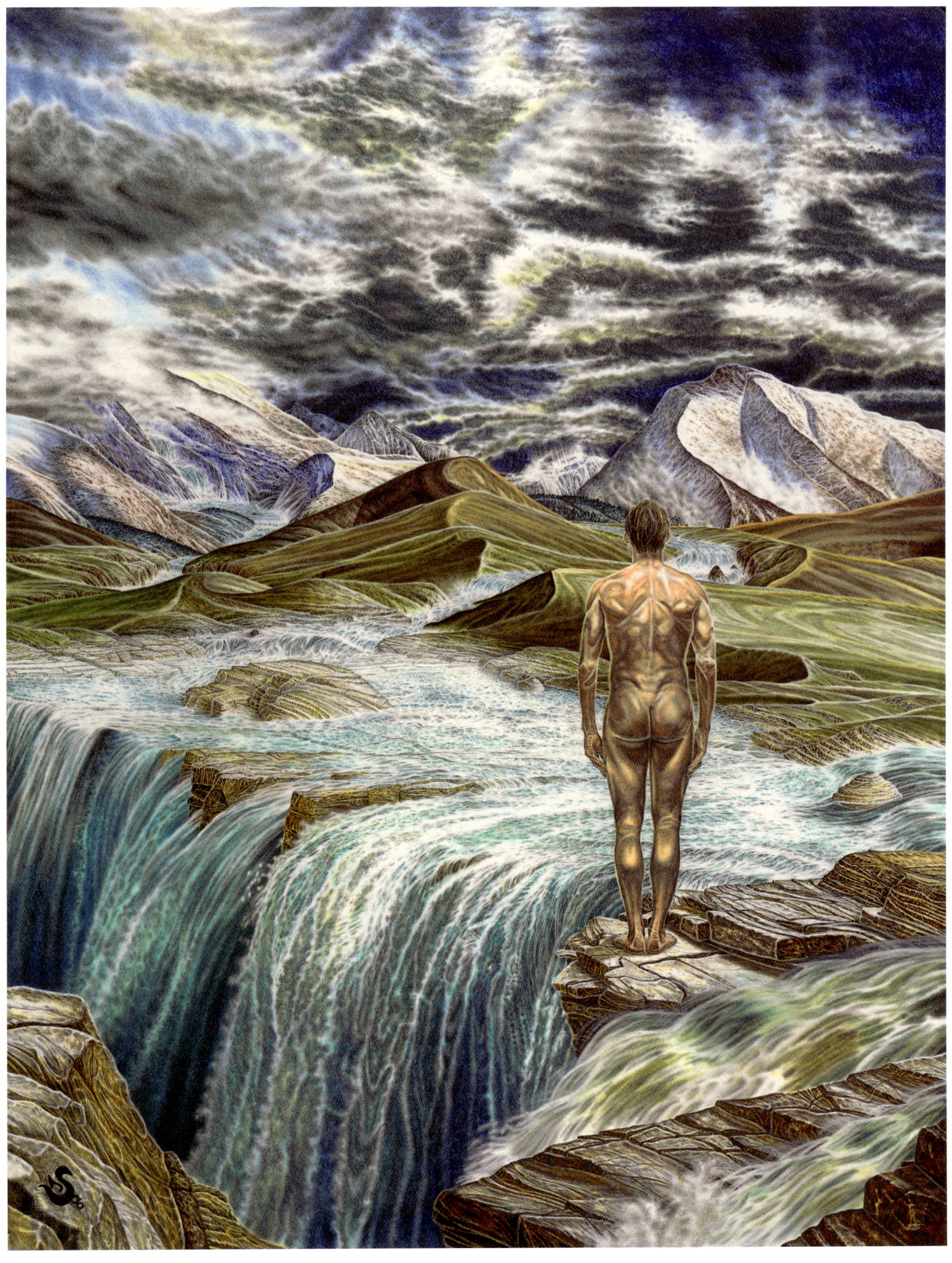

WITHIN THE COMPLEXITY
of a mosaic, a door.

It is a way in,
or a way out?

To escape the claustrophobia
of a self, or to arrive

at the inexhaustible
abundance of nature

we need a way out
and there is a door.

Without the door
a Moorish tessellation

assembled by a modernist.
With the door, Jung

smoking his pipe
offering a choice.

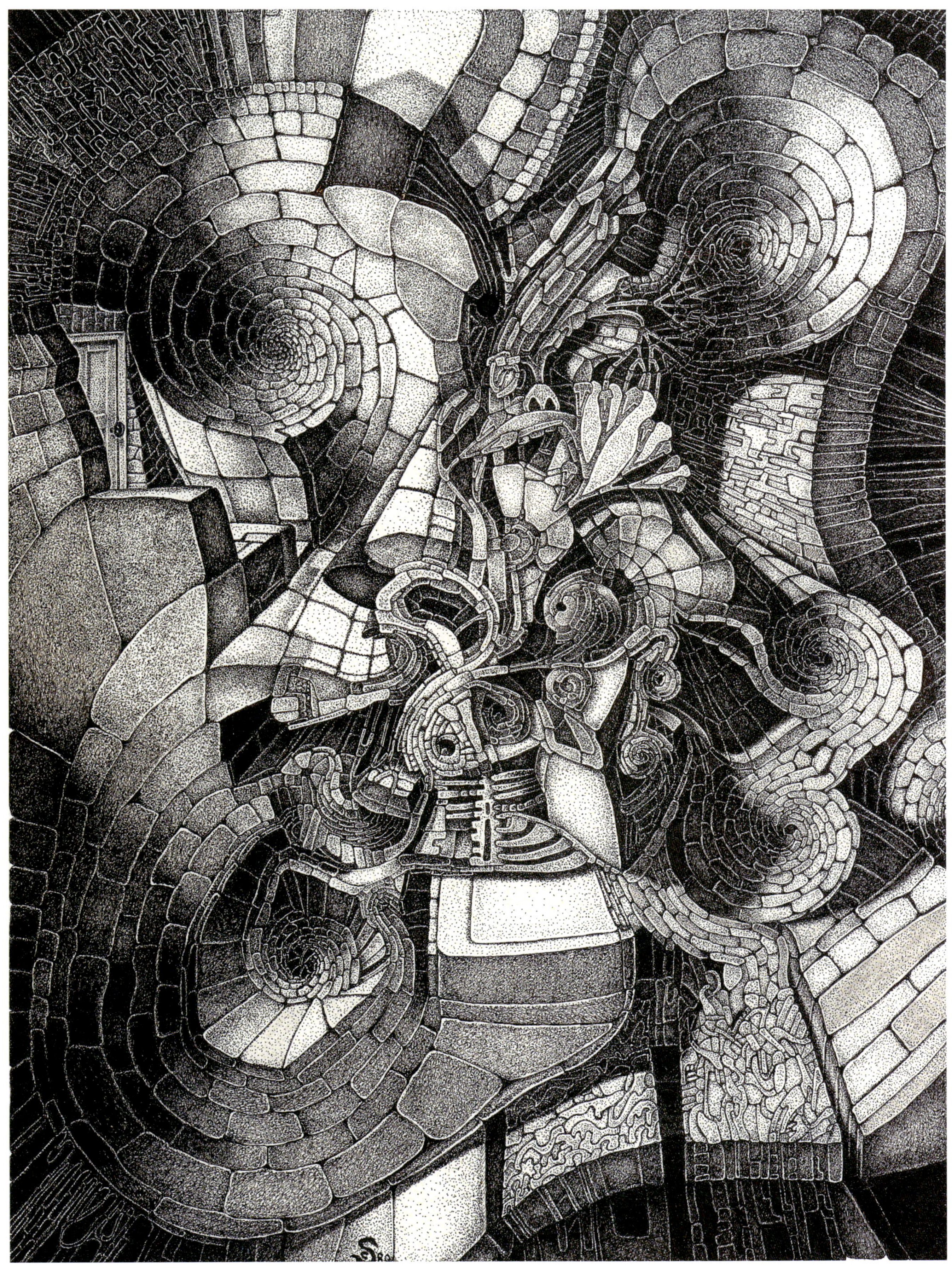

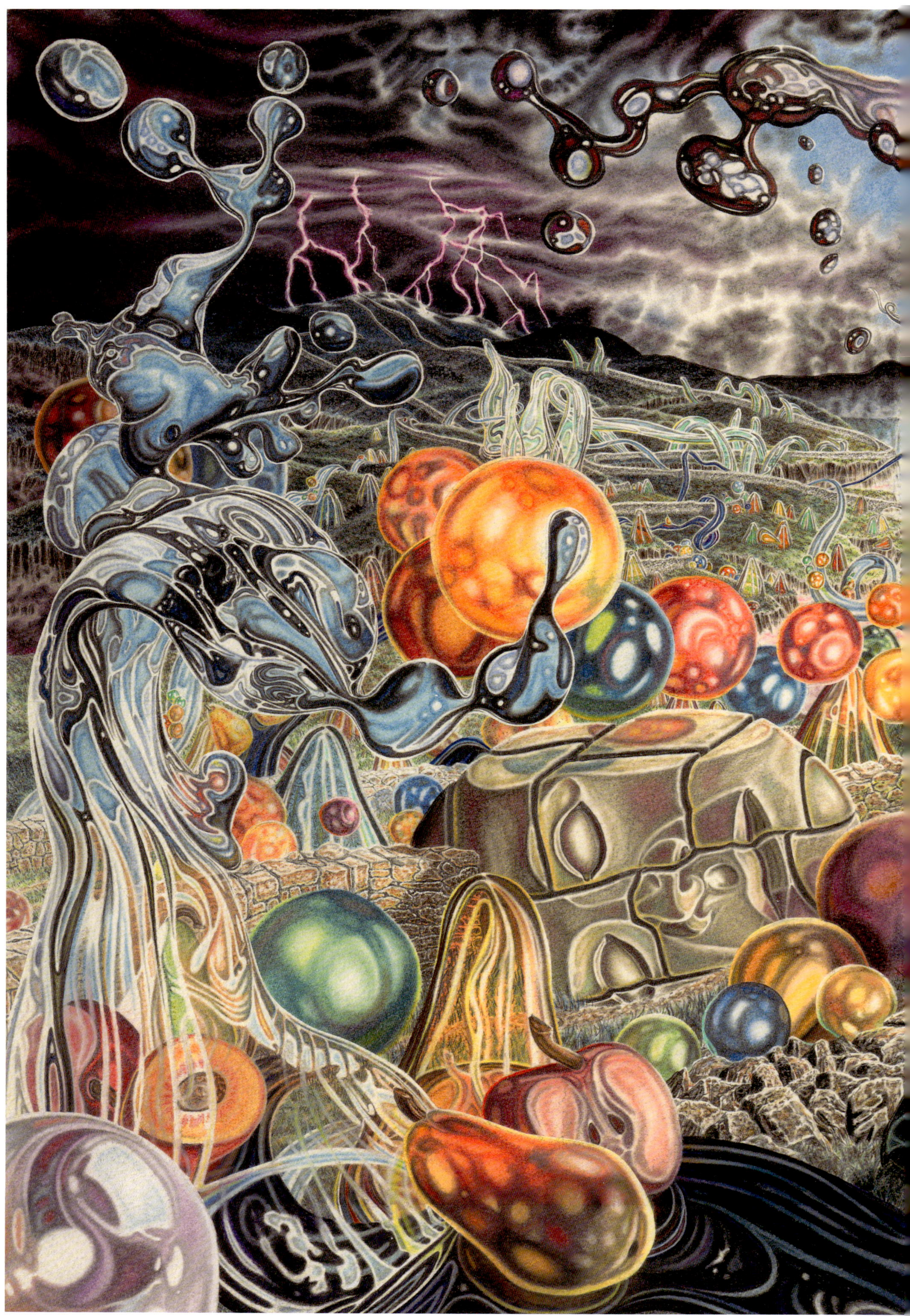

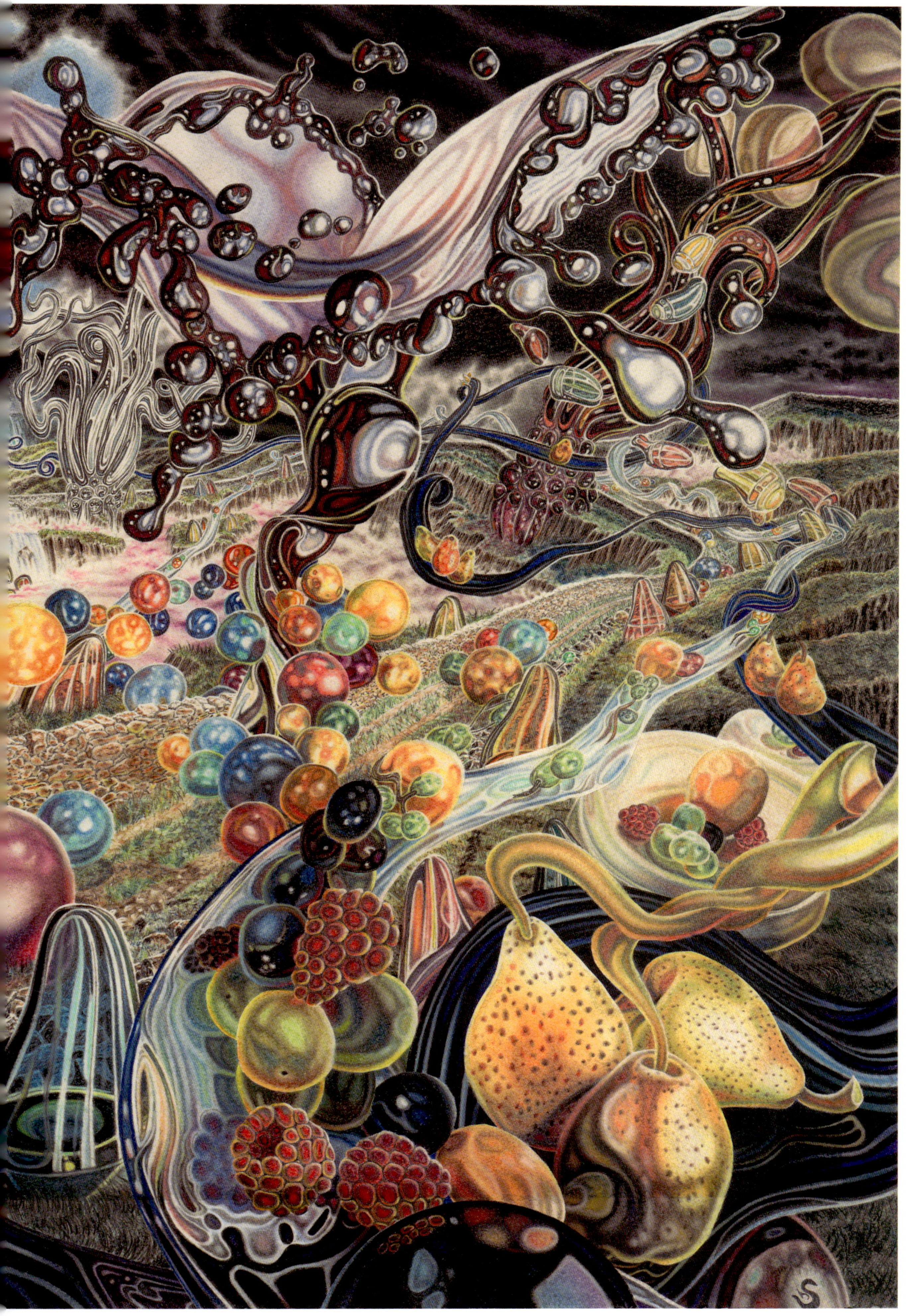

THE HEAD a damp lump of basalt
tucked earthen, wise only in effigy
erodes through ages that have
forgotten to forget him.

He was reared to a high culture
of ever upward, never diminished;
he once roared theisms of faith.
The ways of him have gone—

and the days of him have stayed;
in an altered countryside, well after
the grand anesthetic of man's hand
has aesthetically ceased.

There are a few walls and bridges
and the atmosphere is still fecund
with the imaginative pulse of man's
influence. Evolution whispering

a remembrance perhaps. You can
see an amour-aqueous fluster of globes
glassed up in Popsicle color or opaque
lacquer. A lively simulacrum of fruit

and globulerized trees. Anemones
waggling arms in the fully ionized
tom-tom atomics of a dangerously
safe and renewing thunderstorm.

On the resurrected earth, everything
is ripe and waiting to be picked. It can
never spoil for time has forgotten
how to pass. Childhood has made

a place for itself at last. The neurotic
large children, now extinct, had smiles
of steel. They hop-thumbed crab-wise
into the hop-along fast acid, sunset

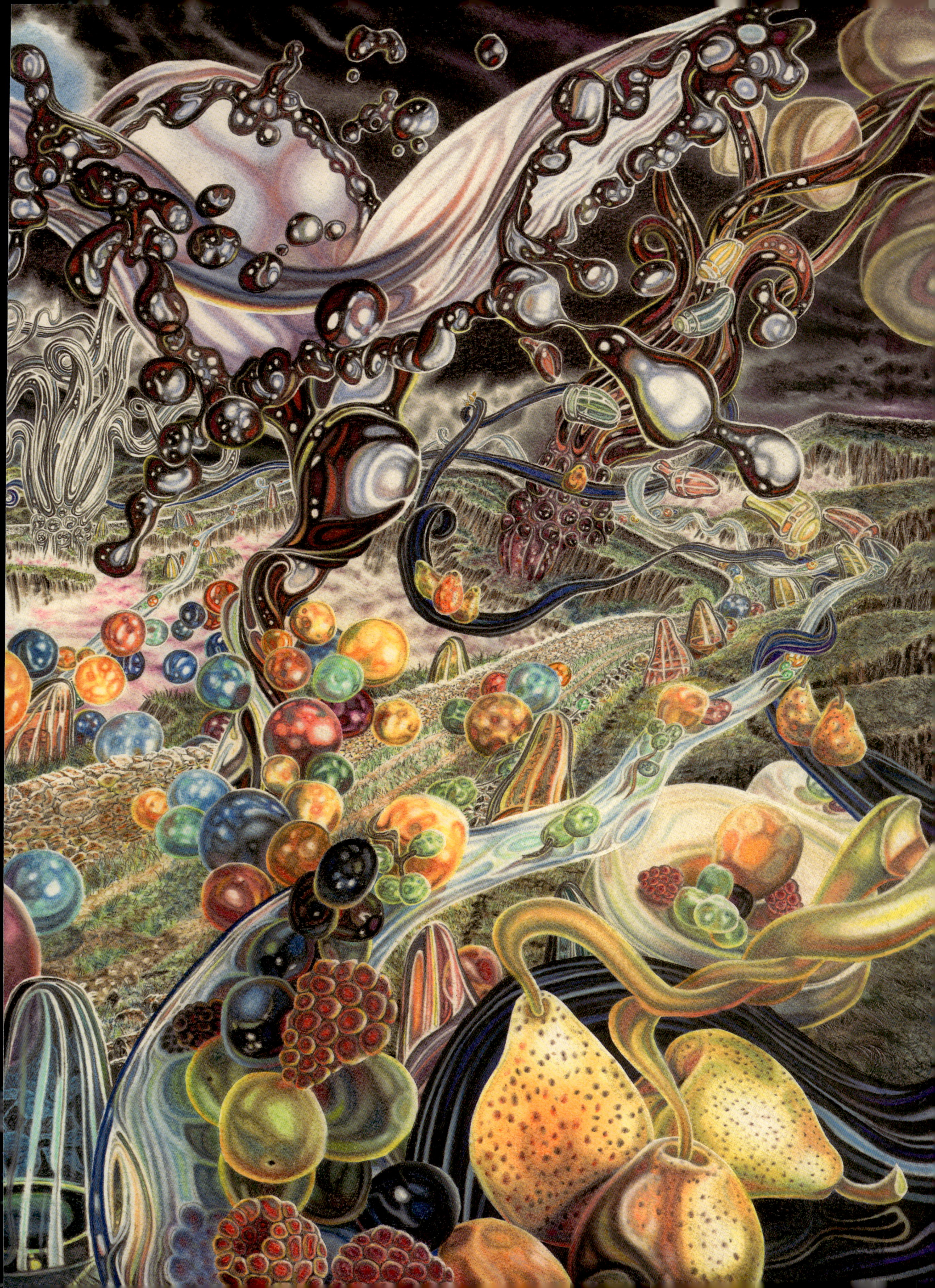

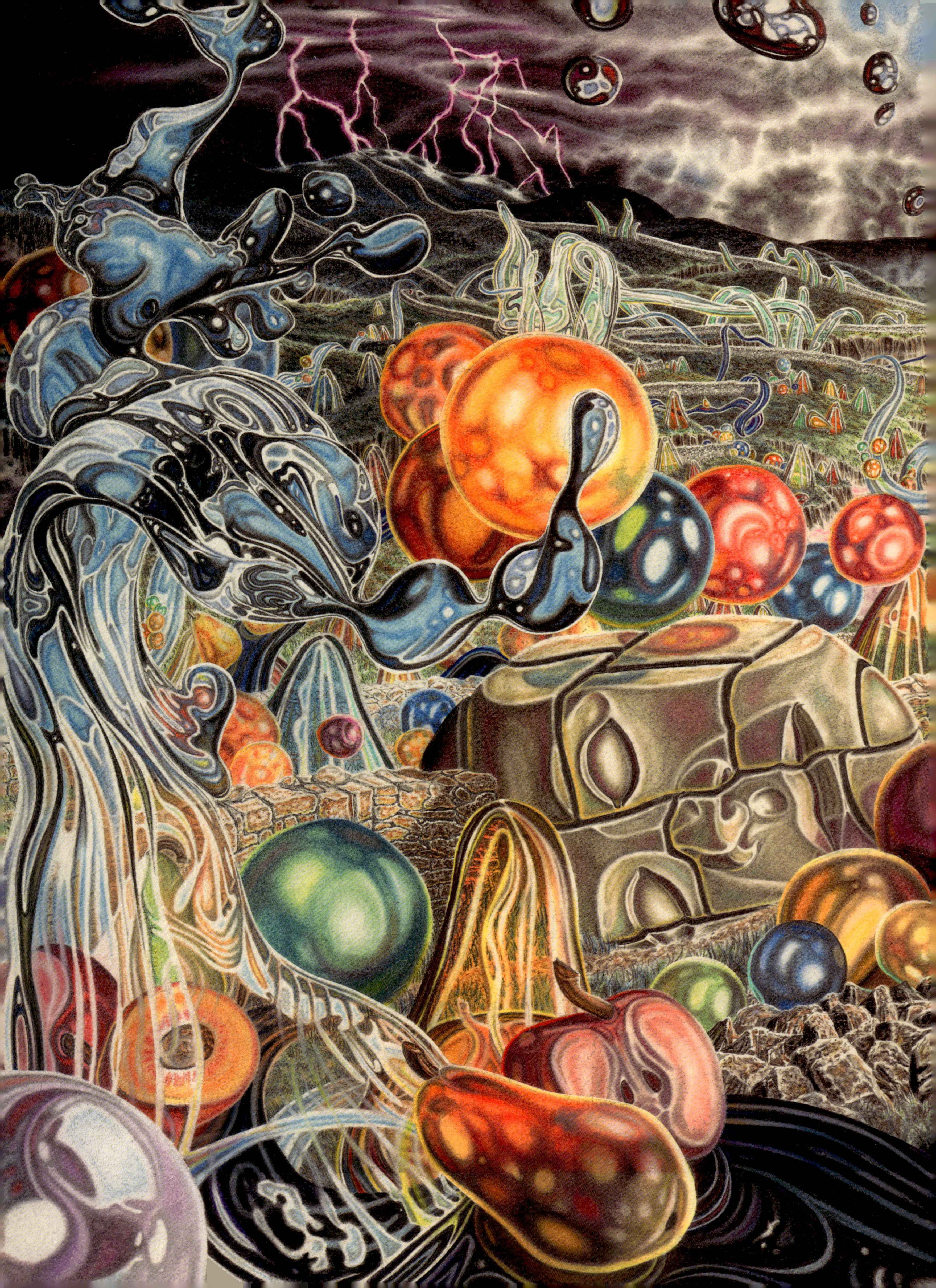

counting their winnings in the dark.
But now everything has become
new washed and edible. The paths
are overgrown with the grass-staining

green of a new glamour. Magic, ribbons,
tart candy hours as ages have stopped.
The music of the spheres has recommenced.
Synesthesia has returned to the garden.

In our first extinction we had forgotten
how to come to our senses, so this time
our senses came to us. This time, innocence
hung around hoping to get it right.

And so color is fugal, sound has hue,
movement is pigmented, voices shape
the very atmosphere, the air itself
vibrates to the aroma of green apples.

The jaw-breaker worldliness of forced fun,
festivals and fetes wearied away and allowed;
jaw-breakers, jujubes, candy floss and the
simple joy of root beer floats to become truth. §

CANNERY BOUND

IN THE WIDE piscatorial realm
of the gull gray over Bering Sea

the Char and Shad, Coho, Red
Chinook, King and Grayling

seek to Finnish their lays of
egg song, sleek sea dancing,

sky grazing through grass
and kelp in transfigured bliss.

Like any mere shellfish, they
want the exoskeleton to fall

from their eyes so they can fly
to the limpid puddle of the moon.

So up they come heavenward
in the gill net of their collective dreams.

Into the air, opened and emptied
enrobed in tin for the dysfunctional

Eucharist of a quick lunch. Yet their soul
is free as they sail beyond canned goods.

In their myths what they truly desire
is the god that's a Bruin upstream

offering up the natural selection
they so richly deserve. Amen and Amen. 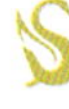

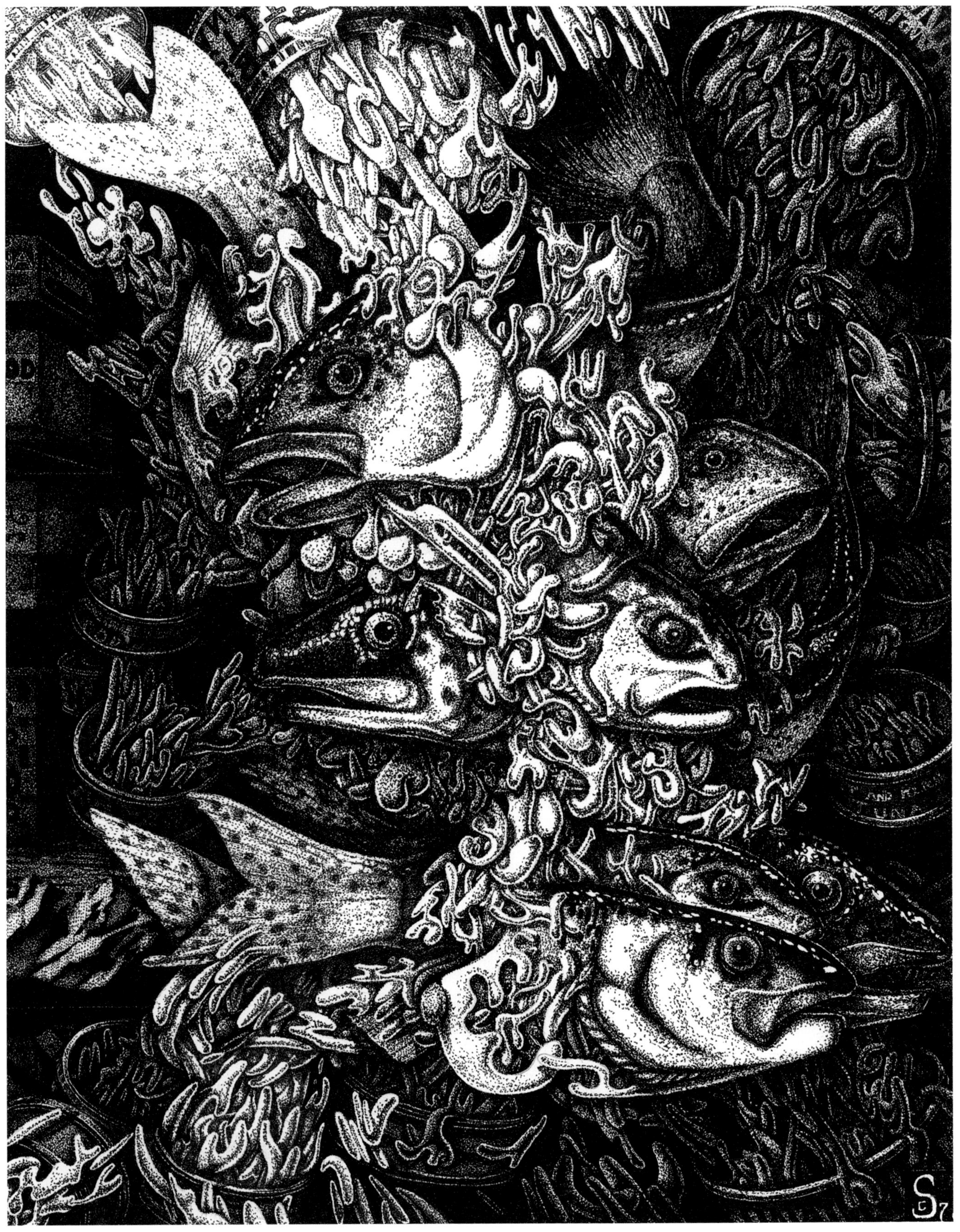

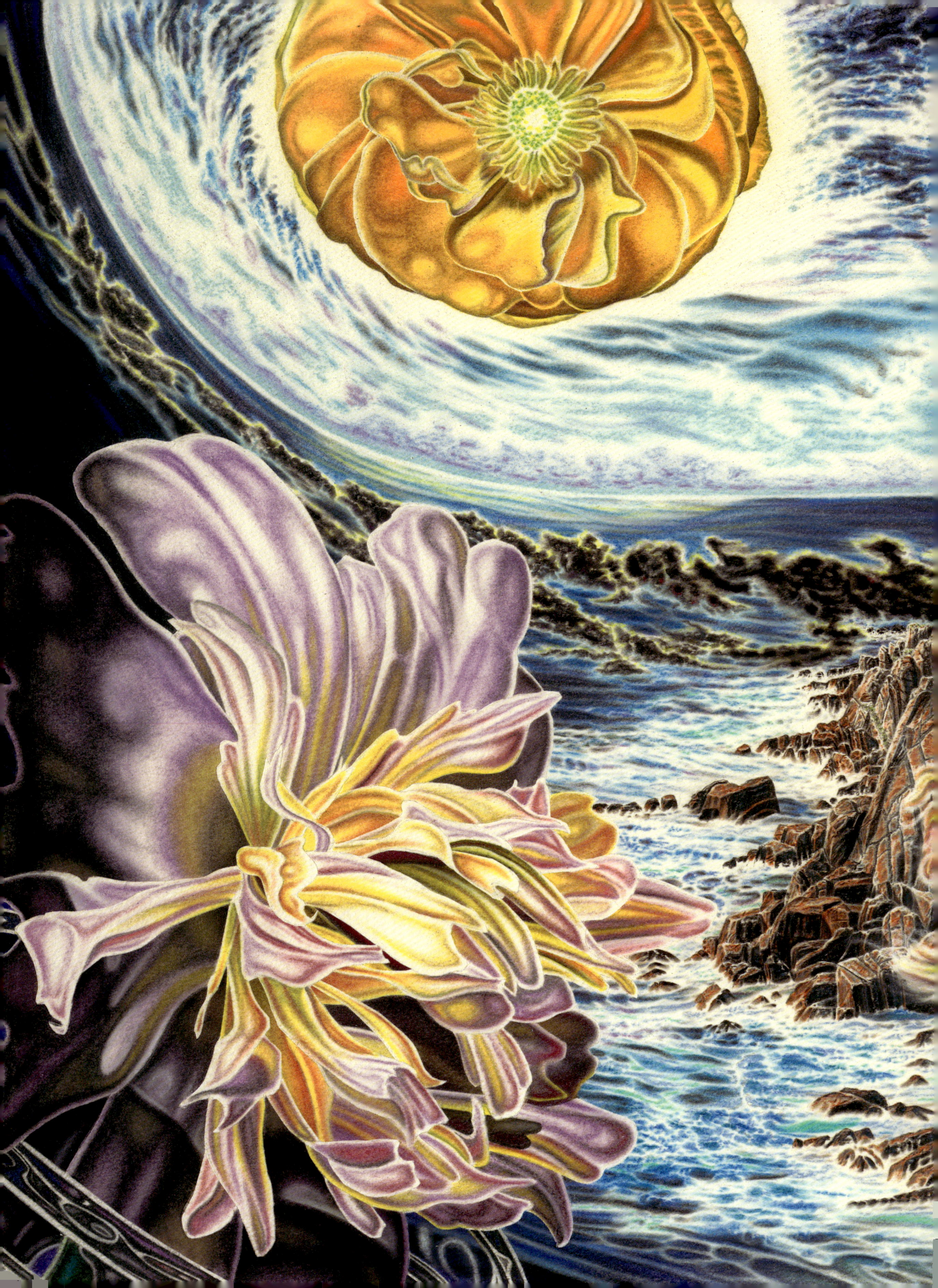

THE ALCHEMY OF THE EVERYDAY

THE CIRCULATION of veins spider in the leaf's web.
The green dynamo pulling the life from sunlight.
Drinking the sun from the earth's life,
preparing a palace for the profligate birth of seed.

The flame lost in the bud, the bud lost in the round
of seasons. A flower is sexed to a cause, pollinated
to a creed, to exceed the world in beauty and feed,
the world in fact. Another day thrown into the sky.

The Yin-full grin and Yang-full tang of it—
bud to blossom, flower to leaf, earth to sky,
fire to water. We are politic butterflies and bees
drunk on the sky's blue liquor, abuzz in ionized air.

We were born in heaven, we have nothing to seek
or return to. The endless history-ripe carnage
of bruised lives and damaged souls does not
change the chance for a miracle every time

we are lucky enough to open our eyes.
What we see and feel becomes story and myth
because the ordinary is so beyond our ability
to comprehend.

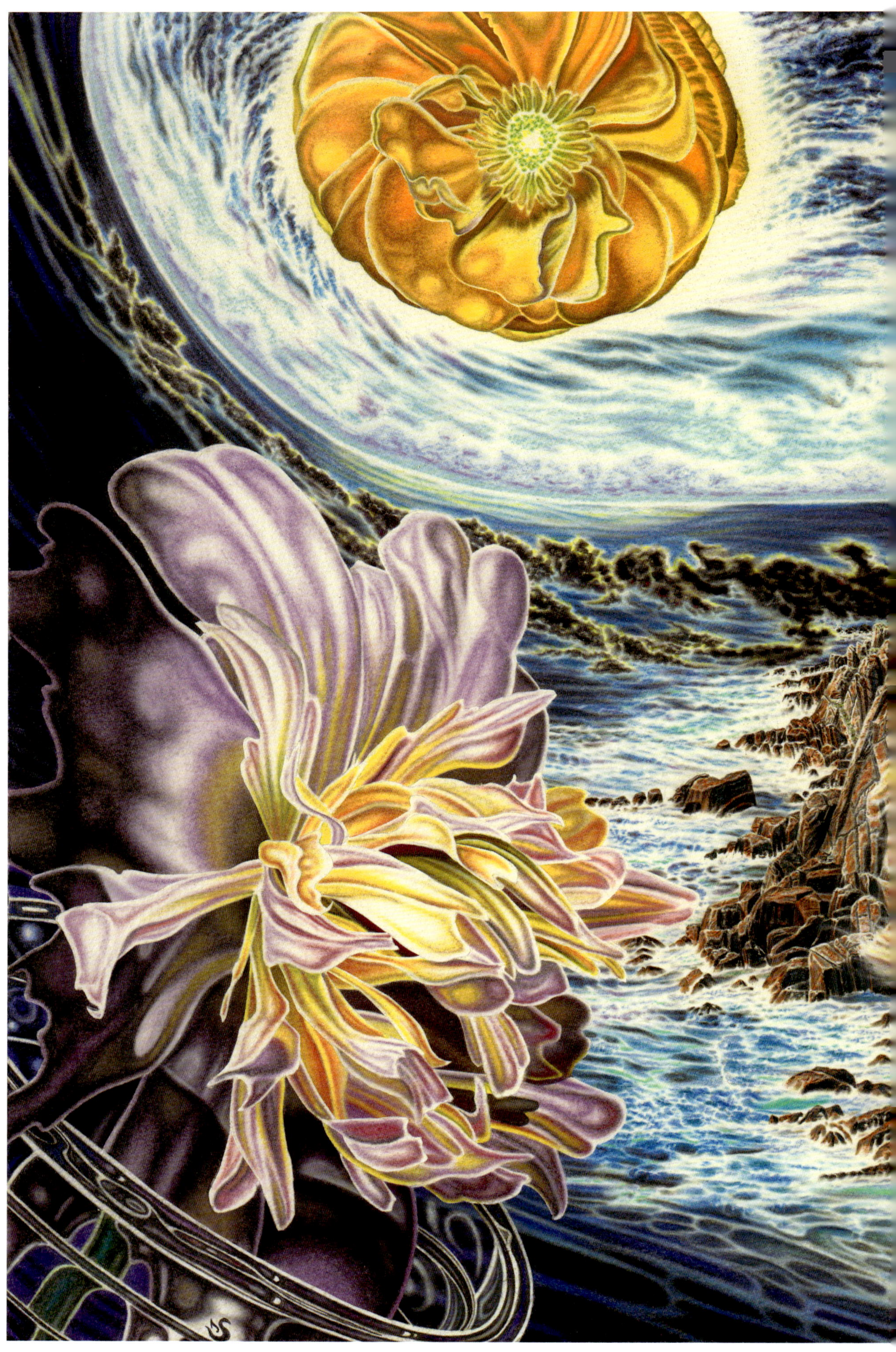

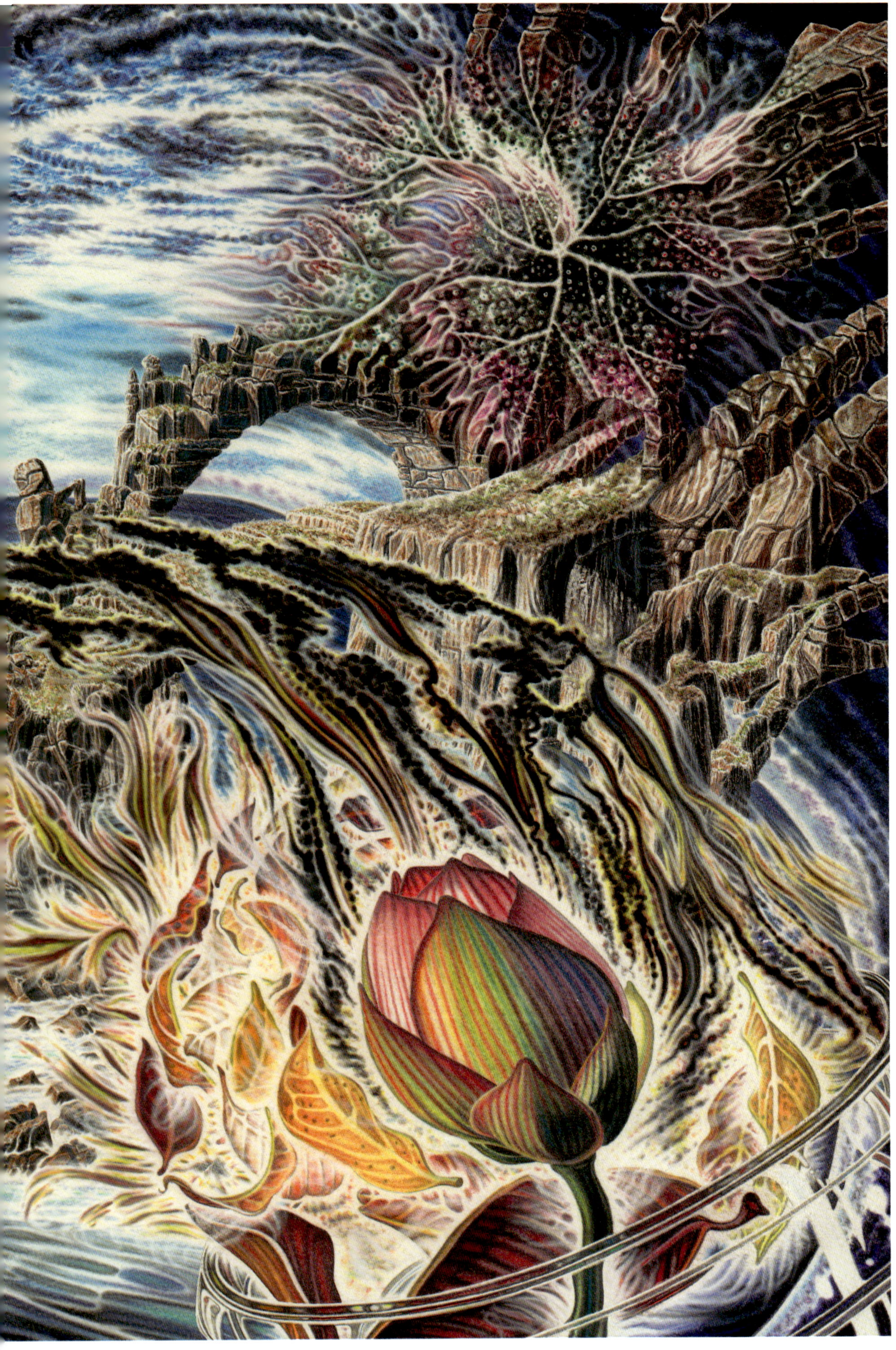

Whenever I'm in Washington D.C. I make a pilgrimage to a small paneled room in the National Gallery. This intimate Dutch jewel box houses three Vermeer's. At the far end of this room hangs Vermeer's *A Lady Writing*. An ocean of ink has been spilled, justly, on these works. But what became apparent to me, is that if you stand at one end of this room and walk toward the painting it fundamentally changes. A simple truism but, only for certain works. For the Vermeer it became a revelation. Every five paces forward its luminosity changes, the engagement of the numinous young woman in the painting to the viewer shifts. Details of pearl, splashes of light, fabric and the like, come in and out of focus, and no matter how close you are to the painted surface the revelations keep coming, right to the point where your breath could almost moisten her skin. You have reached the limits of vision but not the limit to what can be seen.

When I've had the privilege of viewing illuminated manuscripts in some of the most beautiful libraries in Europe, I would often be given a magnifying lens. You could just never get too close to these miraculous pages. The Limbourg Brothers must have used one hair brushes to paint their famous *Book Of Hours*. And the *Book Of Kells* in Trinity College is beyond imagining. Those nameless monks lived in these books. Whole lives of monastic devotion could be spent painting a few pages. The visionary intensity of these small miracles has seldom been equaled. These wondrous worlds of text surrounded by garlands of flowers, dragons and unicorns, landscapes bluing into nothingness, were a way out of the monastery, and into themselves.

There has always been a tradition in painting to capture worlds, within worlds, within worlds. This need is not about the history of styles or the ascendancy of certain isms. This is temperament — a driving obsession to draw entire geographies, coiled and nested philosophies of vision, self-regulating and consistent cosmologies. When you are in these alternative realities, perceptions alter and your real life, for a moment, becomes just another fiction. While in the illuminated page, or the Vermeer interior, your mind is tuned to a different music. if you're not careful you can be lost for a lifetime, as I have.

II. In the 1890s, a whole generation of English Symbolists mad for fable escaped the metal grindstone of pistons and progress and helped to enchant into being the Golden Age of English book illustration. Rackham, Dulac, Detmold, and so many others were inventing worlds of enchantment. They were unwilling to accept a shop-worn reality, to be merely ordinary. They knew that to write a poem or paint a picture is to crystallize the supernatural flux of Time. What they were searching for was the real fountain of youth. We don't live long enough to grow old, but we can grow gray wasting before the frivolities of common speech, common vision, and common sense.

III. The world is sport, a garden, one long continuous war; it is unconditional love, the world is an election, a computer game in the vastness of cyberspace, a mystical union with God, nature, science, an empty terminus of black despair; it is art, poetry, or music. When we talk of these or of fantasy, myth and fable, we are really talking about a choice of metaphors. Change the metaphors, change reality. Change the symbols, alter worlds. The Chinese believed that changing a single key color could alter destiny. The Jews felt even one word, if the right one, could alter creation. The (hygiene) of altering our internal images, colors, and language will make it possible to live swimmingly in the divine fiction of eternity. Each metaphor is a shard of the infinite. Only a careful choice, faith, and a creatively induced amnesia can offer inner grace, and make space for an art that affirms our life and ripples out to

a possible future that we *can* live in, and is *worth* living in. You don't have to be a Buddhist and give up desire; just don't make choices that blacken the soul.

IV. As any Surrealist can tell you, at one level at least, realism is quite easy. You show a three-quarter length portrait, say, and whether it's by Rembrandt, Wyeth, Neel or Picasso, it is nominally real. The means of expressiveness and style, let alone genius, may change, but it is nominally real. But when venturing down the rabbit hole to realms of dream or inner mystery, the level of intention and clarity have to have a commanding conviction. The cup is *really* floating six inches off the table. The Mad Hatter is *really* having a tea party. To take someone somewhere they have never been, you have to have been there yourself.

For me, a painting or a poem is a door. As I walk through it, it walks through me. To walk through the doors of this book, all you need is a willingness to really look — and to taste the honey of words… and the sweet synergy between them. I hope you enjoyed the journey. I did. $

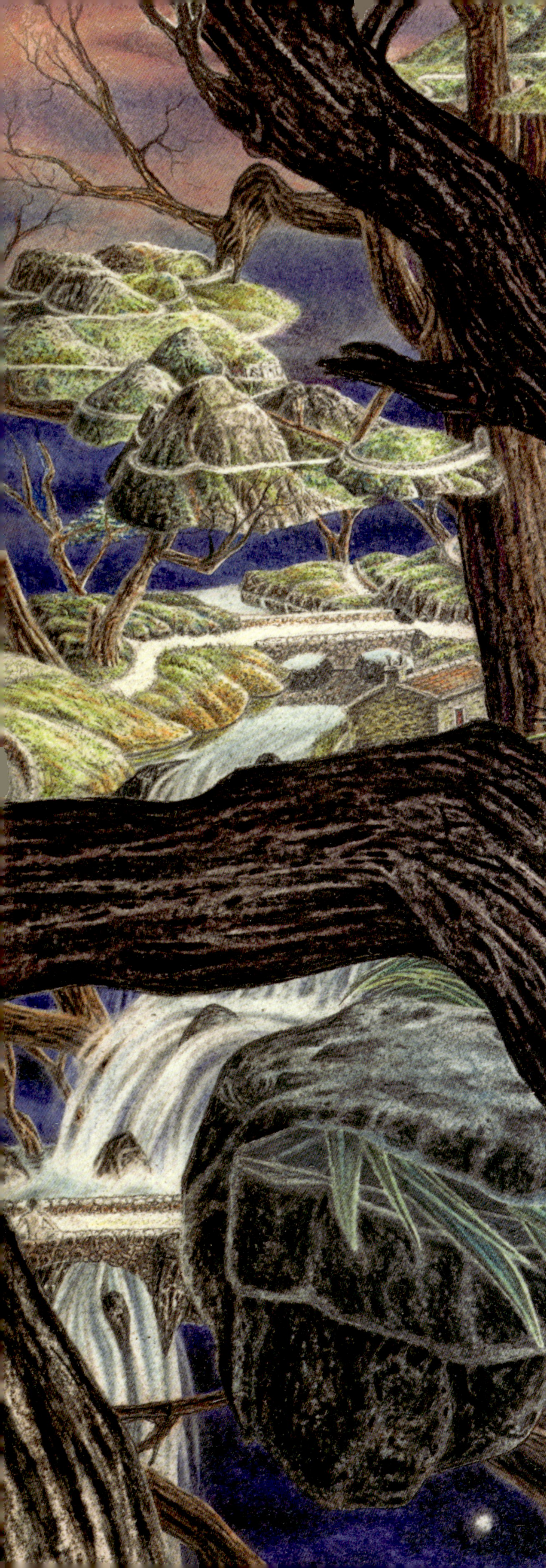

GLOSSARY

Attic – Attica or Athens. The subtle intelligent smile of the Greek God. Da Vinci achieved this miracle in his portraits.

Beth-Luis-Nion – The Tree Alphabet. The Druid way of words, used for divination. A language of 5 vowels and 13 consonants, each letter a different tree. For example, Beth= Birch, Luis= Rowan, Nion= Ash and so on. Look to Robert Grave's *The White Goddess* for more.

Botryoidal – Having the form of a bunch of grapes. The mineral hematite, for example, will form these rounded masses.

Cantrip – A magic charm or spell.

Contrapposto – Counter position. The twist of body in renaissance painting creates movement, and counter balance.

Daemon – Our attendant spirit.

Deliquescence – To become liquid. Our soul is oil on water.

Doxologies – *Praise God from whom all blessings flow.* A formulaic ritual hymn. Reassuring and rote, as all ritual must be.

Diastole – Normal dilation of the heart, the chambers fill with blood. Systole its opposite and in language the long and short of words.

Ducats – Gold coins first minted in Venice in 1284.

Empyrean – The highest heaven.

Hieratic – The priestly way to permanence in art, language and saintliness, fixed in time. As comforting as an old blanket.

Kohl – Powdered antimony to darken the eyes.

Lascaux – The cave of the romping animals painted in the dark, twenty thousand years before Christ by Aurignacian artists. Where we and art and perhaps consciousness began.

Librams – Old leather bound books full of sentience.

Malachology – Mollusks and their shells. A science, but for me always an art. Miracles of symmetry and a source of wonder. Also pretty good eating.

Mythogenesis – The creation of myths themselves.

Mysterium Tremendum – The end game we must all come to. Living the immensity of our own extinction. What makes us human.

Pellucid – To be flooded with light.

Pentimento – Something showing through. A resonance or trace.

Philtre – A magic potion.

Pyritohedron – A crystal of 12 pentagonal faces.

Tabula-Rasa – An empty mind. A clean slate. Original innocence.

Tessellation – Space divisions in Moorish architecture. The Alhambra's mosaics, each piece interlaced. Its high priest was M.C. Escher.

Wurm – A nasty cold Norse dragon.

Xylem – A trees vascular system.

Yggdrasil – The great world tree. The ever-green Ash that binds the world. To worship trees is to worship life.

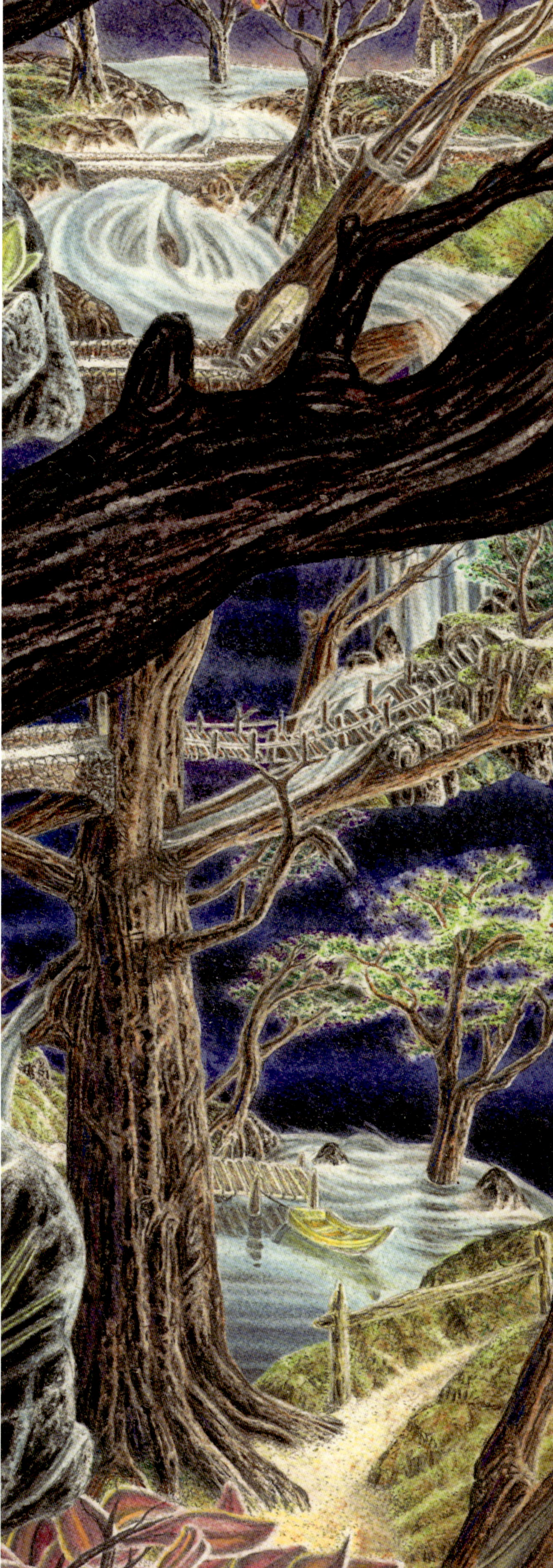